The Science of Self-Actualization:
A Children's Introduction to the Philosophy of Friedrich Nietzsche
by Adeeb Kasem

"What's in a name? that which we call a rose
By any other word would smell as sweet..."
—Shakespeare, *Romeo and Juliet*, II.ii

"We need to interpret interpretations more than to interpret things."
—Montaigne[1]

"O Samas (sun-god), by your light you scan the totality of lands as if
they were cuneiform signs."
—Anonymous Egyptian poet[2]

"The will to power is the very force of life and beauty."
—Dr. Vogelfrei

"Glory and praise to Satan, where you reigned
In Heaven, and in the depths of Hell the same,
Where now you dream in silent reverie!
And may my soul take rest beneath the Tree
Of Knowledge with you, when above your head
Like a new Temple, those great branches spread!"
—Baudelaire, "Les Litanies De Satan," *Flowers of Evil*[3]

"Life is a dice-game played by a child. Kingship belongs to the
child."
—Heraclitus

Table of Contents

Foreword: Directions for Use

"On his standard of proof, *natural* science would never progress, for without the making of theories I am convinced there would be no observation."
—Charles Darwin (1888, p. 315)

This book was originally conceived of as a detailed, systematic, scientific, and comprehensive introduction to the philosophy of Friedrich Nietzsche. However, that endless scientific work of interpretation, a work of scientific interpretation about the science of interpretation itself, remained unfinished due to the sheer scope and magnitude of the task. The present manuscript is much more modest: it is a collection of notes, sketches, drafts, aphorisms, and outlines which focus, for the most part, on two books of Nietzsche's, *Beyond Good and Evil* and *On the Genealogy of Morals*. Elaborating my notes and outlines—at least, elaborating them according to academic standards—would require tens of thousands of pages. Every sentence I write is a thesis unto itself. I have taken no steps to rigorously "prove" the truth of every sentence with the requisite casuistry and baby steps of reasoning, all the while citing every major and minor figure in intellectual history who has said anything even tangentially related to my topic, as demanded by academia. If one needs to justify each and every sentence with an infinite staircase of "reasoning," that is to say, with an infinite staircase of other sentences, which themselves require "justification," it becomes impossible to write anything at all—not to mention that it becomes impossible to think. Simply put, one needs to have courage in order to think for one's self, to dance and leap with one's mind, to invent new thoughts.

However, this book is not, strictly speaking, a study of Nietzsche, because I also extend principles which Nietzsche discovered into territory which Nietzsche did not explore, and indeed could not possibly explore, namely into the territory of the 20th and 21st centuries. I recommend my own book *The Lotus Flower of the Will to Power* as a much more concise interpretation of Nietzsche's philosophy. That being said, I do not think that I have at all improved on anything that Nietzsche has written, with the sole exception of this one minor detail: I have in effect replaced "race" with "culture" in interpreting Nietzsche, but *only* because "culture" is the more empirical and useful concept. (Skin colour is the superficial skin of things. The depths, especially the psychic depths of depth psychology, are *values*. The analysis of values necessitates the genealogy of morals.).

Part of my personal motivation for writing a scientific interpretation of Nietzsche is that I had so greatly and so egregiously misunderstood this thinker in the past. I had once prepared a monograph in which I psychoanalyzed Nietzsche; the book was a thinly veiled work of propaganda in the service of scientism, feminism, and Marxism, and it was filled with the hollowest, tritest, and most nonsensical arguments imaginable drawn from sources as diverse as analytic philosophy, newspapers, and critical theory (particularly, I drew upon the work of such pretentious and pedantic windbags as Bertrand Russell, Slavoj Zizek, and Jacques Lacan). (I have since taken this monograph out of publication, and with good reason). Thus, although I am indeed now a fanatic and militant Nietzschean, I have experienced other perspectives first-hand, and therefore I certainly cannot be accused of never having considered other points of view. It is my guess that Nietzsche will continue to be a widely misunderstood thinker for a long, long time to come; the best cure for such misunderstandings will always be the simple task of actually reading Nietzsche's books—and then reading them *again*.

I confess to being an amateur philosopher, a "bedroom philosopher." However, I am not wholly unfamiliar with the conversations of academics, and much of my book is directed against academia and academic ideas generally. I think that academic ideas are not only completely useless and masks of nihilism and ressentiment, but that even thinking "along the lines" of academics dangerously misleads one from thinking about anything important. For this reason, Shakespeare and Nietzsche—not to mention the Greek and Roman poets—can never be taught in a modern classroom; a professor cannot help but fundamentally misunderstand these thinkers because a professor is limited only to finding himself in everything he reads. As examples of this, as it regards Nietzsche, we have such travesties as Heidegger's *Nietzsche*, Deleuze's *Nietzsche and Philosophy*, and Derrida's *Spurs: Nietzsche's Styles*. If I can be said to have specific academic targets, I suppose it is these three books, which are themselves products of men of ressentiment who are more interested in splitting hairs than they are in life. Although I quote from both Deleuze's and Derrida's texts frequently,

I should never be confused with them; indeed, part of my work is a deconstruction of Deleuze and a deconstruction of Derrida himself. If I can be said to have made an original discovery, it is that Nietzsche was always already a "man of tomorrow," that he has always already been far ahead of even the major continental philosophers of the 20th century.

I do not think that I have at all improved upon the writings of Nietzsche because Nietzsche is much clearer, more precise, more concise, and more effective than these collection of notes and outlines of mine. Moreover, neither I nor Nietzsche am likely to be understood by the vast majority—including the slow wits of analytic philosophers and academics generally—let alone convince them. I have no interest in convincing anyone, and I do not think that Nietzsche had any such interest either. However, as for some time I was deluded by materialism, objectivity, academicism, and morality, I owe it to *myself* to "think through" all my errors and thereby win myself the right to freedom. Freedom for the sake of doing something much more difficult and much more intelligent, not to mention much more amusing, namely creating new values. In this way, I wish to exorcize from myself the follies from which I had suffered, and thereby to forge a memory for myself and make sure that I never believe in such things (materialism, objectivity, the university, morality) ever again. In several senses, then, this book is a work of history, a historiography.

In my book *Whose Unconscious Is It?* I raised the titular question, which is actually several questions: "Whose unconscious do we believe in? Whose theory of the unconscious is the correct one? Who is in control of our own unconscious?" I hinted at something I did not elaborate in that book, namely that the question of which theory of the unconscious is "correct" is a poorly formulated, useless, and erroneous question; that the real question which ought to be asked is how believing in a particular theory of the unconscious affects how we live our lives. Indeed, working with a "neo-pragmatic" epistemology, the only "meaning" of a theory of the unconscious is its *practice* in day-to-day life. We can go on for as long as we like about our "reasons" for this or that theory, but ultimately the test of a theory of the unconscious is whether its practice is healthy or sick. A theory of the unconscious is a form of life, and the ultimate test of such a theory is whether it is a healthy form of life or a diseased form of life. However, in my book *Whose Unconscious Is It?*, I was still a materialist and a cognitive neuroscientist, and thus I was blind to the real question implied by my work. The cognitive unconscious, the neurological unconscious, and indeed materialist theories of the unconscious generally, are diseased forms of life. Indeed, the only healthy theory of the unconscious is Nietzsche's perspectivist psychology, which we have outlined in Part II of the present work.

Explicating Proust's observations in *In Search of Lost Time*, Deleuze writes, "A man can be skillful at deciphering the signs of one realm but remain a fool in every other case: thus Cottard, a great clinician," but a fool in every other case (PS, p. 5). One can be an expert on the brain, an expert on deciphering the signs of neurophysiology, for instance the symptoms of various neurological disorders, the anatomy of the brain, details of neurophysiology such as all the various neurotransmitters, etc., and yet be a complete fool when it comes to deciphering the signs of thoughts and feelings in both one's self and others. Ditto for cognitive science, whose domain of signs is the signs of computer programs, and not the signs of thoughts and feelings. Proust's character Cottard is a symbol, a conceptual persona, embodying the philosophy of materialism, scientism, and objectivity; all materialists are like Cottard to varying degrees, they may be knowledgeable, even experts, in their specialized discipline, but they are more or less stupid when it comes to deciphering thoughts and feelings. More broadly, belief in an objective truth is likewise Cottardian stupidity; cf. Plato's *Republic*, in which, during the cave allegory, Plato presents his ideal of the philosopher, a fool whose senses are dulled, who has almost no practical knowledge about the sensory world, but who instead spends his time fantasizing about abstract ideas. Materialism is still a form of Platonism because it still believes in an objective truth, it mentally superimposes objectalities upon the sensory world, (an "objectality" is an "objectively existing entity"), objectalities which are in actuality nothing but abstract ideas, mere concepts in the mind— thereby the materialist denies the most practical knowledge of all, psychology. Nihilism is precisely this Cottardian stupidity. The essence of Proust's *In Search of Lost Time* is the deciphering of the signs of thoughts and feelings *as thoughts and feelings*; it is this domain of signs which is the domain of the artist, the true artist—the divinely inspired artist-tyrant—who is therefore also the true psychologist, the anti-nihilist par excellence. Proust's *In Search of Lost Time* is in fact a search for power; if it is a search for "knowledge," it is only insofar as "knowledge is power," i.e. it is the search for a form of knowledge which is also a form of power, a search for an effective psychology. Proust's *In Search of Lost Time* is one of the greatest masterpieces of psychology in the entirety of the history of knowledge. It is a testament to the fundamental ignorance and stupidity of academia that real psychology is ignored, especially in psychology departments, in favour of materialist stupidity even greater than Cottard's stupidity.

If *Whose Unconscious Is It?* has any value whatsoever, it is in the fact that I systematically, diligently, and precisely refute the fundamental theories of psychoanalysis, including Freud's theory of repression and his theory of the Oedipus complex, solely by using data from physiology and experimental psychology. Indeed, it was due to the contemplation of memory from a purely physiological perspective that my interest in Nietzsche was rekindled. For one of the best and most concise refutations of Freud, I recommend Kihlstrom's essay "Trauma and Memory Revisited" (2006) (next to my own book, of course). Kihlstrom simply brings attention to the simple fact that pain increases the memorability of an event, i.e. pain *aids* memory. Kihlstrom goes on to point out that not a single credible case of repression and recovered memory exists. Friedrich Nietzsche, on this point and many others, believes in the exact opposite of Freud; Nietzsche does indeed conclude that pain is an aid to memory, and draws further conclusions from this fact (GM, II, 3). That is the origin of my "return to Nietzsche."

Because nearly all of the concepts of psychoanalysis depend on the concept of repression, most prominently the Oedipus complex, all of psychoanalysis (Lacan, Deleuze and Guattari, Zizek, and Solms included) collapses like a house of cards as soon as one realizes that "repression" simply does not exist. That the human race has allowed itself to be deceived so blatantly and thoroughly about so obvious a matter for so long—a little more than a hundred years now—raises the far more interesting question of *why* such a belief was ever necessary. A handful of cognitive scientists are also aware of this great swindle, but cognitive scientists are the victims and priests of other great swindles, e.g. confusing the mind with a computer. Indeed, I even regularly meet academics who continue to believe in repression—and even the Oedipus complex—even after I get them to confess that they remember the most painful events of their lives rather clearly.

As far as I know, Nietzsche is the only psychologist who both has a theory of the unconscious mind and who acknowledges that pain is a mnemonic device. If Nietzschean psychology—that is to say, perspectivist psychology—is to have any future whatsoever, it must begin with the contemplation of pain. Indeed, if amateur philosophy—bedroom philosophy and bedroom psychology—that is to say, the only ones among us who are genuine psychologists and philosophers—is to have any future whatsoever, it must likewise begin with the contemplation of pain. However, such a future is indeed uncertain, because everywhere I look, the theory of an unconscious mind is altogether vanishing from sight, and instead it is replaced by the most vulgar forms of materialism, which on the one hand reduce everything to matter, and on the other hand reduce everything to computer programs. Objects and computers, of course, are incapable of feeling anything, let alone pain. Materialism generally is an ascetic philosophy, a symptom of the diminished capacity to feel and the diminished capacity to empathize with others. If the follies of my past can be summarized in a single word, that word is materialism. Psychology, if that word is to have any meaning whatsoever, must be a science of the *soul*, and the soul is *immaterial*. Materialist psychologies aren't really psychologies at all, nor are they scientific in the strict sense; they are merely fantasies. There are no "immortal souls," such a concept is a laughable superstition of religion. However, there are *mortal souls*, indeed there are *only* mortal souls, and a scientific psychology, in the strict sense, can only ever be the scientific study of mortal souls; but mortal souls require *interpretation* exactly in the same way that art and literature require interpretation.

In this book, my chief allies are Jacques Derrida and Pierre Klossowski. I do not think that my book can be properly understood without also reading Klossowski's *Nietzsche and the Vicious Circle* and at least a study of Derrida's *Of Grammatology*, if not the book itself (I recommend Arthur Bradley's *Derrida's Of Grammatology*). I think that Nietzsche has been largely misunderstood because people have read him too quickly, without properly contemplating him, merely in order to flatter their own vanity and feel superior to everyone all the while remaining just like everyone else. Nietzsche must be read slowly and multiple times in order to be understood; or to say it more briefly, he must be *read* in order to be understood. However, my ideal reader is nonetheless an amateur reader. I confess that I am an amateur writer, consequently I am only interested in amateur readers.

As for the unfinished nature of my work and the host of questions it raises to which at present we have no answers, to paraphrase[4] Freud, it is demanded by the rigorously scientific nature of our work: "We must be patient and await fresh methods and occasions of research. We must be ready, too, to abandon a path that we have followed for a time, if it seems to be leading to no good end. Only believers, who demand that science shall be a substitute for the catechism they have given up, will blame an investigator for developing or even transforming his views. We may take comfort, too, for the slow advances of our scientific knowledge in the words of the poet [al-Hariri]:

'What we cannot reach flying we must reach limping,
The Book tells us it is no sin to limp.'"
(Freud, BPP, pp. 58-59)

The task of a philosophical investigator is precisely to develop and transform his own views. The truly innovative scientific mind recognizes that there is an intellectual trap in every belief. In the science of interpretation, this is all the more true. The science of interpretation perpetually demands patience, fresh methods, and new occasions of research. The science of interpretation perpetually demands that one abandon old, well-worn paths if they fail to bring one knowledge—that is to say, if they fail to bring one power, for "knowledge is power." The science of interpretation, is, after all science—even the most demanding, rigorous, subtle, and scientific of all sciences—and it is *not* religion, and it is especially not the Christian religion. It is precisely for this reason that we have abandoned materialism, which is no better than a religious belief; materialism has failed to bring us power; in fact, materialism weakened us. To interpret more effectively, therefore, we must interpret subjective realities, the realities of subjectivities. The science of interpretation necessitates slow advances in its scientific knowledge of interpretation itself, which is the interpretation of interpretation itself. Our fresh methods and occasions of research must deal directly with subjectivities.

An interpretation is a cartography, a map. Therefore, to paraphrase Guattari, "As in painting or literature, the concrete performance of these cartographies requires that they evolve and innovate, that they open up new futures, without their authors (*auteurs*) having prior recourse to assured theoretical principles or to the authority of a group, a school or an academy" (Guattari, 2000, p. 40). There is no "truth" in science, there are only truths. Therefore, the concrete performance of science, and especially the concrete performance of interpretation, must perpetually evolve and innovate, perpetually open up new futures, and it must do so without any definite guide. No theoretical principles, no group, no school, no academy can ever discover the "true interpretation" or the "true" method of interpretation. All interpretations are subjective, and there are only interpretations. The important question is not that of truth, but the question of effectivity and power. Which interpretation, which method of interpretation, is the most effective, which gives us the most power-over? What are more effective interpretations and methods of interpretation, what give us more power-over? Interpretation opens up new futures, that is to say, interpretation *invents* new futures, it invents the future of the future itself, it invents the future itself. All interpretation is the writing of history, the creation of history itself.

INCIPIT COMEDIA

"Is language the full and adequate expression of all realities?"
—Nietzsche, *On Truth and Untruth*, p. 24

"Words dissemble,
Words be quick,
Words resemble walking sticks.

Plant them,
They will grow,
Watch them waver so."
—Jim Morrison, "An American Prayer"[5]

"I grew accustomed to pure hallucination...Then I explained my magic sophisms with the hallucination of words!"
—Rimbaud, "A Season in Hell"[6]

Of necessity, for diverse reasons, our point of entry into the interpretation of the self, the other, the world, and their relations must be language. In brief, our necessity is motivated by a "crisis," a crisis of language and a crisis of Western discourse, a rupture of Western discourse, a rupture of language itself. Out of this rupture of language itself gushes forth infinite streams of the blood of language itself. Language itself speaks through the mouth of the wound of language itself. In brief, our necessity is the question "What is language?" The question of language is the question of the question itself, it is questionality itself. It is with the scientific analysis of language that post-structuralism begins, and it is also with the scientific analysis of language that *our* theory of social constructionism, metaphorically a "post-post-structuralism," begins. In a way of speaking, the whole of this book is devoted to explicating the following two aphorisms by Nietzsche, and thereby explicating language itself:

"*Language as putative science.*—The significance of language for the evolution of culture lies in this, that mankind set up in language a separate other world beside [and even psychologically superimposed upon] *this* world, a place it took to be so firmly set that, standing

upon it, it could lift the rest of the world off its hinges and make itself master of it. To the extent that man has for long ages believed in the concepts and names of things as in *aeternae veritates* he has appropriated to himself that pride by which he raised himself above the animal: he really thought that in language he possessed knowledge of the world. The sculptor of language was not so modest as to believe that he was only giving things designations, he conceived rather that with words he was expressing supreme knowledge of things; language is, in fact, the first stage of the occupation with science. Here, too, it is the *belief that the truth has been found* out of which the mightiest sources of energy have flowed. A great deal later—only now—it dawns on men that in their belief in language they have propagated a tremendous error. Happily, it is too late for the evolution of reason, which depends on this belief, to be put back.—*Logic* too depends on presuppositions with which nothing in the real world corresponds, for example on the presupposition that there are identical things, that the same thing is identical at different points of time: but this science came into existence through the opposite belief (that such conditions [viz. identity] do obtain in the real world). It is the same with *mathematics*, which would certainly not have come into existence if one had known from the beginning that there was in nature no exactly straight line, no perfect circle, no absolute magnitude."
—Nietzsche, HH, 11

"*Number*.—The invention of the laws of numbers was made on the basis of this error, dominant even from the earliest times, that there are identical things (but in fact nothing is identical with anything else [including itself]); at least that there are things (but there is no 'thing'). The assumption of plurality always presupposes the existence of *something* that occurs more than once: but precisely here error already holds sway, here already we are fabricating beings, unities which do not exist.—Our sensations of space and time are false, for tested consistently they lead to logical contradictions. The establishment of conclusions in science always unavoidably involves us in calculating with certain false magnitudes: but because these magnitudes are at least *constant,* as for example are our sensations of time and space, the conclusions of science acquire a complete rigorousness and certainty in their coherence with one another; one can build on them—up to that final stage at which our erroneous basic assumptions, those constant errors, come

to be incompatible with our conclusions, for example in the theory of atoms. Here we continue to feel ourselves compelled to assume the existence of a 'thing' or material 'substratum' which is moved, while the whole procedure of science has pursued the task of resolving everything thing-like (material) in motions: here too our sensations divide that which moves from that which is moved, and we cannot get out of this circle because our belief in the existence of things has been tied up with our being from time immemorial.—When Kant says 'the understanding does not draw its laws from nature, it prescribes them to nature,' this is wholly true with regard to the *concept of nature* which we are obliged to attach to nature (nature = world as idea, that is as error), but which is the summation of a host of errors of the understanding.—To a world which is *not* our idea the laws of numbers are wholly inapplicable: these are valid only in the human world."
—Nietzsche, HH, 19

   The ground of knowledge is language. All knowledge only exists as linguistic constructs, and all knowledge is communicated only via the mediation of language. The question "What is truth?"—along with the questions "What is knowledge?" and "What is science?", but all three are really the same question—lead ultimately to the very medium of truth, the medium of knowledge, the medium of science: this medium is language. The medium is *not* the message. The message is the use the medium is put to, and the medium can be put to diverse uses. The "message" is the use of the medium because "meaning" is use.[7] The "content" of a medium is its use.
   However, the question of truth is the question of the truth of the medium of truth, the question of the truth of language, because it is only via the mediation of the medium of language that the linguistic constructs of truth, the "messages" that are "truths," are constructed. The truthfulness of truth depends upon the truthfulness of the medium of truth, language: the truthfulness of truth depends on whether the means by which the "messages" of truth are constructed, language, is essentially illusion or essentially reality. Discourse is a particular use of the medium of language, which means that discourse consists wholly of linguistic constructs; therefore, to question the truth of discourse means to question the truth or illusoriness of language and the ground of language.
   But language is never reality. There is an irreducible difference between language and reality, such that language is at

worst a falsification and at best merely a metaphor. All language is falsification and metaphor. Language is essentially illusion. Language is essentially hallucination. Each word is an illusion. Each word is an abyss. With the medium of illusion, one can produce only illusions, "messages" which are only ever illusions because they are constructed out of illusions. Each linguistic construct is an illusion.

With the medium of illusion, how could the "message" ever be "truth"? "Truth," the "message" that is "truth," is only ever a particular use of language, a particular use of an illusion. The essence of truth is illusion. Truth itself is essentially an illusion. All language is fiction, therefore all truth is fiction, truth itself is fiction itself. Language is essentially empty because it is essentially illusion. It is the emptiness of language which gives language its efficacy (its efficacy as language). Logic and mathematics too consist solely of linguistic constructs, solely of illusions, and they are useful precisely because they are falsifications and metaphors, precisely because they never correspond to reality (viz. there is no "identity" in reality). The empirical evidence of this is abundant although often forgotten and ignored: we perceive only change, difference, multiplicity, complexity and flux in nature, but we never perceive identity (we never perceive anything which endures).[8] There are no perfectly straight lines, perfect circles, or absolute magnitudes in nature. There are no numbers in nature. We never perceive unity, we only perceive complexes of difference. Language simplifies the complexity of reality and thereby falsifies reality. Since the medium of language is falsification, any "message" constructed with language, any linguistic construct, including "truth," is necessarily also a falsification.

The world of Ideas constructed by language, which is also the world *as* Idea, is a metaphysical world: this is the world of identities and presence, the world of Beings, the world of the Being of language, because "language is the house of Being,"[9] because it is only via linguistic constructs that there "is" Being, because Being is constructed out of language and is nothing more than a linguistic construct: this is the illusory "other world" which appears to "exist" only via language, this is the "world" other than that of reality, the "world" which is separate from the real world but nonetheless often psychologically superimposed upon the real world such that reality is often confused with mere linguistic constructs. We agree with Plato's fundamental intuition (shared by Parmenides and Heraclitus) that the sensible realm (the physical world, the world of perception, the world as it is perceived, the observable world, the empirical world) is the world of Becoming, the world of change, flux, multiplicity, complexity, and difference, the world which is completely devoid of Being. However, we disagree with Plato upon the existence of a "real" metaphysical world of Beings; the "metaphysical" world of Beings is wholly imaginary, it is the imagination itself, which is thought itself. The metaphysical realm of Beings, which are the same as Ideas, is a symbolic universe,[10] a universe of symbols (imaginary = symbolic), and its space is mind-space, the space of the mind. At best, "beings" are reified (hence the utility of science and mathematics), but in any case they are nonetheless falsifications.

The laws of numbers are not valid in the real world, but they are valid only in the "human world" because the "human world" is itself a symbolic universe, a metaphysical world consisting solely of linguistic constructs. "Human"—this includes both "man" and "woman," typically even when one writes "man"—is merely a linguistic construct, a fiction of the mind. "Man" is, at best, the reification of a cultural construct, but in any case a falsification. It is language which speaks man because man is merely a linguistic construct. The linguistic construct "human" is inextricably linked with, even identical to, the linguistic construct "ego" (or more simply, "I"). Man is an extension of the medium of language. "Man" is a "message" which is an extension of the medium of language. Content determines form.[11] Content = forces. Forces determine form. (Substance determines style). Form is a resultant, a product, of forces. Formlessness is originary.

In the *Tractatus*, Wittgenstein divides reality into three fundamental categories, "thought," "language," and the "world," and these metaphysically "correspond" to each other: words correspond to thoughts, thoughts correspond to the world, and thus the world corresponds to words, words have sense only because they correspond to the world, such that the sense of words, which is a picture of reality, "touches" reality. But the early Wittgenstein's overly simplistic picture of reality is merely a series of metaphysical presuppositions. To begin with, the philosophical investigator may ask: "What is thought? What is language? What is the world? What is reality? What is a picture? What gives one the right to even form these separate concepts of thought, language, and the world to begin with?" To begin with, the linguist, following Saussure, may bring attention to the fact that the relationship between words and the "things" in the "world" they designate is essentially and originarily a relationship of arbitrariness. There is no necessary connection, no "correspondence," between words and things. Arbitrariness is originary. Language, including science and mathematics, never corresponds to the world. The arbitrariness of all language implies that language and the world do not correspond to each other, that language never "touches" the world. There is no inherent "sense" of words; all language is originarily non-sense. Nonsense is originary. The "sense" of a word is always already a construction, a fabrication. The "sense" of a word is determined by how the word is used.

Words are only ever a metaphor for "things." All language is metaphor. Originary arbitrariness is originary metaphor. There is an irreducible difference between words and reality, but there are no "things" in reality, in the world of perception. "Things" only "exist" in the world of thought, in mental space, mind-space. There is indeed nonetheless an irreducible difference between words and "things," but that is the irreducible difference between the signifier and the signified, the signified which is nonetheless and always a mental construct in the space of the mind. To paraphrase one of Derrida's discoveries in *Of Grammatology*, the signified is always already a signifier. We wrote above that "things" are merely linguistic constructs; to be more precise, "things" are merely pictures, pictorial constructs, mental pictures in mind-space. A picture is always already a metaphor because it is always already an arbitrary construction which never actually corresponds to anything else. "Things are symbols of themselves"[12] because "things" are in actuality mental pictures of themselves, mental pictures of mental pictures, mental pictures within mental pictures. However, we may nonetheless continue to use the term "linguistic construct" as a metaphor and an abbreviation because words and "things" are often inextricably linked in the psyche, however arbitrary and artificial that link may be in actuality. In actuality, the link between words and "things" is always arbitrary and artificial.

To overcome humanity and to become the overman, to make the "leap" from "ape" to "overman," it is necessary and sufficient to realize the essential emptiness and falsehood of all language, of language itself: this leap of thought is the psychic emancipation from humanist discourse and humanist culture, which also means psychic emancipation from humanist ethics (e.g., Christian ethics, bourgeois ethics, Marxist ethics, racist ethics, egalitarian ethics), and this psychic emancipation is precisely the actualization of the self, the realization of the self, the metamorphosis of the self into the overman. The overman is indeed a linguistic construct, but it is a linguistic construct whose meaning is the essential falsehood of all linguistic constructs: therefore, to become the overman means to realize the essential falsehood of all language, and thus to arrive at the ultimate truth, "Nothing is true, everything is permitted,"[13] which the overman affirms with joy.

I. The Mediation of the Life-World

"There are still harmless self-observers who believe that there are
"immediate certainties"; for example, "I think," or as the superstition
of Schopenhauer put it, "I will"; as though knowledge here got hold
of its object purely and nakedly as the "thing in itself," without any
falsification on the part of either the subject or the object. But that
"immediate certainty," as well as "absolute knowledge" and the
"thing in itself," involve a *contradictio in adjecto* [contradiction
between the noun and the adjective], I shall repeat a hundred times;
we really ought to free ourselves from the seduction of words!...In
place of the "immediate certainty" in which the people may believe
in the case at hand, the philosopher thus finds a series of
metaphysical questions presented to him, truly searching questions
of the intellect...Whoever ventures to answer these metaphysical
questions at once by an appeal to a sort of *intuitive* perception, like
the person who says, "*I think*, and know that this, at least, is true,
actual and certain"—will encounter a smile and two question marks
from a philosopher nowadays. "Sir," the philosopher will perhaps
give him to understand, "it is improbable that you are not mistaken;
but why insist on the truth?"—"
—Nietzsche, BGE, 16

Husserl fears that if man loses his faith in absolute reason,
then man will also lose his faith in the meaning of history, in the
meaning of humanity itself, and that man will lose faith in his own
freedom because it is by means of absolute reason that the world has
meaning for man (Husserl, 1970, p. 13). By losing the faith in
absolute reason, man would lose "his capacity to secure rational
meaning for his individual and common human existence" (Husserl,
1970, p. 13). But this means that if man loses his faith in absolute
reason, man loses faith in himself—man loses faith in his own
humanity, and consequently, he loses his faith in the existence of
humanity, i.e. man loses faith in his own existence.

However, the faith in absolute reason and man's faith in his
own existence remain matters of faith, and as such they are only of
personal importance to "man" himself, to the creature who believes
himself to be "man." Husserl is an ideologist of humanism, the belief
and faith in man, and in defending man against the forces which

threaten his existence, Husserl explicates the ideology of humanism, thereby inadvertently explicating its weaknesses.

If it is only by means of his faith in absolute reason that "man" secures rational meaning for his own existence and "common human existence," i.e. the concept of humanity itself, then the essential falsehood of absolute reason reveals the essential irrationality of the meaning of humanity. The "meaning" of humanity, without a rational ground, is essentially an illusion, and therefore the concept of humanity is itself an illusion. Therefore, there is no "actual" humanity, no actual "man," for these were nothing more than reifications to begin with.

The social construction of absolute reason, telos ("purpose," viz. the "meaning of history"), and freedom (viz. free will) are all essential to and inextricable from the social construction of man. Absolute reason is the ground of man, and man is the ground of absolute reason. Without man, there is no absolute reason, and without absolute reason, there is no man. Where we and Husserl have written "absolute reason," one may also substitute "absolute truth," or more simply, "truth," and these in turn may also be substituted by "unmediated presence," "immediate presence," "immediate certainty," "self-presence," or more simply, "presence." The interdependence of the concepts "man" and "truth" are most evident in philosophy's anxiety-ridden and neurotic defense of the concept of truth itself, its attempts to ground knowledge in an immediate certainty and thereby to ground the existence of man. From such texts, for example Descartes' *Meditations*, a foundational text of modern humanist philosophy, and Husserl's *Crisis*, one of the last bastions of modern humanist philosophy, the internal logic of humanism reveals itself and deconstructs itself; from these texts specifically, humanist discourse reveals that the faith in man is equivalent to the faith in the ego, since it is the ego which *is* man, and it is the immediate certainty, the unmediated presence, of the ego which grounds all knowledge, all truth, all "absolute reason."

But Husserl himself, inadvertently, also gives us the means to critique all such immediate certainties and unmediated presences, including the existence of the ego, with his concept of the life-world. Husserl writes that the subject lives in a life-world, the world as it is experienced, which is in essence historical and cultural; the subject stands within a "historical horizon in which everything is historical" (Husserl, 1970, p. 369). All experience is always already encultured, always already historical: the horizon of experience is the historical horizon, the horizon of historicity, historicity itself. This means that all experience is social construction, that each experience is always already both a social construct and the process of social construction.

"Meaning" is always already a social construct, including the various "meanings" which Husserl argues is essential for man (viz. the meaning of history, the meaning of humanity, the meaning of the world). Moreover, "absolute reason," "knowledge," "truth," "science," are likewise social constructs, historical and cultural constructs (social construct = cultural construct = historical construct). These concepts, like all concepts, are always already within the historical horizon of the life-world, within the horizon of historicity, and are therefore social constructs.

The problem of radical skepticism, the loss of faith in absolute reason, as Husserl frames it, is a threat to humanism, the belief in humanity and the rationality of humanity, but not only Husserl's conceptual framing of radical skepticism, but the very "fact" that radical skepticism appears as a problem at all, is not truly a fact but an arte-fact, a historical artefact, a social construct within a cultural-historical horizon.

The recognition of the inherent historicity of all concepts and all experiences leads us necessarily to the conclusion that history is inherently meaningless. "Meaning" is only ever a social construct, an artifice, therefore any possible "meaning" of history is likewise a social construct, which means that history is devoid of any inherent meaning. The recognition and comprehension of the inherent meaninglessness of history is the precondition for the production of the overman. Whereas the thought of the inherent meaninglessness of history entails despair for man, it entails joy for the overman because it gives the overman grounds for the construction of infinite interpretations of history, infinite constructions of infinite "meanings" of history. "Man" is essentially a "rational animal," he needs to believe in "truth" and "reason," which means that he is essentially the slave of morality, the slave of slave morality, because his "truth" and "reason" are merely masks of slave morality. The overman has moved beyond the false dichotomies, the false binary oppositions, of "truth" and "falsehood," of "reason" and "unreason," of "rationality" and "irrationality." The overman is essentially a creator, a producer and a constructer of "meanings," a creator of master morality, of "meanings" which are masks of master morality: the overman is a creator of values.

Husserl writes that if man loses his faith in reason he also loses faith in his own true being (1970, pp. 12-13), but that, paradoxically, the true being of man is not pre-given to man but must be attained by him: "This true being is not something [man] always already has, with the self-evidence of the "I am," but something he only has and can have in the form of the struggle for his truth, the struggle to make himself true" (1970, p. 13). It is a contradiction to state that one is capable of losing what one does not have to begin with. If the true being of man is something that man can only attain by means of the struggle for his truth, then it is not something that he can lose because he did not have it to begin with.

` Since the true being of man is, to begin with, absent in man, this calls into question the concept of man, who is evidently always already absent from himself. Husserl writes that man can only attain his own true being via "the struggle to make himself true" (1970, p. 13). The implication, then, is that man is not true to begin with, i.e. that man is originarily false, and that man can only have "true being" by *making* himself "true." That man must "*make* himself true" suggests that man's truth, his "true being," is something which must be made, i.e. that it is a construction, a fabrication.

The epistemological problem here is that "truth" (viz. the truth of man, the true being of man) cannot necessarily follow from falsehood (viz. from "man," who, because he is devoid of his own "true being," is originarily false), at least if by "truth" one means "truth" in the traditional sense, truth which necessarily follows from other truths, and ultimately from an absolute truth which guarantees the truth of all truths.

Man is always already absent from himself, he is always already absent at his own origin, therefore there are no grounds for asserting that "man" exists. Husserl writes that "the self-evidence of the "I am"," i.e. the "self-evidence" of the ego's existence, does not necessarily guarantee the true being of man for man himself (1970, p. 13). Husserl acknowledges that it is "man" who proclaims "I am," that it is man who proclaims the ego's existence with unmediated self-evidence; from this we can conclude the fundamental equivalence of the concepts "man" and "ego" within the humanist cultural matrix of the West—and also that the existence of the ego is not in actuality self-evident because man, who *is* the ego, is always already absent from himself, which means that the ego is always already absent from itself, that the ego is originarily absent, i.e. that there is no ego.

In the terminology of the later Wittgenstein, the ego is merely an element of a language game, i.e. the ego is merely a sign. In *Philosophical Investigations* and *On Certainty*, Wittgenstein argues that knowledge (or certainty) is ultimately neither grounded in an epistemology nor in an ontology, but in praxis (or practice). Wittgenstein explicates "meaning" in terms of praxis, and he describes praxis in terms of "language games." Although a "language game" does not have a formal definition, we define it as a system of uses of signs (or in the singular, a use of a sign). Wittgenstein writes that "meaning is use" because the meaning of a sign is determined by and equivalent to its use, i.e. the meaning of a sign is how it is used in practice. Meaning is praxis.

The ego is used as the subject of many sentences (viz. "subject [insert ego, "I," here] + verb + object"), and is therefore a fundamental element of many language games. The ego only has meaning as part of these language games. However, it does not necessarily follow from the importance of the ego in these language games that the ego exists in actuality. The subject of the statement (the subject of the sentence) is irreducibly different from the ontological-psychological subject (the subject of enunciation).[14] The ego is only ever the subject of the statement. The concept of the ego suggests a particular kind of ontological entity, a self-identical and enduring self, i.e. a Being. Like all Beings, the ego is in actuality a social construct.

To argue that the ego must exist in actuality since it is used in our language games is a circular argument (viz. "It exists because we refer to it, we refer to it because it exists."). Furthermore, such an argument is tantamount to arguing that the ego must exist in actuality because we need it for our language games; this is, obviously, an illegitimate argument because it cannot be legitimately inferred that the ego exists in actuality from the mere fact that the concept of the ego is a fundamental element of many language games.

The ontological-psychological subject is the real subject, the subject which exists in actuality. The ontological-psychological subject is the subject of enunciation (when there is enunciation), the subject which enunciates statements, which means ultimately the subject which exists prior to all possible statements, i.e. the subject which exists prior to the ego. The ontological-psychological subject is a stream-of-subjectivity, a flux-of-subjectivity, a subjectivity-flux, because subjectivity is in "constant change," it is perpetually changing due to its temporality and the infinite flux of its temporality, therefore it is a system of becomings, a system of actions: the ontological-psychological subject is a system of difference, of ontological difference, difference-in-itself, which means it is also a system of multiplicity. To clarify, humanist discourse asserts that the ontological-psychological subject is the ego (which is an identicality), but the discourse of the overman, post-human discourse, asserts that the ontological-psychological subject is a system of difference. (*Difference-in-itself* designates pure difference, difference absolutely devoid of identity. Difference-in-itself is Deleuze's concept, developed in his book *Difference and Repetition*. However, our concept of difference-in-itself differs from Deleuze's concept.).

Humanist discourse is the discourse of the ego, and therefore egoist discourse, whatever it may claim to the contrary, because the belief in the existence of the ego is egoism. As we mentioned above, this is most evident in one of the foundational works of humanist discourse, Descartes' *Meditations*. Descartes establishes the foundation of all knowledge, the foundation of truth itself, in the concept of the ego: the "existence" of the ego is the "immediate certainty" which serves as the "one firm and immovable point" upon which Descartes builds all knowledge, knowledge itself. The concept of the ego is the centre, the "ex-centric centre" (as Derrida might say; Derrida writes that the "ex-centric centre" is a centre which is merely illusory, and consequently it is a centre which is both a centre and not a centre, cf. WD, pp. 278-279), of the humanist episteme (which is the same as the Western episteme) because the concept of the ego orients and supports the totality of humanist discourse. This is to an extent a tautology since the concept of the ego is equivalent to the concept of man and since humanist discourse is by definition the discourse of man.

Descartes argues that the ego, the "I am," is the cogito, the "I think," on the grounds that if the existence of everything, including the existence of the ego itself, is doubted, the ego must necessarily exist in order to be able to doubt itself to begin with. Husserl calls Descartes' method of doubt a "radical, skeptical epoche" and, alternatively, the "Cartesian epoche" (Husserl pp. 75-76). Husserl's term "epoche" means the suspending of judgement on the existence or non-existence of a given phenomenon. Husserl accepts Descartes' method of radical, skeptical epoche for the acquisition of knowledge, even claiming that it and the initial result it yields, namely the indubitable proof of the existence of the ego, is essential to the task of philosophy (Husserl, 1970, pp.75-78).

Recapitulating Descartes' argument for the cogito, Husserl writes, "I, the ego carrying out the epoche, am not included in its realm of objects but rather—if I actually carry out the epoche radically and universally—am excluded in principle. I am necessary as the one carrying it out" (1970, p. 77). Husserl writes that it is the ego which carries out the task of Cartesian epoche, and it is only on that basis that the ego can be claimed to indubitably exist. The ego can only be excluded from the epoche in principle if and only if it is the ego which performs the epoche. As soon as the distinction is made between the subject of the statement and the subject of enunciation, the existence of the ego can once again be doubted, because it is the subject of the enunciation which is performing the epoche while the ego is merely the subject of the statement.

Furthermore, Wittgenstein argues that even skeptical statements, however radical, nonetheless presume the certainty of one proposition or another, and that these presumed propositions are themselves exempt from doubt in order for there to be doubt at all. Wittgenstein calls such propositions "hinge propositions." Wittgenstein writes that "the *questions* that we raise and our *doubts* depend on the fact that some propositions are exempt from doubt, are as it were like hinges on which those turn" (1969, 341). Just as a door must have hinges in order to be moved and function as a door functions, so does doubt need hinge propositions in order to function as doubt functions.

To clarify, hinge propositions are purely linguistic constructs and they do not necessarily imply the existence of ontological entities (viz. there are no "hinge phenomena," no "hinge beings"). Wittgenstein develops the concept of hinge propositions in order to explicate the activities of questioning and doubting in terms of language games. That is to say, questioning and doubting are each forms of language games, and hinge propositions are fundamental elements of those language games. Doubting is merely a particular use of language, it neither proves nor disproves anything. Knowledge itself is merely a language-game.

Wittgenstein's concept of hinge propositions may be used to explicate and critique the Cartesian epoche, and epoche more generally. Epoche is a form of doubt, at least in the Cartesian sense of "doubt," and Husserl's explication of Cartesian doubt in terms of "Cartesian epoche" testifies to this. In the Cartesian epoche, the proposition of the ego's existence is the hinge proposition upon which the door of the Cartesian epoche moves. The Cartesian epoche, after all, is not a naive argument that everything is indeed an illusion; rather, it is a strategic argument employed by Descartes, and recapitulated by Husserl, in order to "refute" radical skepticism. In the Cartesian epoche, it appears as if the ego must necessarily exist because the proposition that the ego exists, implicit in the statement "I think" (viz. the proposition "I am" is implicit in the "I" in "I think" and also in the "I" in "I doubt"), is required for performing the language-game of the Cartesian epoche.

Husserl himself offers a critique of Descartes' epoche and even of his own epoche. Husserl writes, "It is obvious that Descartes, in spite of the radicalism of the presuppositionlessness he demands, has, in advance, a *goal* in relation to which the breakthrough to this "ego" is supposed to be the *means*. He does not see that, by being convinced of the possibility of the goal and of this means, he has already left this radicalism behind. It is not achieved by merely deciding on the epoche, on the radical withholding of [judgement on] all that is pregiven, on all prior validities of what is in the world; the epoche must seriously *be* and *remain* in effect" (1970, p. 79).

Husserl argues that the epoche of Descartes is repudiated in effect by Descartes' use of the epoche as a means to an end. To posit the goal, Descartes is certain of the goal, and thus is not, in effect, suspending judgement. In Wittgenstein's terms, Descartes' overarching goal is a hinge proposition of his epoche. Generalizing from his example of Descartes, it is evident that Husserl is arguing that epoche can only be effective, that there can only be an actual epoche, in the total absence of a goal because a goal serves an implicit certainty and thereby renders the epoche ineffective and non-actual. Husserl argues that for epoche to be effective, it does not suffice for it to be stated that epoche is being employed, but epoche must be employed in effect and in practice. However, Husserl's critique of Descartes' epoche opens the question of whether Husserl himself actually employs the epoche in effect or merely claims that he does so, and it gives us the grounds to judge such a claim, namely whether or not Husserl employs the epoche as a means to an end.

Husserl does indeed employ the epoche as a means to an end. To begin with, Husserl subscribes to the same methodological assumptions of Descartes, namely that "immediate and apodictic knowledge whose self-evidence excludes all conceivable doubt" is possible and desirable, and that a radical, skeptical epoche analogous to the one employed by Descartes is the means by which such immediate, apodictic, and indubitable knowledge may be attained (Husserl, 1970, pp. 75-76). Husserl goes so far as to prescribe a radical, skeptical epoche for all philosophers: "Once in his life every philosopher must proceed in this way; if he has not done it, and even already has "his philosophy," he must still do it. Prior to the epoche "his philosophy" is to be treated like any other prejudice." (1970, p. 76). The irony, of course, is that neither Husserl nor Descartes question themselves enough, as is evident from their writings they still harbour presuppositions, and their goals are examples of such presuppositions.

In Wittgenstein's terms, here Husserl and Descartes play the same language game, that of Cartesian doubt or Cartesian epoche. Both use doubt for the same end, the establishment of an immediate certainty, the existence of the ego. Moreover, as it regards the *Crisis* in particular, Husserl employs phenomenology and the method of epoche for the clearly stated purpose of defending man's faith in himself. Husserl writes that his purpose in writing the *Crisis* is "the reestablishment of philosophy with a new universal task and at the same time with the sense of a renaissance of ancient philosophy [viz. Platonic philosophy]—it is at once a repetition and a universal transformation of meaning. In this it feels called to initiate a new age, *completely sure* of its idea of philosophy and its true method, and *also certain of having overcome all previous naivetes*, and thus all skepticism, through the radicalism of its new beginning" (1970, p. 14; my emphasis). These goals and the certainty of their possibility and their desirability precede any possible epoche, and indeed they could not be established if there were a suspension of judgement as to their possibility and desirability. Husserl's own words attest that he has goals to achieve in the *Crisis*, and his own words also argue that epoche is impossible where there are goals. This means that although Husserl himself proclaims to employ epoche, he himself fails to employ epoche in effect and in practice according to his own standards. More generally, a total and genuine epoche is never possible because there are always hinge propositions and there are always goals.

More fundamentally, the concept of language games implies ends and means because the concept of use implies ends and means. When a sign is used, there is an end for which it is used, and that which is used is a means to an end. In a language game, signs are always a means to an end, and it is only in the practice of being used for an end that a sign has any meaning at all; this is implicit in Wittgenstein's phrase "meaning is use."

Husserl further undermines his concept of epoche, not to mention the concept of the ego and even his very conception of philosophy itself, with his concept of the life-world. The life-world is the "ground" of all the practical and theoretical activities of the subject. Husserl writes that the life-world is the world "pregiven to us," and that to live, which means invariably to live in the life-world, "is to live-in-certainty-of-the-world" (Husserl, 1970, p. 142). The life-world is the ground of all the activities of the subject and the ground of subjectivity itself, from thought to praxis. Living, which invariably means living in the life-world, necessarily entails certainty within the subject that there is a life-world and that there are "things" in the life-world (Husserl, 1970, pp. 142-143). The certainties entailed by living in the life-world also preclude epoche: in this regard, it may be argued that the hinge propositions of doubting and questioning are not only elements of language games, but are also the certainties entailed by living in the life-world.

While explicating the Cartesian epoche, Husserl does mention the life-world in relation to the task of the Cartesian epoche. Husserl writes that the Cartesian epoche places into question the existence of everything, including "even the validity of the pre-[scientific] and extra-scientific *life-world, i.e. the world of sense-experience* constantly pregiven as taken for granted unquestioningly and all the life of thought which is nourished by it—the unscientific and finally even the scientific" (1970, p. 76; my emphasis). Since Husserl considers the existence of the ego to be immediate and apodictic knowledge but considers the life-world to be something whose existence can be doubted, the implication is that the certainties of the life-world, including the living-in-certainty-of-the-world of the life-world, are essentially *mediate* knowledge (mediate certainties), i.e. forms of mediation, and that life-world itself is essentially a system of mediation.

Husserl writes, "It is experience in the usual sense which is thus called into question, "sense" experience—and its correlate, the world itself, as that which has sense and being for us in and through this experience, just as it is constantly valid for us, with unquestioned certainty, as simply there, having such and such a content of particular real objects, and which is occasionally devaluated as doubtful or as invalid illusion only in individual details" (Husserl, 1970, p. 76). Furthermore, the life-world encompasses all the activities of subjectivity, from perception, thought, imagination, and emotion to action.

The life-world, therefore, encompasses all experience, including sense-experience, and the "world itself" which Husserl refers to is none other than the life-world, since both the life-world and the "world itself" are the world which "has sense and being for us in and through" experience, i.e. the world as it is experienced by the subject. Because subjectivity is a system of experiences, the life-world is subjectivity itself. The world itself is subjectivity itself. Subjectivity is essentially a system of mediation.

The unquestioned certainty of the life-world does not mean *unquestionable* certainty since Husserl does indeed question it and does argue that the life-world is "occasionally devaluated," presumably by experience in the life-world itself, "as doubtful or as invalid illusion," albeit only "in individual details" and not in its totality. The life-world, which has sense and being for the subject only through the experiences of the subject, is itself mediated by other experiences in the life-world.

The concept of the life-world is not the concept of a world external to subjectivity, but of "the world as experienced," therefore the life-world is the world dependent upon subjectivity, the subjective world. On the one hand, the life-world only exists insofar as the subject experiences it, and on the other hand, the life of the subject presupposes the life-world. The life-world, which consists of experiences, only has sense and being for the subject in and through the subject's experience of the life-world. There is no objective world, there is only an infinity of life-worlds, there is only an infinity of subjective worlds.

The life-world is essentially both a system of mediation and a system of experiences. The experiences of the life-world mediate and are mediated by other experiences. The life-world is a system of difference, the essential ontological difference of experience. It is within this totality of mediated experiences, experiences of mediation, this totality which is the life-world, that the fluxes of subjectivity flux.

The life-world, even considered as a totality, does not qualify as immediate knowledge because it is a totality only by being a totality of mediations. Here we encounter yet another problem with positing the existence of the ego: there is an ontological problem of how the unmediated presence of the ego could arise from the life-world, which is a system of mediation.

Although the existence of the life-world does not necessarily entail immediate certainties, it nonetheless entails "mediate certainties," and on this basis Husserl himself recognizes the shortcomings of the method of epoche: "We notice thereby that the first step which seemed to help at the beginning, that epoche through which we freed ourselves from all objective sciences as grounds of validity, by no means suffices. In carrying out this epoche, we obviously continue to stand on the ground of the world; it is now reduced to the life-world which is valid for us pre-scientifically" (1970, p. 147).

All subjective activity, including the activity of epoche, takes place within the life-world, and thus assumes the certainties, however mediate, doubtful, or even illusory, of the life-world—at the very least, the certainty of being-in-the-life-world ("to live is to live-in-certainty-of-the-world"). The method of epoche does not suffice because during the use of epoche the subject continues to inhabit the life-world and thus to assume the certainties of the life-world. In other words, epoche fails to suspend judgement regarding the existence or non-existence of entities because being in the life-world necessarily entails certainties, however mediate, dubious, or illusory, regarding the existence or non-existence of entities.

This shortcoming of the method of epoche brings into question whether it was valid to use the method of epoche to begin with. Husserl writes that the epoche does not suffice because the subject continues to be grounded in the life-world even as it employs epoche. This implies that the epoche was insufficient to begin with because the life-world was always already the ground of the epoche and this ground necessarily entailed mediate certainties. Just as Wittgenstein writes that doubt always presupposes certainties in the form of hinge propositions, so does epoche entail hinge propositions, at the very least the certainties necessitated by being in the life-world.

Husserl attempts to surmount the contradiction between the method of epoche and the necessary mediate certainties of the life-world by inventing a new form of epoche, which he calls the "transcendental epoche" (Husserl, 1970, pp. 148-152). Husserl asserts that via the transcendental epoche a "*total change* of the natural attitude" is possible such that subjects can cease living "as human beings within natural existence, constantly effecting the validity of the pre-given world," effectively constantly denying natural existence in the life-world (Husserl, 1970, p. 148). Husserl writes that the transcendental epoche allows the philosopher to evade the certainties entailed by the life-world: "An attitude is arrived at which is *above* the pregivenness of the validity of the world, *above* the infinite complex whereby, in concealment, the world's validities are always founded on other validities" (1970, p. 150). But this merely means the denial of mediation ("the world's validities are always founded on [and thus mediated by] other validities,") and thus the denial of subjectivity itself. The denial of the life-world is the denial of subjectivity itself because the life-world itself *is* subjectivity. The denial of the life-world is self-denial, and self-denial is the denial of the life-world. It is impossible for the subject to divorce itself from the life-world because the subject *is* the life-world and the life-world *is* the subject.

Subjectivity is essentially an infinitely complex and infinitely concealed system of mediation, originary mediation, the world's mediations (which are always "founded" on other mediations). Subjectivity is itself essentially the infinity of the life-world, it is infinity itself, originary infinity, the infinite system of difference which is always already a differential system of infinity. Subjectivity is essentially originary complexity, complexity itself.

Contrary to Husserl's claims, it is only through the radical affirmation of mediation, the affirmation of originary mediation, that the subject can in actuality cease being human. But to cease being human does not mean to cease being in the life-world. To cease being human means to affirm the subjectivity of the subject and therefore it means to affirm the life-world. To cease being human is to become the overman, to produce the overman. The production of the overman is not the "transcending" of the life-world. On the contrary, the production of the overman is the metamorphosis of the life-world, the production of a new life-world, the life-world of the overman.

It must be remembered that insofar as Husserl's analysis presupposes goals and means, that epoche, whether transcendental or not, remains non-functional, since epoche can only function in the absence of goals. However, there are additional problems with the concept of transcendental epoche. The means that Husserl gives for achieving his otherwise inexplicable "*total change* of the natural attitude" is merely a mental act, more specifically, an act of self-denial ostensibly willed by the mind: "here, situated *above* his own natural being and *above* the natural world, [the philosopher] *loses nothing of their being and their objective truths* and likewise nothing at all of the spiritual acquisitions of his world-life *or those of the whole historical communal life*; *he simply forbids himself*—as a philosopher, *in the uniqueness of his direction of interest*—to continue the whole natural performance of his world-life; that is, he forbids himself to ask questions which rest upon the ground of the world at hand" (1970, p. 152; my emphasis). An obvious indication that Husserl's discourse is firmly grounded in his life-world comes from his own admission that despite his transcendental epoche one retains one's "objective truths" and the "spiritual acquisitions" of one's "historical communal life." Moreover, as we have mentioned above, the transcendental epoche is posited by Husserl as a means to an end, and this is made abundantly clear by Husserl himself when he writes that the philosopher who employs transcendental epoche has a unique "direction of interest," a "direction of interest" being an apt description of a goal. Husserl asserts that the transcendental epoche is not an interpretation of the world, since an interpretation would necessarily be grounded in the life-world; Husserl asserts that he has freed himself from the very ground of the life-world by means of the transcendental epoche (Husserl, 1970, p. 152). However, that the philosopher does indeed have a goal, his unique direction of interest, means that he still harbours certainty (viz. of the goal) and thus he is still grounded in the life-world and not at all performing a genuine epoche according to Husserl's own standards. Despite himself, Husserl proves that his alleged "transcendental epoche" is indeed merely an interpretation of the world, another perspective among other perspectives.

Husserl provides no grounds for asserting how the philosopher can indeed free himself from the life-world merely by the mental act of self-denial. To the contrary, Husserl, in his description of the life-world, provides support that it is impossible, while alive, to escape the life-world, whether by the means described by Husserl or by some other means. Husserl himself writes that the life-world, "for us who wakingly live in it, *is always already there, existing in advance for us, the "ground" of all praxis whether theoretical or extratheoretical*," and that the life-world "is pregiven to us, the waking, always somehow practically interested subjects, not occasionally *but always and necessarily as the universal field of all actual and possible praxis*, as horizon" (Husserl, 1970, p. 142; my emphasis).

The life-world is *always already* pregiven for the subject, thus it is not a mode of being that the subject can possibly escape.

The life-world is originary, it is always already there at the origin. Just as the life-world is dependent upon the subject, the subject is dependent upon the life-world; insofar as the subject exists, the subject exists in the life-world (just as, conversely, the life-world exists only as the subjectivity of the subject). The life-world is the ground of all thought and praxis whatsoever. Whether the praxis of transcendental epoche is theoretical or extra-theoretical is irrelevant because either way transcendental epoche is a praxis, and as such its ground is ultimately in the life-world. The transcendental epoche is merely a mental act of self-deception and self-denial.

Furthermore, Husserl writes that the pregivenness of the life-world is not an occasional phenomenon, but that the life-world is always already and necessarily the "universal field of *all* actual and possible praxis." In other words, the life-world is originary, by which we mean that the life-world is always already pre-given, its pregivenness is always already there at the origin. As it regards the originariness of the life-world, it must also be remembered, as we have established above, that the life-world is a system of mediation and that the life-world is essentially cultural and historical, which means that the originariness, or pregivenness, of the life-world is always already the originariness of history, the originariness of historicity itself, the originariness of culture, the originariness of enculturation, and the originariness of social construction.

To explicate our use of Husserl's concept of the life-world, a use which is grounded in Husserl's own writings on the life-world, it is instructive to compare it with Wittgenstein's writings on certainty and forms of life, but in order to do so we must first briefly discuss Moore's writings on certainty. Moore's answer to radical skepticism is to, in a deceptively simple and self-deceptively simple manner, claim that one does indeed have immediate and certain knowledge: as examples, Moore advances seemingly everyday proclamations such as "I know that here is a hand," and "I know the earth has existed long before my birth." The first presupposition we might question here is the existence of the ego: "What is this "I" you speak of, Moore?" Moore and Descartes both consider radical skepticism to be problematic, and both arrive at the conclusion that there is immediate knowledge, although the respective essences of their "immediate knowledge" are at least superficially different—ultimately, both Moore and Descartes ground their discourse in the existence of the ego. Moore's "immediate certainties" are the "immediate certainties" of the ego, which ultimately means that they are the "immediate certainty" of the existence of the ego itself. (All "immediate certainties" and all "mediate certainties" are merely social constructs).

Wittgenstein takes a different approach to the problem of radical skepticism. Wittgenstein neither tries to argue that radical skepticism may be sound, nor does he try to dispel radical skepticism by means of an appeal to an immediate certainty. Instead of laying a claim to immediate certainty, Wittgenstein argues that both doubt and certainty are only applicable in certain contexts, viz. in the operations of certain language games, i.e. that doubt and certainty are themselves merely language games, and consequently that both radical skepticism and the appeal to immediate certainty are therefore misguided.

Wittgenstein introduces Moore's immediate certainty about having a hand by writing, "If you do know that *here is a hand*, we'll grant you all the rest" (1969, 1). That is to say, if it is indeed immediately certain that "here is a hand," then it is also certain that there is immediate certainty. However, a statement such as "here is a hand," according to Wittgenstein, cannot be proved (1969, 1). Wittgenstein does not mean that it cannot be derived from other propositions, since like all propositions it may be (1969, 1). Rather, the proposition "here is a hand" is in itself no more immediately certain than any other proposition (1969, 1). All propositions are mediate, mediated and mediating, propositions: all propositions are forms of mediation.

Wittgenstein argues that statements such as "I know I have a hand," like other seemingly common-sense propositions which may serve as Moorean immediate certainties, are unclear propositions, and that one may comprehend their lack of clarity by considering their negations (1969, 4). For example, "I do not know if I have hands" is an unclear proposition. Just as Wittgenstein argues that doubt is a language game, so does he argue that certainty too is a language game. Just as radical skepticism is merely a language game which ultimately proves nothing (and rests upon implicit assumptions, hinge propositions), so too are alleged "immediate certainties" merely language games which ultimately prove nothing.

To clarify, by rejecting immediate certainties, Wittgenstein rejects the epistemological claim of immediate certainties (namely, that they constitute immediate and apodictic knowledge), and he does not directly engage with the ontological content of alleged immediate certainties. Wittgenstein rejects radical skepticism (since it always has implicit assumptions) and propositions such as "I do not know if I have hands" (since they are unclear propositions), but *not* in favour of immediate certainties and especially *not* in favour of the ontological claims of immediate certainties. The ontological claims of immediate certainties are by implication rendered irrelevant and false because what formerly appeared as a question of ontology now appears as merely a question of the use of signs; there are no ontological problems as such because questions of ontology only arise due to the misunderstanding of language, i.e. due to the confusion of language with reality.

Wittgenstein's argument is that knowledge, whether one means the everyday knowledge required for everyday life in a given culture, scientific knowledge, or specialized philosophical "knowledge," consists of language games, and that the concept of immediate certainty is entirely superfluous and practically useless. Situations could be imagined in which "immediate certainties" such as "here is a hand" are stated, but such situations would be anomalous and perhaps even be symptomatic of mental disturbance. It is only in the specialized context of "doing philosophy" that "immediate certainties" are uttered, but they have no practical value. For example, Husserl himself, as quoted above, prescribes the radical skeptical doubt of the Cartesian epoche as a necessary task for all philosophers in order to arrive at immediate knowledge (which for Husserl meant specifically the "immediate certainty" of the existence of the ego, just as it did for Descartes), but the concept of the ego has no practical value in terms of a pragmatic psychology, a psychology useful for having power over one's self and others.

Wittgenstein himself explicitly rejects the concept of immediate certainties: "Giving grounds, however, justifying the evidence, comes to an end;—but the end is not certain propositions' striking us *immediately as true*, i.e. it is not a kind of *seeing* on our part; it is our *acting*, which lies at the bottom of the language-game" (1969, 204; my emphasis). Since language-games are neither immediate certainties nor founded upon immediate certainties, they are by implication systems of mediation. The ground of language-games is action, and all action is mediation, just as all mediation is action. The originariness of action is the originariness of mediation. Writing is, as Derrida defines it, essentially a system of mediation and difference. Language-games are writing-games because they *are* writing, they are always already writing and always already writing-games. Language-games are ultimately grounded in forms of action, what Wittgenstein describes as "forms of life," systems of actions, always already encultured systems of actions, sociocultural modes of becoming-in-the-world which are also themselves systems of mediation. The life-world is essentially writing and forms of life are forms of writing. The mode of living in the life-world is essentially writing: a form of life, a form of writing. To live is to write: to live is to write with life itself, to write with writing itself.

On the essential enculturation and historicity of the life-world, Husserl writes, "We stand within the horizon of [a] human civilization, the one in which we ourselves now live...To the one [given] human civilization there corresponds essentially the one cultural world as the surrounding life-world with its [particular] manner of being [form of life]; this world [this life-world], for every historical period and civilization, has its particular features and is precisely the tradition. We stand, then, within the historical horizon in which everything is historical, even though we may know very little about it in a definite way...Here we are led back to the primal materials of the first formation of meaning, the primal premises, so to speak, which lie in the prescientific cultural world. Of course, this cultural world has in turn its own questions of origin which at first remain unasked." (Husserl, 1970, p. 369)

In brief, the concept of the life-world suggests a necessity for psychology and a theory of the unconscious. History and culture, which consist of signs, are implicit in the life-world, which means that each life-world is also an implicit code of signs. Because we know little about the life-world in a "definite way," these implicit signs are only ever partially explicit in consciousness, i.e. they are of necessity largely unconscious; the unconscious is the code of signs of the life-world, the signs of culture and the signs of history. The life-world is encultured, it *is* culture, in all its implicit historicity. Therefore, we are constantly, vitally *unconscious* of this horizon—the horizon of culture, the horizon of history, the horizon of historicity itself—and specifically as a temporal-historical horizon implied in our given "present" horizon.

The life-world is a system of experiences, therefore experience is always already encultured, and culture exists only via the mediation of experiences. All experience is dependent upon culture and ultimately *is* culture. We know very little about our own enculturation because culture is largely unconscious; the origin of culture is the unconscious, an unconscious which is always already encultured. Each civilization, each culture, has its own life-world, its own unconscious system of experiences, its own unconscious system of signs. (Experience = mediation = sign). The unconscious is a code of signs, and this code of signs is equivalent to culture: culture and the unconscious are equivalent to each other. Culture is a system of meanings, therefore culture is a system of uses of signs. Culture consists of language-games. The history of culture is the history of language-games.

Even though forms of life are similar to life-worlds in that both are systems of mediation, we have been speaking as if there were a difference between the two: a form of life consists of practices, whereas the life-world consists of experiences, the life-world is the ground of forms of life, a form of life is a practice (or system of practices) in the life-world. However, this distinction, although it may retain some value as a way of speaking, ultimately does not suffice. By "practices" we have ostensibly meant "external practices," practices in the "external" world, whereas the life-world refers to the "internal" or "inner" world of experience; however, "external world" is merely a metaphor since there is no such thing strictly speaking, and the "external world" is dependent upon subjective experience, i.e. it is part of the "inner world" of subjectivity. (Experience = subjectivity = action = praxis).

The unconscious is a system of signs and its semiotics are essentially Wittgensteinian: "meaning is use," even and especially in the unconscious. Since the unconscious is a system of signs, it is also an unconscious system of uses of signs, an unconscious system of "inner" practices, unconscious practices, practices of the unconscious, the unconscious practices of the inner world, of subjectivity. The unconscious, a code of signs, is always already a form of life: the unconscious *is* a form of life. A life-world *is* a form of life, a form of life *is* a life-world. Experience is praxis, praxis is experience. Thought *is* praxis. A life-world ultimately refers to the praxis of the unconscious, the unconscious code of signs which is always already an unconscious system of uses of signs, unconscious writing-games, the writing-games of the unconscious. The unconscious is a form of writing, a writing-game.

Furthermore, it is important to note that although discourse is essential to culture, culture is not essentially discourse. Culture, the cultural world, the symbolic universe of culture, is primarily, essentially, and originarily pre-scientific, whereas scientific discourse is itself a product of the pre-scientific cultural world. Culture is primarily, essentially, and originarily transcursive,

transcursive writing. Transcursive writing is the writing of difference, whereas discursive writing is the writing of identity. The ground of discourse is transcursive writing because identities are always fabricated by systems of difference. Identities are always fictions because the hyle of identicalities is always transcursive writing. Transcursive writing soars, groans, swings, sings, solos, intones, and scampers. Discourse is the writing of uniformity, continuity, linearity, and repetition. Discourse is the product of the unconscious transcursive writing of culture, the transcursive code of signs of the unconscious. The transcursive code of signs of the unconscious is "the primal materials of the first formation of meaning, the primal premises," of a culture. To paraphrase Nietzsche, science never creates values, but science is always already in the service of a system of values which is itself pre-scientific; and moreover, Western science is the product of the ascetic ideals of Christianity and Platonism (Christianity is essentially a vulgarized Platonism), which can be inferred from the fact that they both rest upon the same foundation, they both have the same infrastructure, "the belief that truth is inestimable and cannot be criticized," i.e. the logocentric faith in unmediated presence (GM, III 25). The system of values of a culture is an infrastructural system of signs, or code of signs, located in the unconscious.

Wittgenstein writes that the originary form of life of mediate knowledge is biological: certainty is "something that lies beyond being justified or unjustified" because certainty is "something animal" (1969, 359). However, we think that mediate knowledge is more generally something organic and biological rather than merely something animal; we think that all life thinks, that life is essentially subjectivity, that all life fabricates mediate knowledge, that the mental construction of mediate knowledge is essential to life. Epistemology is ultimately a question for psychology. A life-world is both cultural and biological: physiology is always already encultured and culture is always already physiological. Since a form of life is a set of practices, the originary form of life, as something biological, is the practice of being an organism, which is equivalent to the life-world of being an organism, the life-world of organismality, biologicality; however, the originary form of life is also originarily encultured, i.e. the biological is always already cultural, the biological is always already a biosemiotic system, i.e. the biological is always already psychological, always already an unconscious transcursive system of signs.

The biological necessity of mediate knowledge is also the biological necessity of mediation. The mental construction of identicalities (which does not necessarily imply the mental construction of an "unmediated presence"), i.e. discursive writing, as well as transcursive writing, is essential to life. Life essentially writes, life essentially writes both discourse and transcourse. In other words, mediation and difference are both the ground of the life of the organism (in terms of both form of life and the life-world) and a biological necessity of all life (because to live is to write).

Because the only actual form of certainty is mediate certainty, certainty is essentially mediation, which also means that certainty is essentially deception, that deception is the essence of certainty. Deception is essentially mediation and mediation is essentially deception. The traditional concept of truth refers to an indubitable truth, an immediate certainty, i.e. an unmediated presence, that which is present to itself without mediation; however, there is no such thing in reality. Reality is mediation, and mediation differs and defers onto other mediations; because there is only mediation, there is only différance, reality *is* différance, ontological différance, différance-in-itself. *Différance*, or the *originary trace*, is "the essential or constitutive process by which every sign is related to every other" in a context (Bradley, 2008, p. 69), "the movement by which any language, or any code, any system of reference in general, becomes "historically" constituted as a fabric of differences" (Derrida, SP, p. 141). Différance is essentially both difference and mediation. Therefore, the very ground of "truth," unmediated presence, is evidently merely mental construction, merely fiction. There is no truth. Moreover, the essential mediation of a sign averts a sign from itself, a sign is always already itself and not itself, itself and an other, therefore a sign is always already and essentially a metaphor. I.e. there are only metaphors, only fictions.

The equivalence of deception and mediation is also suggested by the etymology of "deception": from the Latin "decipio" [I catch, ensnare, entrap, deceive, mislead, beguile, elude, cheat], in turn from the Latin "de [of, or from] + capio [I capture, seize, take; I take on; I take in, understand]." *De capio*, of or from capturing, seizing, taking, taking on, taking in, understanding: a trace of this etymology is suggested by *decipio*, which can mean either catching (taking, taking in, understanding) or mis-leading, beguiling, eluding, cheating. All understanding, all interpretation, is mediation, which means that it is also deception, it is both a form of capturing and seizing (viz.

appropriating signs-qualia) and mis-leading and eluding (i.e. mediation, being averted from itself, differing and deferring infinitely).

Since forms of life and the life-world are both systems of mediation, they are systems of deception, and the biological necessity of mediation is also the biological necessity of deception. Deception is both a biological necessity of all life and the ground of the life of the organism. The originariness of deception merely means that writing is originary and that life *is* writing. Deception, fiction, falsehood, fabrication are originary. Art is originary. "To imagine a language is to imagine a form of life" because life is always already writing. To imagine a form of life is to imagine a language. Life *is* art, art *is* life: life and art are one (life = art). If it appears that we say that "reality is language," it is merely as a metaphor, it is never in the sense that reality consists of words, but it is only in the sense that reality is *writing*, which means precisely that reality is a system of mediation and difference, that reality is a system of signs, that words are empty and never reality, that metaphor is originary, that reality is metaphor, that reality itself is metaphor itself: which means precisely that there is no truth, that there never was any truth, that there never can be any truth, that all truth is deception because all life is deception.

<u>II. Chaos and Its Power</u>

[In the original Ancient Greek sense of the word, in the way that Hesiod meant it, *Chaos* is "void," "chasm," "abyss," "nothingness," "emptiness." But it also has another meaning in Ancient Greek, given to it much later by the philosopher Anaxagoras, *Chaos* as "disorder." That Chaos has two possible meanings is itself an example of Chaos.]

"I say unto thee: one must still have Chaos in oneself to be able to give birth to a dancing star. I say unto thee: thou still havest Chaos in thyselves."
—Nietzsche, *Thus Spoke Zarathustra*, I, 5

"Tell me these things, Olympian Muses, tell
From the beginning, which first *came to be*?
Chaos was first of all..."
—Hesiod, *Theogony*, ln. 114-116, trans. by Wender, 1973, my emphasis

"When the engineer joins spokes together in a wheel,
He also makes the centre hole
In which the axle goes,
The empty hole
That makes the wagon move.

When the sculptor shapes clay into a pot,
He also shapes the emptiness inside
That holds whatever we want.

When the architect designs a house,
He also designs empty spaces for windows and doors,
And the empty space in between walls and ceilings,
That make the house liveable.

Wherever there is existence, there is emptiness,
It is emptiness which is efficient,
Emptiness is efficiency itself,
Efficiency is emptiness itself."
—Lao Tzu, *Tao Te Ching*, 11, my translation

"Chaos is the will to power, the will to power is Chaos."
—Dr. Vogelfrei

1.

Foucault writes, "Order is, at one and the same time, that which is given in things as their inner law, the hidden network that determines the way they confront one another, and also that which has no existence except in the grid created by a glance, an examination, a language; and it is only in the blank spaces of this grid that order manifests itself in depth as though already there, waiting in silence for the moment of its expression" (Foucault, OT, p. xx).

Foucault envisions two forms of order: particular orders, which he also calls epistemes (these are quasi-a-prioris inculcated by particular cultures), and the universal of order, the true a-priori idea of order. Whereas particular orders are evident in particular epistemes, which can be delineated by a collection of texts from a given time and place in a given culture, the universal of order, like all universals, is an abstraction, an intangible metaphysical entity. There is a sheer difference between one particular order and another, and it is by way of forgetting and ignoring these differences that the universal of order can be constructed.

The universal of order is a metaphysical entity which can only be constructed *after* the observation of particular orders. On the other hand, it is only by way of a "pure reason," whose very foundations are questionable, that one can posit a universal of order which is the cause or origin of all particular orders. It is only by way of "pure reason," which is without foundation, that one can insert the universal of order into the "beginning" of a mental construct of a causal chain, such that it appears as if all particular orders resulted from this universal.

Foucault's error is symptomatic of the deeply rooted Platonism at the heart of Western culture, and whose vestiges survive in all the diverse epistemes of the West. Foucault himself writes that order has existence only through particulars: "[order] has no existence except in the grid created by a glance, an examination, a language." But if this is the case, then it would be impossible for order to simultaneously be a universal which functions as the "inner law, the hidden network that determines the way [particular orders] confront one another," because there is no universal of order which exists apart from particular orders and therefore there is no universal of order with an independent existence which would be able to function as the inner law of diverse particular orders.

Particular orders each function according to their own internal logic. There is a sheer difference among these internal logics which excludes the possibility of their transcendental unity. If identical cases, cases of identity, are essential to each episteme, it is nonetheless the case that the concept of identity itself, the universal idea of identity, can only be derived as an abstraction from particular cases of identity, particular identicalities which are themselves mental constructions to begin with.

In order to posit a universal "inner law" of order, the irreducible differences among epistemes would need to be ignored and a new metaphysical entity would need to be constructed. The universal of order described by Foucault is just such a mental construction, and it is an a-posteriori construction, whether or not he was conscious of this fact.

Let us consider Foucault, like all animals, as possessing his own episteme. In Foucault's episteme, all particular orders, all epistemes, exist as "things" which can be organized in diverse ways, and alongside these particular orders, as another thing alongside other things, there is the universal of order. The universal of order is merely a "thing" alongside the other "things" upon the table knowledge, the space of knowledge, and it can be arranged, re-arranged, and de-ranged in infinite possible combinations with other "things."

In the blank spaces of a "grid of knowledge," an episteme, there lies in wait *nothingness*, as if it were a positive substance. In the blank spaces of knowledge, there is an encroaching void, with all its sheer terror to the order-loving mind, an encroaching void which reveals itself as the totality of the space of knowledge itself: the blank spaces of a grid of knowledge reveals that the space of knowledge is itself a blank space in all its parts and in totality, that the ground of all knowledge is this empty space, this nothingness, which means that all knowledge is empty, that all knowledge is nothingness: the space of knowledge is nothingness, the nothingness which is *Chaos*. Chaos is the originary atopia, the essential and originary non-space of space itself, and the originary aphasia, the essential and originary non-name of names themselves: the space of nothingness, the originary namelessness, the unnameable ultimate reality. In the blank spaces of a grid of knowledge, indeed even in the blank spaces of the space of culture more generally, there lies in wait a primordial, originary, and ultimate Chaos which threatens to undo the comfort of order and culture and unravel the essential emptiness of all possible orders and all possible cultures. Chaos is the productive and positive unconscious of all knowledge and all culture.

2.

Nietzsche describes the Anaxagorian Chaos as a pell-mell mixture of objects, a pell-mell of surreal juxtapositions of objects: "a mixture which [Anaxagoras] imagined as a total pell-mell of even the tiniest particles, the result of mixing, as though with mortar and pestle, all the elemental substances until they were like dust motes and could be stirred about as in a mixing-cup" (Nietzsche, PTG, p. 102). Ovid describes just such an Anaxagorian Chaos as his original Chaos: a raw mass, a "lifeless bulk, with warring seeds/ of ill-joined elements compressed together," wherein "nothing kept its form,/ all objects were at odds, since in one mass/ cold essence fought with hot, and moist with dry,/ and hard with soft and light with things of weight" (trans. by Melville, 1986, p. 1).

Anaxagorian Chaos may also serve as an apt metaphor for the space of the mind: the space of the mind is a raw mass wherein all "objects" coexist simultaneously in a pell-mell confusion and disorder, a mixture of surreal juxtapositions wherein opposites coexist in the same mixture whose ground is formlessness: all "objects" coexist simultaneously in a pell-mell confusion upon the table of knowledge in a surreal juxtaposition of everything all at once. But the space of knowledge is "lifeless" because knowledge is the domain of identity, whereas life is the domain of difference, the space of difference itself. However, ultimately, the space of the mind is the space of nothingness because all the "objects" contained within it are mere mental constructs and the table of knowledge itself, the space of knowledge itself, is a mental construct, hence the emptiness of all Beings and the emptiness of all knowledge.

3.

Foucault writes, "The fundamental codes of a culture—those governing its language, its schemes of perception, its exchanges, its techniques, its values, the hierarchy of its practices—establish for every man, from the very first, the empirical orders with which he will be dealing and within which he will be at home. At the other extremity of thought, there are the scientific theories or the philosophical interpretations which explain why order exists in general, what universal law it obeys, what principle can account for it, and why this particular order has been established and not some other. But between these two regions, so distant from one another, lies a domain which, even though its role is mainly an intermediary one, is nonetheless fundamental: it is more confused, more obscure, and probably less easy to analyse. It is here that a culture, imperceptibly deviating from the empirical orders prescribed for it by its primary codes, instituting an initial separation from them, causes them to lose their original transparency, relinquishes its immediate and invisible powers, frees itself sufficiently to discover that these orders are perhaps not the only possible ones or the best ones; this culture then finds itself faced with the stark fact that there exists, below the level of its spontaneous orders, things that are in themselves capable of being ordered, that belong to a certain unspoken order; the fact, in short, that order *exists*. As though emancipating itself to some extent from its linguistic, perceptual, and practical grids, the culture superimposed on them another kind of grid which neutralized them, which by this superimposition both revealed and excluded them at the same time, so that the culture, by this very process, came face to face with order in its primary state. It is on the basis of this newly perceived order that the codes of language, perception, and practice are criticized and rendered partially invalid. It is on the basis of this order, taken as a firm foundation, that general theories as to the ordering of things, and the interpretation that such an ordering involves, will be constructed." (Foucault, OT, pp. xx-xi).

Foucault claims that the universal of order is distinct from the scientific theories and philosophical interpretations "which explain why order exists in general [and] what universal law it obeys," i.e. that the universal of order is distinct from the discourse about order. Foucault argues that the universal of order lies in a region between the particular orders of a given culture and that culture's discourse about order. Foucault's own discourse, however, is *precisely* a philosophical interpretation "which explain[s] why order exists in general [and] what universal law it obeys," i.e. Foucault's very own discourse constitutes, for his culture, a major part of the discourse about order. Therefore, according to Foucault's own discourse, the universal of order is inaccessible to his own discourse, because the universal of order lies in a region into which his discourse can never enter.

The universal of order functions in Foucault's discourse as what Derrida calls an "ex-centric centre." An ex-centric centre a contradictorily coherent concept, a concept which is perceived as being coherent despite in actuality being contradictory, which orients and supports a structure and is simultaneously absent from that structure (Derrida, WD, p. 278). All a-priori ideas, in the strict sense (as in Plato and Kant), function as ex-centric centres: they are both at the centre of a psychological structure because they determine, support and orient that structure, and they are simultaneously absent from that psychological structure because they exist prior to it. This raises the problem, among other problems, of their origin: because a-priori ideas are by definition prior to all experience, their origin remains inexplicable since no possible experience can exist prior to an a-priori idea. By contrast, there is no such contradiction with the concept of a "quasi-a-priori," or as Derrida calls it, a "quasi-transcendental," an "idea" which exists prior to a given set of experiences but which itself has its origin in other experiences, because a quasi-transcendental is indeed part of the structure it orients and supports (e.g an episteme is a quasi-transcendental, the values of a given culture are also quasi-transcendental).

Derrida himself recognizes that the concept of the origin and the concept of the transcendental (the transcendental in the strict sense) are both forms of the ex-centric centre (WD, pp. 279-280). Derrida argues that the ex-centric centre is a transcendental signified, an unmediated presence: "the centre receives different forms or names" in the history of Western culture, but it is nonetheless essentially "the determination of Being as *presence* in all senses of this word" (WD, p. 279). The concept of the transcendental, of a-priori ideas, is essentially the concept of unmediated presence: an a-priori idea is present to itself without mediation (if it were mediated, it would not be truly a-priori, since there would be something prior to it). However, because there is no unmediated presence in reality, there are no a-priori ideas in reality.

Because there is only mediation in reality, the ground of knowledge is mediation and deception, the ground of knowledge is the emptiness of all knowledge, or more simply put, the ground of knowledge is emptiness: the total absence of presence, a positive absence, the "presence" of absence, the nothingness of mediation and difference, the epistemological nothingness whose ground is ontological becoming, flux, mediation, and difference: Chaos. Chaos is both being and non-being: Chaos is neither being nor non-being, nor both, nor neither. Chaos is the originary paradox, paradox itself. Chaos is simultaneously the negative difference of negative becoming, the negative difference of positive becoming, the positive difference of positive becoming, the negative difference of positive becoming, the negative mediation of negative nothingness, the negative mediation of positive nothingness, the positive mediation of positive nothingness, and the negative mediation of positive nothingness. Chaos is negative space. The point is that Chaos is a positive and productive multiplicity of forces. Emptiness is something which is *used*, which means that it is a system of mediation and difference; in fact, it does not matter whether we say "nothingness" or "existence" as long as we are affirming mediation and difference because the ultimate nature of reality is mediation and difference. In any case, the ultimate nature of reality is transcursive writing.

In Foucault's discourse, the universal of order fulfils the function of an ex-centric centre by being the basis and origin of all possible orders and, simultaneously, existing in a region outside of all particular orders and even outside discourse about order. Although this arrangement of "things" upon the table of knowledge (the "things" are particular orders, the universal of order, and discourse about order) is coherent from the perspective of Foucault, it is nonetheless contradictory since these three "things" are apparently independent of each other, lying in different regions, such that the universal of order is located in an altogether separate, distinct, and independent region from particular orders and yet somehow serving as their basis, their infrastructure and structural centre. Yet, at the same time, as Foucault writes in an earlier passage, the universal of order has no existence apart from a particular order (p. xx). This creates a contradiction characteristic of an ex-centric centre: now not only is the universal of order existent in a region distinct from particular orders, but the universal of order is also inseparable from particular orders, thus making it impossible for the universal of order to be existent in a region beyond particular orders since the universal of order is by implication inextricably linked with particular orders.

This irreconcilable internal contradiction in Foucault's text suggests that the universal of order is not an a-priori idea of the mind, as Foucault claims, but in actuality merely an abstraction, a mental construct among other mental constructs; and here more specifically, Foucault's mental construct, heavily informed by Kant, of a universal of order which serves as an a-priori idea. To be more precise, it is not only Foucault's mental construct, but the mental construct of a Western discourse of which Foucault is only a symptom; a Western discourse which is in turn itself a symptom of a disease of the unconscious.

Moreover, a given culture's particular order and its discourse about order inhabit the same region. They are inseparable, not altogether distinct, and inextricably linked, i.e. they both together form the particular order. The discourse about order is itself ordered, i.e. discourse involves an arrangement of things and therefore discourse about order is always already also a particular order, a particular arrangement of things. This is all the more apparent given the fact that one of the primary functions of the discourse about order is to explain "why this particular order has been established and not some other." By explaining why the particular order of its culture is the established order, the discourse about order links itself inextricably to that particular order, at least if it is the case that the discourse about order justifies and rationalizes that particular order. If the discourse about order is a critique of a particular order, then that means merely that the discourse about order is distinct from that particular order but belongs to an other particular order with which it is inextricably linked (an other particular order which, however, depending on the circumstances, may or may not have grown out of the critiqued particular order). A radical critique of order, not only of a particular order but of order itself, is an overcoding and an overcoming of knowledge and culture, the code of signs that is knowledge and culture, it is a new use of old signs, it is a new power dominating the old signs: it is an affirmation of Chaos, the production of the overman, the production of a new knowledge and a new culture (the knowledge of the overman, the culture of the overman), the production of the episteme of the overman, a perspectivist episteme, the episteme of perspectivism.

In any case, a discourse about order is inextricably linked with a particular order, and therefore these two interdependent constructions are located in the same mental region. Therefore, it cannot be said that there is a region between these two, since they are not two separate regions but are two interdependent constructions within one and the same region.

The universal of order also functions, in Foucault's episteme, as a transcendental signified because Foucault posits the universal of order as an entity with an unmediated presence. Culture, or what amounts to the same thing, the "individual" within a culture, can come "face to face with order in its primary state," i.e. there is a "pure experience of order" (Foucault, OT, p. xxi), an unmediated and direct experience of order in which order has pure and immediate being, i.e. presence. The presence of order itself guarantees that all things have an inner law (Foucault, OT, p. xx), that particular orders are supported, and that Foucault's own discourse has a "firm foundation" (ibid, p. xxi). Foucault's universal of order serves the function of anchoring all meaning in itself, which is exactly the function of what Derrida describes as the transcendental signified. In Foucault's discourse, the ultimate significance of all things, orders and discourse, including Foucault's own, is the a-priori idea of order itself. In other words, Foucault's entire project remains a metaphysical project because it depends upon his concept of the universal of order, which is an unmediated presence.

Foucault himself writes that the universal of order has no existence except in liaison with particular orders, which would mean that the universal of order can only be known by and through mediation. Foucault also acknowledges the necessity of mediation, and thus by implication the impossibility of the unmediated presence of an a-priori idea of order, when he writes that for culture to come face to face with the universal idea of order, it must first construct a special kind of episteme (grid of knowledge): "As though emancipating itself *to some extent* from its linguistic, perceptual, and practical grids [codes of signs], the culture *superimposed on them another kind of grid [episteme]* which neutralized them, *which by this superimposition both revealed and excluded them at the same time*, so that culture, by its very process, *came face to face with order in its primary state*" (Foucault, OT, p. xxi; my emphasis).

A special kind of episteme, superimposed upon a "conventional" kind of episteme "neutralizes" the "conventional" episteme, and this process according to Foucault, is what allows the unmediated experience of the allegedly a-priori idea of order, "order in its primary state." Foucault offers no explanation of how this neutralization is possible, it simply inexplicably occurs, and in this his transcendental method resembles the transcendental epoche of Husserl: this transcendental act is in actuality a self-deception and a self-denial, a mental act of self-denial, a denial of the essential mediation of the self. As long as the belief in the transcendental, in a-priori ideas (a-priori in the strict sense, prior to all possible experience), survives, the Western episteme (whose roots and foundations are in Plato) survives, albeit via diverse disguises, diverse masks. It is only by affirming mediation and originary mediation that the Western episteme can be neutralized because the concept of originary mediation has its roots and foundations in a philosophy of becoming (viz. the philosophies of Friedrich Nietzsche and Heraclitus, who are themselves merely symptoms of particular unconscious psychic forces), a Dionysian philosophy, which is fundamentally antithetical to the roots and foundations of the Western episteme (viz. Plato); these two plants, the Platonic and the Dionysian, are deadly enemies engaged in combat, one must kill the other.

Foucault himself also writes that the special, transcendental episteme of his is emancipated "*only to some extent*" from the "conventional" episteme, which is tantamount to arguing that the special episteme is *not* emancipated from the conventional episteme. Since the special episteme is "only to some extent" emancipated from the conventional episteme, the implication is that the special episteme is largely unemancipated from the conventional episteme, i.e. that it is largely inextricable from and thus identical with the conventional episteme. The "special" episteme is merely an extension of the conventional episteme, and is therefore not really "special" at all, but an extension and outgrowth of the conventional episteme.

Furthermore, according to Foucault himself, it is only through the mediation of the "special" episteme that culture experiences the a-priori idea of order. More precisely, it is only through the mediation of the "special" episteme that the conventional episteme is "both revealed and excluded at the same time." Therefore, it is only via mediation that culture allegedly "comes face to face with order in its primary state," the a-priori idea of order. The a-priori idea of order is not an actual unmediated presence, for there is no such thing in actuality, but the mental construct of an which means that difference is not only the total absence of all possible origins, but also that difference itself has no origin: difference-in-itself is infinite and eternal. That there are no a-priori ideas means that there is only experience, that experience is originary, that experience is infinite and eternal difference-in-itself. Difference-in-itself *is* experience, experience *is* difference-in-itself.

Originary difference-in-itself is originary Chaos. The blank spaces of an episteme are spaces of difference-in-itself, and the space of knowledge itself is a blank space, a space of difference-in-itself. Originary difference is the mediation of difference-in-itself by difference-in-itself, it is mediation and différance, différance-in-itself: différance-in-itself is originary deception, that which is averted from itself in infinite mediations, the infinity of mediation itself, mediation-in-itself. Originary différance is the total absence of presence, the total absence of presence which *is* nothingness, originary nothingness (nothingness is always already there at the origin, especially because the origin itself is always already absent, non-existent), the infinite mediation of infinite nothingness, i.e. originary mediation *is* originary Chaos, the infinity of Chaos, the infinite which is always already Chaos. The originary surplus of mediation is equivalent to the originary surplus of nothingness, the infinity of nothingness; there is an originary surplus of nothingness because nothingness is the total absence of presence, an "absence" which is equivalent to the originary surplus of difference-in-itself and mediation. That nothingness is originary merely means that all language is fiction. The originary surplus of différance is equivalent to the originary surplus of Chaos. Nothingness, or Chaos, is the positivity of, the positive mediation of, originary difference.

6.

In contrast to his own description of the space of knowledge, Foucault describes a different kind of space when discussing the works of Borges, a *heteroclite* space, a *heterotopia*, which for us serves as a much more accurate and precise description of the space of knowledge itself: "...there is a worse kind of disorder than that of the *incongruous*, the linking together of the inappropriate; I mean the disorder in which fragments of a large number of possible orders glitter separately in the dimension, without law or geometry, of the *heteroclite* [the perspective of difference]; and that word should be

55

taken in its most literal, etymological sense: in such a state, things are 'laid,' 'placed,' 'arranged' in sites so very different from one another that it is impossible to find a place of residence for them, to define a *common locus* beneath them all...*Heterotopias* [places of difference] are disturbing, probably because they secretly undermine language, because they make it impossible to name this *and* that, because they shatter or tangle common names, because they destroy 'syntax' in advance, and not only the syntax with which we construct sentences but also that less apparent syntax which causes words and things (next to and also opposite one another) to 'hold together'...heterotopias (such as those found so often in Borges) desiccate speech, stop words in their tracks, contest the very possibility of grammar at its source; they dissolve our myths and sterilize the lyricism of our sentences." (Foucault, OT, pp xvii-xviii).

An unmediated presence, e.g. Foucault's concept of a-priori order, if it existed, would be a "common locus," an ex-centric centre, beneath all possible orders, a transcendental organizational entity, a "universal syntax" or "universal grammar" by which all discourse would "hold together"; such a universal grammar would run "with the very grain of language" and permit, sanctify, rationalize, justify, legitimate, and produce discourse. It would give language "mass" and "density," whereby language would have an ultimate, inherent, and originary "sense" or "meaning," and thereby it would bestow certain comforts, especially the comfort of immediate certainty, upon those who believe in it, because it would provide the illusion of a fundamental, foundational, and omnipresent stability not only of language, but of all existence, to the entire universe of words *and* "things." But in reality, meaninglessness and nonsense are originary.

The limits imposed by Foucault's concept of a-priori order excludes the heteroclite from the space of knowledge in favour of the illusion that the space of knowledge is homoclite (the perspective of the same, of unity, identicality, and homogeneity), and thereby the space of knowledge as a totality appears as if it were a homotopia (a place of the same, of unity, identicality, and homogeneity). But sameness (or identicality) *presupposes* difference, a system of difference which constructs identical cases, since all identical cases are mental constructs. Through this artificially constructed limit, which we can always already see beyond, even if only by a little distance, the deconstructive danger of the heterotopia is "fended off," as if by a magic circle drawn with chalk, since the heterotopic is excluded from the space of knowledge by means of a limit that amounts to nothing more than fantasy, and the space of knowledge is thus confined to homotopia, the space of presence, which is itself also a space of fantasy. Through this manoeuvre, the entire domain of the knowledge is represented as the illusion of a fundamental and foundational stability, such that even if a particular order is rendered "partially invalid," the a-priori idea of order, order itself, which governs all particular orders, is given a "firm foundation."

There is indeed a real experience of order in its primary state, but because order in its primary state is a mental construction, this experience is the experience of the essential emptiness of order itself, the essential emptiness of knowledge itself, the experience of emptiness itself, the experience of Chaos. With the artificial limits of all transcendental signifieds dissolved, identical cases appear as they are, as merely mental constructs, and therefore the space of knowledge appears as it is, the space of difference and mediation, the scene of writing, the space of literature, a heterotopia. The space of knowledge and the space of the mind have no centre, therefore they are each a system of difference unto themselves; they never possess a "common locus" (all their "centres" are illusions, merely ex-centric centres, viz. they are mental constructs).

The heteroclite is the perspective of difference and mediation, the perspective of différance, and the heterotopia is the space of difference and mediation, the space of différance, the space of knowledge, which is always already the space of the mind. The heteroclite is the perspective of writing because it *is* originary writing, which means the originary absence of law or geometry, the absence which is the precondition of the construction of laws or geometries: the heteroclite is the geometry of différance, the geometry of originary difference, the geometry of difference-in-itself: the unwritten and unwritable law, the unwritten and unwritable writing of writing itself: it is the fragments of writing, of mind-writing, of the writing of the psyche, which are the fragments of possible orders which glitter separately in the dimension of the heteroclite, which is the dimension of writing, which is writing itself. In the dimension of the heteroclite, the signs of writing are arranged in irreducibly different scenes of writing without centre; structures of writings, arrangements of signs, of mediations, without centre, differ and defer endlessly onto other structures of writings ad infinitum, all written by writing itself.

A heterotopia is a space of difference and mediation, a space of writing, it is space itself, but space itself is always already writing unmediated presence, the fantasy of an unmediated presence constructed by a system of mediation, as is the case for all transcendental signifieds.

4.

Deleuze also believed in a-priori ideas and in doing so he denied difference despite himself: "Ideas contain all the varieties of differential relations and all the distributions of singular points coexisting in diverse orders 'perplicated' in one another. When the virtual content of an Idea is actualised, the varieties of relation are incarnated in distinct species while the singular points which correspond to the values of one variety are incarnated in the distinct parts characteristic of this or that species. The Idea of colour, for example, is like white light which perplicates in itself the genetic elements and relations of all the colours, but is actualised in the diverse colours with their respective spaces; or the Idea of sound, which is also like white noise. There is even a white society and a white language, the latter being that which contains in its virtuality all the phonemes and relations destined to be actualised in diverse languages and in the distinctive parts of a given language." (Deleuze, DR, p. 206).

In *Difference and Repetition*, Deleuze straightforwardly announces his philosophy to be a transcendental philosophy and he aligns himself fundamentally with Kant. Deleuze is fundamentally a Kantian philosopher, not a Nietzschean philosopher. This means that Deleuze suffers from the disease of Platonism; this is all the more evident in the early Deleuze's alignment with structuralism (cf. Deleuze's "How Do We Recognize Structuralism?"), and even the later Deleuze, with his theory of "machines" in *Anti-Oedipus* is altogether too reminiscent of structuralism, even despite himself, insofar as Deleuze and Guattari reduce desire into an objectality, the objectality of "machines" or "production" (cf. *Anti-Oedipus*, p. 311, my emphasis: "desire is shifted into the order of production...it is defined as the natural and sensuous *objective being*, at the same time as the Real is defined as *the objective being of desire*."; strictly speaking, desire is a completely and essentially *subjective* phenomenon, there is absolutely nothing "objective" about it whatsoever, therefore Deleuze and Guattari fundamentally and egregiously misunderstand desire); moreover, keeping in mind that structuralism is basically a pseudo-empirical Platonism (cf. Derrida's "Force and Signification"), Deleuze reproduces structuralist discourse with his theory of Ideas, to the extent that *Difference and Repetition* is essentially a structuralist philosophy, an epistemological and ontological grounding of structuralism.

However convoluted Deleuze makes his concept of perplication in order to appear as if he is affirming difference, what it amounts to in effect is a denial and negation of difference and an affirmation of identity and homogeneity; e.g. the multiplicity and difference of colours are denied by the Deleuzian Idea of colour, which is "like white light," meaning that the multiplicity and difference of colours are dissolved in the unity and the homogeneity of a kind of "white light." Ditto for the Deleuzian Ideas of sound, society and language, which are akin to white noise, "white society," and "white language" (no pun intended). Deleuzian Ideas are virtualities which are actualized: this is analogous to Plato's metaphysics, in which metaphysical ("virtual") Ideas are actualized in the physical world. Indeed, Deleuze even goes so far as to write that the virtual content of Ideas are "incarnated" in actualities.

Thus, Deleuze denies the actuality of difference by placing its origin in the virtuality of the same (in the perplication of "white" Ideas, which is a convoluted concept of unity and sameness). Deleuze concept of the virtual, like Plato's (and not only Plato's) concept of the metaphysical, is a fiction, a mere mental construct which evinces a misunderstanding, whether conscious or unconscious, of the fact that universals are mentally constructed only a-posteriori via the forgetting of difference-in-itself, the forgetting of experience.

5.

That difference is originary means precisely that there are no a-priori ideas. Difference, difference-in-itself, is merely quasi-transcendental. A-priori ideas are origins, origins of knowledge, origins which precede all possible experience. That difference-in-itself is always already there at the origin means that there is no "origin" as such, that "origin" is at best merely a metaphor and at worst a falsification, since the "origin" is always already different from itself, that the origin is the origin and not the origin, i.e. there is always already a difference-in-itself prior to all possible origins, itself. Writing—a system of difference and mediation, a system of différance—secretly undermines language itself, because the différance of writing makes it impossible to name this *and* that (a thing is always itself and an other thing, ad infinitum), because the différance of writing shatters and tangles common names, because différance, by functioning as the precondition of all syntax, destroys all syntax in advance (the essential emptiness, arbitrariness, historicity, and plasticity of all syntax), "and not only the syntax with which we construct sentences but also that less apparent syntax which causes words and things (next to and also opposite one another) to 'hold together'" (since there is an irreducible difference and infinite mediation between words and things, and also since "things" are themselves mental constructions, products of mind-writing, products of the différance of mind-writing). Writing desiccates speech (because speech is a form of writing, as Derrida discovers in *Of Grammatology*), stops words in their tracks (because originary writing is prior to and beyond all possible words), contests the very possibility of grammar at its source (there is no universal grammar because the mediation of writing is originary). Writing dissolves our myths and sterilizes the lyricism of our sentences.

The genesis of writing, the genesis of genesis, genesis itself, is Chaos, which is the total absence of genesis. Chaos is the scene of writing, the space of literature, the origin of writing, but Chaos is writing itself, originary writing itself. Chaos is the originary heteroclite, the originary heterotopia of writing, of originary writing. Chaos is the originary perspective, the multiplicity and infinity of perspectives, the essential différance-in-itself of perspective itself. Chaos is originary emptiness, the originary emptiness of all laws and of all transgression (law and transgression are both empty fictions, fictions of language). Chaos is the originary dimension, the dimension of writing, in which infinite fragments of infinite systems of writing glitter darkly bright in their essential différance.

Chaos is the infinite space of infinite différance, the emptiness of all language and of all writing, it is the writing of emptiness, emptiness itself, which is writing itself, because writing itself is always already the emptiness of all writing. Chaos is infinite writing, the infinity of writing itself, which is infinity itself: it is writing itself which deconstructs the signification of writing itself, it is writing itself which shatters and tangles the signification of writing itself, it is writing itself which deconstructs all the possible orders of writing itself, which deconstructs possibility itself, the possibility of writing itself, because writing itself is beyond the artificial and mentally constructed false binary opposition of possible or impossible: it is ontological writing which deconstructs ontology itself, which means it deconstructs ontological writing itself: it is writing itself which desiccates and destroys writing itself while also producing writing itself in an infinite and eternally returning vicious circle with no centre and an infinite, theologically immanent, and originary circumference, the circumference which is the writing of Chaos, originary writing and originary Chaos.

7.

Derrida writes, "Now, stricto sensu, the concept of structure refers only to space, geometric or morphological space, the order of forms and sites. Structure is first the structure of an organic or artificial work, the internal "unity" of an assemblage, a *construction*; a work is governed by a "unifying" principle, the *architecture* that is built and made visible in a location...How is this history of metaphor possible? Does the fact that language can determine things only by spatializing them suffice to explain that, in return, language must spatialize itself as soon as it designates and reflects upon itself? This question can be asked in general about all language and all metaphors [and about language itself and metaphor itself]...One risks being interested in the figure itself to the detriment of the play going on within it metaphorically." (Derrida, WD, pp. 15-16)

"Nothingness" is metaphor, "construction" is metaphor, "topology" is metaphor, "morphology" is metaphor, "architecture" is metaphor, "geometry" is metaphor, "space" is metaphor, and ultimately even "mind" is metaphor. The metaphoricity of space is the metaphoricity of structure, but the metaphoricity of structure is, to use a metaphor, a structure without a centre, *the* structure without a centre, the différantial structure of différance itself. The metaphoricity of différance is the metaphorizing construction of différance, the metaphoricity of multiplicity and the multiplicity of metaphoricity, merely the metaphor of metaphoricity (metaphoricity itself is only ever a metaphor), the metaphor of a metaphoricity which exists only and always already through multiplicity and variety. Likewise, the metaphoricity of différance, the originary metaphoricity of différance, is a différantial multiplicity, a multiplicity constructed out of genetic différantial "space" with the différantial geometry of originary différance. Space itself is metaphor itself.

History is metaphor, history itself is metaphor itself. Historicity itself is metaphoricity itself. Language can determine things only by metaphorizing them: this is sufficient to explain the fact (all facts are merely metaphor, facticity itself is metaphoricity itself) that language necessarily metaphorizes itself as soon as it designates and reflects upon itself, indeed language even necessarily metaphorizes itself even prior to designating and reflecting upon itself: whenever language determines, designates, or reflects, indeed even whenever language signifies (language always and always already signifies, it is infinite signification of infinite signification, it is the infinite signification of infinity itself; infinity itself is infinite signification itself) it necessarily metaphorizes itself. Therefore, language always and always already fictionalizes and it always and always already fictionalizes itself. Language is always already self-referential and self-reflexive: language is always what Hofstadter describes as a "strange loop," a self-referential system. The figure is always already the play of metaphor going on within it: the figure is always already the play of metaphor itself: play is always already the play of metaphor itself, play itself is metaphor itself.

The space of writing is the space of metaphor: space is metaphoricity, space itself is metaphoricity itself. The metaphor of space is the metaphor of extension, mutability, malleability, and complexity. The metaphoricity of space is originary: extension, mutability, malleability, and complexity are originary. Not only is all space dependent upon subjectivity, an artefact of subjectivity, but the mind itself is a space, the metaphor of space, metaphor itself. Space is always already empty space, the nothingness which is extended, mutable, malleable, and complex: space is always already the absence of space, the absence of space which is space itself. The mind, which is Chaos itself, is extended, mutable, malleable, and complex.

Space is essentially force, a multiplicity and complexity of forces, the deconstruction, destruction, and construction of forces. Force *is* the extensionality (or extentionality) of space, force *is* the mutability of space, the malleability of space, force *is* the complexity of space. The infinite divisibility of space and time is the infinite divisibility of forces. Force is originary. (Force = energy = action = becoming = time = difference = space = mediation = subjectivity = metaphor). The différantial structure of originary différance itself, the originary architecture of originary différance itself, is a system of forces, the originary deconstruction of force itself.

Force *is* signification, signification is the signification of forces. The structure of a sign is a system of forces. The elements of a sign are forces. Forces construct signs. Forces are the genetic signification of signs and the productive signification of signs: forces are signifiers which signify signifiers: the originariness of the signifier is the originariness of force (force = signifier). Forces differ and defer infinitely onto other forces. To be more precise, force and sign are equivalent to each other (force = sign). All structures are always already structures of forces. Structures are the products of forces, the resultants of forces. Force is writing, force itself is writing itself. Force is the construction of writing, the writing of construction: force is construction itself, and construction itself is writing itself. The structure of force is a complex of forces: forces construct structures. Forces construct forces.

8.

To use Foucault's metaphor, the space of knowledge is the table of knowledge, the tabula of knowledge: "What has been removed [from surreal juxtapositions], in short, is the famous 'operating table'; and rendering to Roussel a small part of what is still his due, I use the word 'table' in two superimposed senses: the nickel-plated, rubbery table swathed in white, glittering beneath a glass sun devouring all shadow—the table where, for an instant, perhaps forever, the umbrella encounters the sewing-machine; and also a table, a *tabula*, that enables thought to operate upon the entities of our world, to put them in order, to divide them into classes, to group them according to names that designate their similarities and their differences—the table upon which, since the beginning of time, language has intersected space." (Foucault, OT, p. xvii).

The beginning of time is a metaphor, the metaphor of genesis (the genesis of metaphor is itself a metaphor), originary metaphor: it is originary metaphor which intersects space, space itself which is always already metaphor itself: the table of knowledge, the table of space itself, is the inexistent or non-existent table of originary metaphor, the metaphor of a table, the mental construct of a table. Because the table of knowledge is metaphor itself, the objects upon the table of knowledge are also metaphor itself, they are inexistent or nonexistent objects fabricated by the mind. Just as the table of knowledge is a social construct made by psychic forces, so are the objects upon it social constructs made by psychic forces.

The table of knowledge is a game-board, the game-board of writing, the game-board of metaphor, upon which mentally constructed "objects" are used in the language-games of knowledge. The surreal juxtaposition of the sewing-machine and the umbrella upon the table of knowledge, the game-board of knowledge, is a form of transgression of the rules of the language-game of knowledge: the disorder of the *incongruous*, "the linking together of the inappropriate." But transgression is a fiction because law is a fiction. The dangerous liaison of the sewing machine and the umbrella is always already the fiction of a transgression because the rules of knowledge are always already fictions: knowledge is a fiction, knowledge itself is fiction itself.

The eternal copulation of the sewing machine and the umbrella upon the operating table of knowledge is the eternal copulation of two mental constructs upon the table of Chaos within the primal scene of writing wherein writing intersects writing in an endless interplay of metaphor. The table of knowledge is the table of difference, the game-board of difference upon which the language-games of knowledge, knowledge-games, are fabricated: the language-games of knowledge are the language-games that enable the subject to operate upon the reified entities of the reified world, the language games that enable the ordering of mental constructs, and the language games that enable the categorization and classification of mental constructs. However, these knowledge games are preceded by more fundamental knowledge games played upon the gameboard of difference: the language games which mentally construct "entities," the language games which designate the similarities and differences among mental constructs, and the language games of culture.

In a parable which describes the history of knowledge, Foucault describes a certain kind of aphasiac, an epistemologically disordered aphasiac: "It appears that certain aphasiacs, when shown various differently coloured skeins of wool on a table top, are consistently unable to arrange them into any coherent pattern; as though that simple rectangle were unable to serve in their case as a homogeneous and neutral space in which things could be placed so as to display at the same time the continuous order of their identities or differences as well as the semantic field of their denomination. Within this simple space in which things are normally arranged and given names, the aphasiac will create a multiplicity of tiny, fragmented regions in which nameless resemblances agglutinate things into unconnected islets; in one corner, they will place the lightest-coloured skeins, in another the red ones, somewhere else those that are softest in texture, in yet another place the longest, or those that have a tinge of purple or those that have been wound up into a ball. But no sooner have they been adumbrated then all these groupings dissolve again, for the field of identity that sustains them, however limited it may be, is still too wide not to be unstable; and so the sick mind continues to infinity, creating groups then dispersing them again, heaping up the diverse similarities, destroying those that seem clearest, splitting up things that are identical, superimposing different criteria, frenziedly beginning all over again, becoming more and more disturbed, and teetering finally on the brink of anxiety." (Foucault, p. xviii).

The history of knowledge is the history of knowledge games, the history of the writing games played upon the table of Chaos. Western discourse, anthropomorphized as a conceptual persona, is Foucault's epistemologically disordered aphasiac, anxiously constructing various language games only in order to de-construct them and construct new ones, but constructing new knowledge games only as ways of denying mediation and difference-in-itself, thereby re-constructing Western discourse. From the historian's perspective, Western discourse is unable to consistently arrange its language games in any coherent pattern, ultimately because there is no actual transcendental signified, no actual ultimate identity, which can bind together the writing of identity. The table of knowledge ultimately cannot be used as a simple and geometric space, a logical space, an analytical space, "a homogeneous and neutral space in which "things" could be placed so as to display at the same time the continuous order of their identities or differences as well as the semantic field of their denomination," ultimately because the table of knowledge is itself a table of fiction, it is the table of Chaos upon which all identities and meanings had to be fabricated to begin with. Knowledge is fundamentally unstable because its categories, connections, and even its objects are merely fictions: the emptiness of categories, connections, and objects is the essential dis-order of all orders, of order itself, because it is the implicit fictionality of categories, connections, and objects which is the ground of their potential and inevitable dissolution, the dissolution into nothingness which is merely the recognition that they were always already fictions. The field of identity is essentially unstable because it is, in totality and in all its parts, a field of emptiness. The essential fictionality of truth is the essential disorder of order, the essential groundlessness of order which threatens to undo all orders and order itself because ultimately there is no centre (the centreless centre, the centrelessness, of all order is nothingness, Chaos) which orients and supports order: the fundamental instability of all order is the immanence of Chaos.

What Derrida describes as the logocentrism of Western discourse, its essential fantasy of unmediated presence which denies mediation and difference, is evidence that it is the product of sick minds: the logocentrism of Western discourse is a denial of difference and Chaos, a defense mechanism against reality itself, a denial of reality itself (because reality itself *is* difference and Chaos), hence why over the course of history the sick mind of Western discourse continues constructing, de-constructing, and re-constructing the knowledge games of identity to infinity, "creating groups then dispersing them again, heaping up the diverse similarities, destroying those that seem clearest, splitting up things that are identical, superimposing different criteria, frenziedly beginning all over again, becoming more and more disturbed, and teetering finally on the brink of anxiety." The arbitrary divisions of identity and the arbitrary constructions of identity which proliferate in Western discourse are all motivated by anxiety insofar as they are denials of difference-in-itself. The arbitrary differentiations of identity are all nonetheless reliant on identity and thus are proliferations of identity just as much as the construction of identities, the superimpositions of categories upon "objects," and the superimposition of categories upon categories. Identities are fictions because they are constructed by and out of difference, because systems of difference are the elements of identity, the elements out of which identities are constructed. The anxiety and sickness of Western discourse is weakness, weakness in the face of reality, weakness in the face of difference, weakness in the face of the ontological difference which is reality itself.

1. Introduction

What is social constructionism? To be more precise, what is *our* theory of social constructionism? To be brief, it is the science of construction, the genealogy of morals and perspectivist psychology, the science of deconstruction and new construction, the science of drive psychology, the psychology of the drives, i.e. the science of psychic forces. Our answer must necessarily be a work in progress for diverse reasons, including the inherent historicity of our answer, the infinity of possible interpretations, and the perpetual deconstruction inherent to science itself. Social constructionism grew out of diverse movements in philosophy, linguistics, and social science, out of several events which may be described as "crises," or at least symptoms of "crises," crises of science which are ultimately crises of language: social constructionism grew out of the empty spaces of the ruptures of knowledge, the ruptures of a knowledge which was always already empty space, the ruptures of the void out of which gushed the infinite reservoir of Chaos, the infinite gushing of infinity itself.

Samples of these ruptures include: the linguistics and semiology of Wittgenstein's *Philosophical Investigations* and Derrida's *Of Grammatology*; the sociology of Berger and Luckmann's *The Social Construction of Reality* and Pierre Bourdieu's *Outline of a Theory of Practice* and *The Logic of Practice*; the psychology of Pierre Klossowski's *Nietzsche and the Vicious Circle*; the philosophy of Friedrich Nietzsche, renewing historiography, the scientific method, and experimental anthropology; a Kantian philosopher like Gilles Deleuze, once again taking up the problem of the interpretation of Kant; the historiography of Michel Foucault, renewing epistemology; the literary criticism of Maurice Blanchot; poets such as those among the symbolists, surrealists, and the dadaists. Of these, none use the word "social constructionism" in our sense of the term, and although the term "post-structuralism" has been applied to them, many of them have rejected it. Some use the word "structure" whereas others prefer the word "system," but both of these have the same meaning and are in effect used to mean the same thing (structure = system). To paraphrase Deleuze, "These are all very different kinds of thinkers, and from different generations, and some have exercised a real influence on their contemporaries [especially Friedrich Nietzsche, who is the mother of them all]. But of more import is the extreme diversity of the domains they explore. Each of them discovers problems, methods, solutions that are analogically related [and more than analogically related], as if sharing in a free atmosphere or spirit of the time [the freedom disclosed, opened up, by the ruptures of Chaos, the freedom disclosed by the ruptures of historicity itself, the ruptures of temporality *by temporality itself*], but [a free atmosphere] that distributes itself into [differential] creations and discoveries in each of these domains.—*Ism* words, in this sense, are perfectly justified" (Deleuze, DI, p. 170). Nietzsche is a sociologist and anthropologist par excellence, and this study of Nietzsche is likewise a work of sociology and anthropology. Sociology is the scientific interpretation of formations of domination. Anthropology is the scientific interpretation of culture.

There are sufficient and necessary reasons to ascribe the origin of social constructionism to linguistics: not only Derrida, but the entire French school of critical theory. And if social constructionism then migrates to other domains, this occurs not merely as a question of analogy, nor merely in order to apply the methods of post-structural linguistics, methods which succeeded in the analysis of language, that is to say the deconstruction of language itself. In fact, writing is the only thing that can properly be said to have structure, all structures only exist in and through writing, as writing, and the structure of writing itself is originary writing: the originary structure of originary writing is always already originary writing, ad infinitum. There are structures of the unconscious only to the extent that the unconscious is writing and that the unconscious constructs structures. There are structures of bodies only to the extent that bodies are writing: bodies are the writing of the unconscious, the subjectivity of the body *is* the unconscious. Writing is always already the language of forces. So the question *What is social constructionism?* is further trans-formed—it is better to ask: What do we recognize in those that we call social constructionists? And *what* do they themselves recognize? How do the social constructionists go about recognizing writing in something, the writing proper to a domain? What do they discover in this domain?

2. First Criterion: The Symbolic

The imagination, the image, is originary. Reality is always already imaginary, which means that the ultimate nature of reality is the psychic drives. Reality is a multiplicity of subjectivities, and each subjectivity is a multiplicity of images, a multiplicity of forces which are always already images. Reality is a bestiary and a garden of images, a forest of symbols. The following equivalences suggest the fundamental equivalence of reality and the imagination: thought = emotion; thought = image; thought = subjectivity; reality = subjectivity; subjectivity = force; reality = signs. The essential and originary subjectivity of reality is the originariness of the imagination because subjectivity is the construction of images. Subjectivity is imaging (image-ing), the construction of images by forces which are themselves always already images. The image *is* imaging, the image is always already imaging. The real, the imaginary, the symbolic, and the semiotic are one: reality = images = symbols = signs.

The total absence of truth is precisely the originariness of subjective reality, which means the originariness of the imagination. Even the understanding, the intellect, the faculty of reason, is in actuality the imagination, the synthesis of images. Images are constructed and de-constructed from images by images ad infinitum in an endless interplay of mediation. The image is mediation itself, mediation itself is imaging itself. The originariness of the symbolic is the originariness of mediation. The symbol, the symbolic, *is* imaging (mediation = imaging = symboling). The depths of the real are the depths of subjectivity, which is the depths of the imagination itself. The power of reality is the power of intersubjectivity, the power of images, the power of imaging. Reality itself is always already image itself, imaging itself.

The poetry of the symbolists, surrealists, and dadaists also suggest that reality is always already image, at least if the interpretation of their poetry is pushed to the point of deconstruction, to the point of the self-deconstruction of their own texts. Baudelaire writes, "Man walks through a forest of symbols/ Each of which regard him as kin" [*L'homme y passe à travers des forêts de symboles/ Qui l'observant avec des regards familiers*]. In fact, "man" is himself merely a symbol in a universe of symbols, in a universe which is originarily symbolic, in a reality which consists in its totality and in all its parts of symbolic intersubjectivities which mentally construct symbols. Each symbol is a subjectivity unto itself, hence why, as Baudelaire writes, each symbol regards "man" as kin, for "man" is a symbol-subjectivity among symbols-subjectivities. The overman walks through reality itself having realized that the ultimate nature of reality is symbolic, thus the overman walks through a forest of symbols.

The first criterion of social constructionism is the discovery and re-cognition of the semiotic essence of reality, the originary semiotic essence of reality. (Semiotic = symbolic = imaginary = reality). The affirmation of the originary symbolism of reality itself constitutes the first dimension of social constructionism. In this case again, everything begins with linguistics: beyond the word in its sur-reality and its semiotic elements, beyond mental pictures and the pictorial constructions associated with words, the social constructionist linguist discovers elements of quite another nature: forces, constructive forces. The productive and positive unconscious mind consists of psychic forces, i.e. of wills to power. Force is always already a multiplicity of forces. It is in this symbolic element that symbolist poets such as Arthur Rimbaud wish to locate themselves in order to renew the reality of subjectivity itself, which is reality itself, as well as the associated forms of life. Beyond the history of men, beyond the history of ideas, beyond humanistic historiography and beyond idealistic historiography, Friedrich Nietzsche discovers a deeper, subterranean ground that forms the object of both a genealogy of knowledge and a genealogy of culture. Behind reified men and their reified relations, behind ideologies and their imaginary relations, Friedrich Nietzsche discovers a deeper domain as the domain of a gay science and a new philosophy which he calls alternately "perspectivism" and the "genealogy of morals."

The first criterion of social constructionism consists of this: that the regimes of the real, the imaginary, and the symbolic are always already reducible to the regime of forces. Force is originary. This forcial element consists of psychic drives. Forces construct structures, forces construct sensible forms, forces construct figures of the imagination, forces construct intelligible forms. "Content" *is* force. Forces determines form (content determines form = forces determine form). Forces are the elements of a structure. Forces produce variation. Social constructionism sometimes ventures into reflections on rhetoric, metaphor, and metonymy because truth itself is always already rhetoric, metaphor and metonymy, and because these are all products of forces. A form is a combination of forces.

The qualitative relations of forces are the qualitative-algorithm of qualia supporting formal elements: forces, which always already means the relations of forces, produce forms. As Deleuze writes, formal elements by themselves have "neither form, nor signification, nor representation, nor content, nor given empirical reality, nor hypothetical functional model, nor intelligibility behind appearances" (Deleuze, DI, p. 173). Forces construct formal elements, and forces construct forms, significations, representations, metaphors, abstractions, contents, given empirical realities, perceptions. "Hypothetical functional models" are merely mental constructs. Forces *are* the "essences" of "appearances," and forces *are* the "appearances" as well. Emotions *are* the essences of existents; it is in this sense only that we can say that "essence precedes existence," or that "essence determines existence." No one has better determined the status of force as identical to the will to power itself than Friedrich Nietzsche—and the will to power must be understood as the production itself of construction itself. The originariness of the will to power is originary production and originary construction.

Structuralism, by constructing arbitrary distinctions between the real, the imaginary, and the symbolic, fundamentally misunderstands the essence of language.

Force is always already interpretative and interpreting: force is interpretation itself. The originariness of force is originary interpretation. Social constructionism renews our interpretations, our interpretations of "things" and our interpretations of interpretations, and claims to discover the originariness of the will to power. Signs are the genetic and differential elements of forces, the genetic and differential elements of the will to power. More precisely, signs *are* the will to power, the will to power *is* signs (signs = the will to power). Wills to power are the genetic and differential elements of signs. The will to power constitutes language, the will to power elaborates works themselves, the will to power constructs ideas, and the will to power produces actions. Symbolism and surrealism, but also post-structuralism and Machiavellianism, thus become the objects of profound reinterpretations. Not to mention the mythical, poetic, philosophical, or practical works which themselves are subjected to social constructionist interpretation. To paraphrase Deleuze, "But this reinterpretation [of social constructionism] only has value to the extent that it animates new works which are those of today, as if the symbolic were the source, inseparably, of living interpretation and creation" (Deleuze, DI, p. 173). Social constructionism is the construction of new works, new works animated by the will to power. The new work of social constructionism is the construction of the overman, the construction of the culture of the overman. The interpretations and re-interpretations of social constructionism are new constructions. All interpretation is essentially social construction. Interpretation is always already a creative act, an act of literature. (Each mental act is an act of literature, always already an act of literature. The unconscious mind is essentially literature, the writing of literature, the writing itself of literature itself. All actions are writing-acts, acts of literature. All relations are intertextual relations, intertextuality is originary, and all intertextual relations are power relations.). To interpret is to create, to live is to interpret, to live is to create. Life itself is the interpretation of life itself. Interpretation itself is life itself. Social constructionism is living interpretation and creation, the interpretation and creation of life itself. The source of social constructionism is the symbolic, it is the will to power itself.

3. Second Criterion: The Positionality of Forces

The symbolic elements of a structure consists of forces, which are always already actualities. Equivalent to the real and to the imaginary, the symbolic is defined either by the pre-existing realities which determine it, or by the imaginary or conceptual contents which determine it, and which give it a signification. Forces, the elements of a structure, have both extrinsic designations to other forces and intrinsic significations to the mediations within themselves. It must be recalled rigorously that forces determine a *sense* [*sens* = meaning and direction]: a sense which is necessarily and uniquely the positionality of forces.

It is a matter of location in the real spatial expanses of the *mind*, and of sites in imaginary extensions, which are determined by forces; it is a matter of the places and sites of mind-space, the topology of the mind, which are determined by forces. Space is what is forcial, an extended and extensive space, the differential *spatium* constituted multiplicity by multiplicity as a complex of mediation, in which the actuality of mediation has precisely both an ordinal sense (an ordinal sense is a sense of hierarchy) and a signification in extension. In short, real forces, the forces of reality, are primary in relation to structures. In micro-sociological, socio-psychological, and anthropological analyses, real forces, the forces of reality, are also primary in relation to the imaginary roles and effective events which necessarily "appear" when they are constructed by forces.

The scientific ambition of social constructionism is qualitative, topological, and relational, a principal that Nietzsche constantly affirms and re-affirms. In terms of the political economy of the psyche, it must be specified that the real "subjects" are neither "structures," nor the "ego," nor the "individual," nor "human beings," because these, just like the roles they fulfil and even "events" themselves, are merely ideological constructs, constructions of ideology. Rather, the real subjects are above all forces themselves: forces determine all the places in the topology of the mind, all the structures of mind-space, and even the relations of psychic production. "Death," "desire," "work," and "play" are determined by forces, both in the sense that they are mental constructs determined by forces and in the sense that they are dimensions of empirical experience—dimensions of empirical experience are always already dimensions of metaphor—determined by forces. Death, desire, work, and play are primarily the forms of life and the experiences of subjects, subjects which are always already animated by a motivation (force *is* motivation), motivations which animate them as "mortal and dying," or "desiring," "workman-like," or "playful." Subjects are equivalent to a hierarchy of mediation and difference, a hierarchy of mediation and difference which determines the construction of structures, a hierarchy of mediation and difference which is construction itself. Structure, however, is only secondarily constructed (especially because "structure" is always already merely an abstraction, a fiction). It is only secondarily that the forces which animate a subject construct the qualifications of places and positions of forms of life, qualifications of places and positions which are necessarily ideological constructs of forms of life, e.g. the qualifications of the places and positions of forms of life such as "mortal and dying," or "desiring," "workman-like," or "playful." That is why we can propose the social constructionist distribution of the empirical and the quasi-transcendental: the quasi-transcendental is defined and determined by empirical motivations and empirical forms of life. The empirical is originary. The originary empirical is originary mediation and originary subjectivity. Social constructionism is inextricably linked with a new empirical philosophy, or empiricist philosophy, in which force prevails over structure. Kinship terms such as "father," "mother," etc. are first of all social constructs, the products of forces; likewise, kinship systems are first of all social constructs, the products of forces. We are mortal primarily due to the combat of forces, the movements of forces, movement itself (which is becoming itself, time itself), and it is only secondarily that forces, the topological hierarchy of mediation and difference of forces, produce social constructs of death, the limits of death, the sites of death, and the structures of death.

A subject is always already a multiplicity of subjects, always already an intersubjectivity unto itself. The self is always already an other unto itself, the self is always already a system of others unto itself (an intersubjectivity is a system of subjectivities, a system of others). Subjectivity is always already the subjectivity of a signifying chain, a chain of signs wherein each sign is subjectivity. Subjectivity is equivalent, originary, and immanent to signifying chains. A signifying chain is a subjectivity-ing chain, a chain of subjectivities. The displacements of signs *are* the displacements of subjectivities: the actions of subjectivities *are* the actions of signs, of signs which are always already forces. Forces determine subjects in their acts, in their will, in their refusals, in their ignorances, in their conquests, in their innate gifts, in their social acquisitions, in their sex, and in their character: in sum, forces determine the fate of subjects, forces determine fate itself. Fate itself is force itself. "Character is fate" only because fate determines character, fate itself determines character, which means that force itself determines character. We have attempted to explicate as clearly as possible how and why quasi-transcendental psychology is not only founded and grounded in, but determined by an empirical topology, a psychology of forces, a perspectivist psychology.

All relations among forces are power-relations, relations of positionality. Positionality is originary. The originary positionality of forces is the originary ensocialment of forces, originary ensocialment itself, which is originary hierarchy itself. The originary ensocialment of forces is the fact that forces are always already immersed in a specific environment of forces, a specific environment of intersubjectivity, in which the antecedent power relations among forces determine subsequent power relations among forces. The originary positionality of forces is the fact that forces are always already placed in a particular position in relation to other forces, that forces are always already embedded in a hierarchy of forces, in relations of domination and submission. An intersubjectivity is a hierarchy of subjectivities, is always already a hierarchy of subjectivities. Each force is always already embedded in a network of power relations, a network of relational positions.

Several consequences follow from this criterion of the positionality of forces. First of all, because the symbolic elements, forces, have extrinsic designations to other forces, intrinsic signification to itself (to force itself, which is mediation itself), and a positional sense, it follows necessarily that *sense always results from the combination of forces which are always already signifying other forces, from the combination of forces which are always already the signifying of originary différance.* Sense is force, force is sense. Sense is always a resultant, an effect: a positional effect, a product, a perspective, an effect of writing, an effect of difference-in-itself. Sense itself is difference itself, which means that sense is always itself and not itself: nonsense is originary, sense is always already nonsense. To paraphrase Deleuze, "There is, profoundly, a nonsense of sense, from which sense itself results" (DI, p. 175). The nonsense of sense, the originary nonsense of sense, is difference-in-itself, originary difference: nonsense itself is difference itself, difference-in-itself, and différance. We return in this way to an aspect of Eastern philosophy, to what is often called a philosophy of emptiness: for such a philosophy, sense itself is in essence the negative space of conceptualization because sense itself is essentially constituted by systems of negative spaces of conceptualization. For social constructionism, likewise, sense itself is essentially empty, but this also means that there is always too much sense, an overproduction, an over-determination, and an over-differentiation of sense, always produced in excess by a combination of forces, by a combination of the positionality of forces, by forces themselves. It is not only the case that, to paraphrase Deleuze, "Nonsense is that which gives value to sense" (ibid), but it is also the case that nonsense produces sense by circulating forces among forces: but forces are what give value to sense, therefore nonsense itself is force itself, and nonsense necessarily implies a multiplicity of nonsense, just as force necessarily implies a multiplicity of forces: forces produce both nonsense and sense simultaneously by circulating forces among forces. Social constructionism owes much to both Franz Kafka (cf. *The Trial*, "The Metamorphosis," "The Hunger-Artist," "The Great Wall of China," "In the Penal Colony," as well all of his other works) and Lewis Carroll (cf. *Alice's Adventures in Wonderland* and

Through the Looking Glass; cf. also Deleuze's *The Logic of Sense*, but only when considered from the perspective of its own self-deconstruction).

The second consequence is social constructionism's inclination for language games, differential games, the theatre of the absurd, and the theatre of cruelty. Wittgenstein's concept of language games is itself undefinable because definitions are forms of language games. Derrida's concept of différance is itself undefinable because of the difference-in-itself inherent to each definition, the difference-in-itself which makes each definition itself and not itself. The metaphor of the game is the game of metaphor: the game itself is metaphor itself, metaphor itself is the game itself. The noblest games such as writing-games are those that construct a combinatory system of forces in the space of Chaos, the space of Chaos which is an infinitely deep complexity of infinity within infinity, with the game-pieces of writing, forces themselves, which are infinitely extended images, the infinite extension of the imagination itself. Or when Derrida ruptures *Writing and Difference* with his essay on Artaud's theatre of cruelty, a rupture of writing out of which gushes the blood of writing itself; the theatre of cruelty is a theatre of both dream and reality simultaneously, an originary theatre of mediation and difference, the principle of which is in Dionysus, and that would today find its most extreme expression in life itself. In short, the very manifesto of social constructionism is Mallarmé's famous formula, eminently poetic, gameic (game-ic), and theatrical: "thought is a dice-throw"[16] [*penser, c'est émetre un coup de dés*].

The third consequence is that social constructionism is inseparable from a new empiricism, a new atheism, a new anti-nihilism, a new anti-Christianity, a new gay-scientism, a new post-humanism, a new transhumanism, a new overhumanism, a new superhumanism. Because force is originary in relation to language games, it does not matter much whether one says "Christianity" or "humanism" because their respective language games are motivated by the same forces, the forces of ressentiment, bad conscience, guilt, and nihilism. Christianity and humanism are in actuality not opposed to each, despite the claims to the contrary made both by Christians and by humanist atheists, because they both embody the same values, the values of ressentiment and nihilism, the slave values of slave morality. The death of God foreshadowed the death of man, and the death of man has come: the birth of the overman has come, the birth of the overman out of the spirit of power, out of the forces of genesis and the genesis of forces, out of the forces of difference and mediation, the transformation of forces out of the forces of transformation. It is only in the context of the production of the overman that we understand the imaginary character of man for Foucault, the ideological character of humanism for Althusser, the ontological originariness of difference-in-itself for Deleuze, and the originariness of writing for Derrida.

4. Third Criterion: The Differential and Multiplicity

Reality is actuality, actuality is reality: there are only actualities, the actualities of difference-in-itself. Subjectivity is actuality, actuality is subjectivity (reality = actuality = subjectivity). If we ever make a distinction between the "real" and the "imaginary" it is only as a way of speaking, a metaphor, partly because it is sometimes pragmatic, and partly because we lack the language to express reality itself, which is inexpressible difference-in-itself, but we nonetheless attempt to express the inexpressible. In actuality, the real is always already the imaginary, an infinity of images and imagings: always already the symbolic, an infinity of symbols and symbolings.

We call the determination of the difference-in-itself of a force by a force of difference-in-itself *differentiation*; we call the actualisation of difference-in-itself into an other system of difference-in-itself by a force of difference-in-itself *différantiation*. Differentiation is the production of difference-in-itself by difference-in-itself. Différantiation is the production of différance-in-itself by différance-in-itself. Differentiation and différantiation imply each other and are ultimately and primordially equivalent to each other (differentiation = différantiation). Differentiation and différantiation are originary. The reality of the actual consists of the differential elements of forces (which are forces themselves) and the differential relations of forces along with the multiplicities (of forces) which correspond to them. The reality of the actual is force, the multiplicity of forces.

The relations of forces are power relations and social relations, always already power relations and social relations (forcial relations = power relations = social relations). The relations of forces are never the "pure logic of relations" of formal logic and mathematics; the "pure logic of relations," "pure relations," are always relations of identities, they are the purely artificial relations of systems of identity, i.e. they are purely fictional relations, the fictional relations of fictions, that never correspond to reality. By contrast, the relations of forces are always already the differential relations of differences, the différantial relations of différances, the mediate relations of mediations: the différantial logic of différantial relations of systems of différance: actual relations. Differential relations are power relations and social relations, always already power relations and social relations (differential relations = power relations = social relations).

Forces are the elements of a relation. Forces always determine the values of a relation. Moreover, the elements of a relation, forces, determine each other reciprocally. The superiority of the superior force is determined by the inferiority of the inferior force, and the inferiority of the inferior force is determined by the superiority of the superior force. Relationality is originary: relations always already determine relations. Forces are dynamic and ordinal, diachronic and positional. This process of differential determination and reciprocal determination is the essence of a relationship that allows one to define the regime of the symbolic in terms of forces.

To use a mathematical metaphor, the metaphor of mathematics and the mathematics of metaphor: the metaphor of calculus, the metaphorical calculus of metaphor itself: social constructionism is the superior mathematics, the mathematics of superiority, the superior calculus, the calculus of superiority: the différantial calculus of writing itself, the diachronicities of sensitivities and the sensitivities of diachronicities: the mathematics of social constructionism is the différantial calculus of différance, the integral calculus of integral différance, the qualitative calculus of qualia, the forcial calculus of forces: the aleatoric calculus of aleatoricality itself, the aleatoric calculus of aleatoric forces, forces of aleatoricality itself, aleatoricality itself is force itself: the qualitative, forcial, aleatoric, and différantial calculus of power, of the will to power: the interpretive calculus of interpretation, the différantial calculus of the dynamic, the diachronic, hierarchy, and positionality: the liberating calculus of liberation, liberation itself, the infinite calculus of infinity, infinity itself: the social-constructive calculus of social construction.

Corresponding to the determination of differential relations are mediations, distributions of mediating forces which characterize différance-in-itself. The reciprocal determination of forces continues henceforth into the differential determination of mediations that constitute the systems corresponding to these elements. Mediation is crucial to the construction of structures: the domain of mediation is the domain wherein structures are constructed. Construction is always already social construction.

The general formula, "thought is a dice-throw," itself refers to the inherent and originary multiplicity of the dice-throw, to the inherent and originary multiplicity of the dice-throw's mediation, to originary multiplicity itself which is always already originary mediation itself, to mediation itself which is always already multiplicity itself: the general formula, "thought is a dice-throw" itself refers to the mediations, the de-structive mediations and the con-structive mediations, the mediations of chance itself (mediation itself is chance itself), out of which the dice of différance are thrown: as Mallarmé writes, "a dice throw at any time never will abolish chance...a dice throw/ at any time/ even when cast in/ everlasting circumstances/ from the depths of a shipwreck"[17]: the dice-throw of thought is the dice-throw of force, the dice-throw of the will to power, the will to power which is always already chance itself because chance itself is power itself, the power of différance and the différance of power: the dice-throw of force is the dice-throw of temporality itself, force itself is temporality itself, thus temporality itself is chance itself, the différance of chance: the dice-throws of forces, the dice-throws of temporality itself, de-struct and con-struct and de-construct, but de-struction and de-construction is always already con-struction and social construction, always already the dice-throws of forces, always already the dice-throws of thought, hence why the dice-throw born from the bottom of a shipwreck is always already an affirmation of chance, of the originary multiplicity of chance, always already an affirmation of deconstruction and social construction: to con-struct is to de-construct and to de-struct: to de-construct or to de-struct is to con-struct: out of the mediations of the de-structions, de-constructions and con-structions of force, différance is generated.

Inherent in every force are the following two aspects: a system of différantial relations according to which the symbolic elements determine themselves reciprocally, and a system of multiplicities corresponding to these relations and constructing the mind-space of the system of difference. To paraphrase Deleuze, "Every structure is a multiplicity," a multiplicity within multiplicity generated by multiplicity within multiplicity (DI, p. 177). The question "Are there forces in any domain whatsoever?" must be specified in the following way: in a given domain, can one uncover symbolic elements, différantial relations, and sets of multiplicities which are characteristic of it? In every domain, we discover exactly all of these, therefore we discover forces in every domain. Forces are incarnated in the symbolic elements and différantial relations of the domain considered; the différantial relations are actualized in the power relations between the symbolic elements; the multiplicities are the multiplicities of the mediations of forces, the distributions of mediations, the distributions of symbols, the distributions of différance, the distributions of constructions, the distributions of construction itself. Force is the multiplicity of infinity, the infinity of multiplicity: multiplicity itself is infinity itself.

In each domain, one must find symbols, relationships, and mediations. The symbolic elements, elements of symbols, forces, and their relations always determine the nature of the structures which come to realize them, while the multiplicities of forces form a hierarchy of positions that simultaneously determines the multiplicities of structures. The determination of the structure is therefore completed in a theory of forces which explains its functioning.

Multiplicities correspond with the symbolic elements and their relations because ultimately multiplicities are equivalent to the symbolic elements and their relations (multiplicity = symbol = relation). One could say, rather that multiplicities "symbolize" with symbolic elements and their relations, derive from them, construct them, since every determination of differential relations entails a distribution of multiplicities and mediations. The values of differential relations are incarnated in structures, the values of multiplicities are incarnated in structures. Difference-in-itself and multiplicity are each both variables and functions. Difference-in-itself and multiplicity are each both derived yet irreducible. The symbolic elements of the unconscious necessarily refer to the power relations within the body itself, incarnating multiplicities of forces in such and such structures. In this sense, every force is psychosomatic, or rather, the psychosomatic is a system of difference and mediation.

Let us consider the political economy of the unconscious using Althusser's interpretation of Marxian political economy: above all, the relations of production are determined as différantial relations that are established between forces, between forces which are both the "objects" of production and the "agents" of production, which, first of all, have a symbolic value "(object of production, instrument of production, labour force, immediate workers, immediate non-workers, such as they are held in relations of property and appropriation)" (Deleuze, DI, p. 178). Each mode of production is thus characterized by multiplicities corresponding to the values of the power relations. And if it is obvious that this is merely a metaphor, that is because this is merely a metaphor: the production of metaphor, the metaphor of production: production itself is metaphor itself. The true subjects are the forces themselves: the différantial and the multiplicitous, the differential mediations and the multiplicitous mediations, the reciprocal determination of forces and the complete determination of forces by forces.

5. The Différanciator, Différanciation, Diachronicity

Différanciation is another way of writing différantiation (différanciation = différantiation). The différanciator is another way of writing the différantiator (différanciator = différantiator). The arbitrary substitution of "c" for "t" in the concepts of the différanciator and différanciation signifies the arbitrariness of all writing, the originary arbitrariness of writing itself, originary arbitrariness itself. To write différance is to write writing itself: the différantiator is ontological writing: the différantiator itself is writing itself, the writing itself of writing itself, the writing itself of writing itself always already within the writing itself of writing itself ad infinitum.

Difference-in-itself is always already subjectivity itself, therefore it is always already the difference-in-itself of a multiplicity of subjectivities, which is precisely hierarchy. Difference-in-itself produces difference-in-itself, the subjectivity itself of difference-in-itself produces the subjectivity itself of difference-in-itself, which means precisely that the subjectivity itself of hierarchy itself produces the subjectivity itself of hierarchy itself. The subjectivity itself of hierarchy itself is the will to power, the drive for power. Differentiation is the production of hierarchy by hierarchy: differentiation is the production the will to power by the will to power. Difference-in-itself *is* the will to power. A system of difference is always a system of will to power. The differentiator *is* the will to power. The originary differentiator itself is the originariness of the will to power itself. The will to power is originary: originary writing itself is the originariness of the will to power itself.

Forces are necessarily unconscious, by virtue of the elements, relations, and mediations which compose them. Each system of forces has differential forces, différantial forces, and a multiplicity of mediating forces, all of which are actualities. The actualities of forces construct the structures which they are incarnated in; forces constitute the structures in which they are incarnated. The concept "actuality" precisely designates the modes of forces and the motivations of forces, on the condition that we remember that potentialities are also actualities and that potentialities are fully actualized at the given moment of their existence. Actuality itself has a temporality and a diachronicity which is proper to it, a temporality and diachronicity which exists prior to the mental constructions of the "past," "present," and "future." Actuality itself is always already subjectivity itself, which is always already imaging itself, always already force itself. We will say of actuality: *simultaneously reality itself and subjectivity itself, simultaneously image itself and force itself.* Force is an actual reservoir, a reservoir of actuality, an actual repertoire, a repertoire of actuality, in which deconstruction and social construction coexist simultaneously in actuality, and where actualization is necessarily carried out according to the simultaneous chance and necessity of différance, always implicating partial combinations of forces and the unconscious decisions of forces. To discern the forces of a domain is to determine an entire actuality of coexistence which pre-exists the structures and microstructures of the domain. Every force is a multiplicity of actual coexistence. A force is always already a social system of forces, and a social system is always already a system of forces: a social system is defined by a coexistence of elements (the elements of a social system are forces) and economic relations (a political economy of forces), but these are themselves différantials which are engendered by différance-in-itself. A social system is always already a system of writing, and a system of writing is always already a social system: a writing system defined by a coexistence of différantials, a political economy of writing: ontological writing engenders the writing of writing itself.

It is forces which coexist in a structure. The forces which coexist in a structure are its elements, its relations, its relational values, its multiplicities, its domain itself. The relationships of forces and the différantial elements of a structure coexist in a completely determined whole determined by forces themselves. Forces are actualized in particular relations, relational values, and distributions of multiplicities; but these consist of forces themselves and in turn actualize forces. Each society, each social form, is produced by particular elements of given forces, particular relationships of given forces, and particular production values of given forces (the hyle of all of these are also forces).

As it regards language, to paraphrase Deleuze, "There is no total language [*langue*], embodying all the possible phonemes and phonemic relations" (DI, p. 179). Forces construct and actualize particular phonemes and phonemic relations. Forces construct and actualize the actual totality of the language system [*langage*]. Forces construct and actualize syntax. Forces construct and actualize the diversity of specific languages, the relationships of each, the relational values of each, and the multiplicities of each. The writing itself of writing itself constructs and actualizes all systems of language, all systems of signs and all elements of semiology.

We must therefore distinguish between the totality of forces of a domain as an ensemble of actual coexistence (the coexistence of actualities), and the diverse sub-structures that are constructed and actualized by their corresponding différantial forces. Of forces as actualities, we must say that they are always already différantiated and différantiating, that they are totally and completely différantial. There is no genuine "undifferentiated'; the concept of the "undifferentiated" is a logocentric concept, the concept of a fictional unmediated presence which is magically devoid of difference. Structures embody the forces which construct and actualize them: because the elements of a structure are forces, structures are always already différantiated and différantiating, they are always already différantials. Force is equivalent to this double aspect, or this complex: différantial and différantiation.

Social constructionism explicates systems of différance which have their origins in différance-in-itself and which produce différance-in-itself. All differentiation, all actualization (actualization = differentiation) is carried out along multiplicitous paths, along paths of multiplicity, the transcursive writing of multiplicity, the multiplicity of transcursive writing: transcursive writing itself (which is always already writing itself) is multiplicity itself. The différantial relations are incarnated in qualitatively différantiated multiplicities, while the corresponding multiplicities are incarnated in the transcursive writing and intentions of forces (or intentionalities of forces) which construct each sign. Forces construct "individuals," which are always already mental constructs, and forces construct "species," which are likewise mental constructs, but ones which, since they are abstracted from "individuals" via the forgetting of difference, are even more abstract and even moreso mental fabrications than "individuals," which are abstractions and mental fabrications to begin with. Each part of a structure is always already a multiplicity, always already différance-in-itself. Each part of a "species" is always already a multiplicity, always already différance-in-itself. Forces construct structures, forces construct parts, forces construct individuals, and forces construct species: hence linguistic structures and the language species, and the parts of each one (which are always already systems of multiplicity, systems of différance, they are writing itself); hence the specifically defined social modes of production within the unconscious itself and the organized parts corresponding to each one of these modes, etc. all of which are writing itself. One will readily notice that the process of actualization always implies diachronicity, and the variability of diachronicity according to what forces are actualized. For example, not only does each type of social production have a global diachronicity, but its organized parts have their own specific diachronicities. As regards temporality, historicity, and diachronicity (temporality = historicity = diachronicity), the position of social constructionism is thus quite clear: actualization is always already a time of diachronicity, the diachronicity of time, the différantial genesis of forces is always already the elements of actual coexistence différantiated by the forces of diachronicity, the diachronicity of forces: force itself is diachronicity itself. The genesis of forces is always already diachronic, diachronicity is originary, it is always already at the origin of forces and their actualizations, and of forces and their constructions. Writing itself is diachronicity itself. Diachronicity is the actualizations of actualities by actualities: it is the différantiation of forces by the différantials of forces. Diachronicity is the relations of successions of forces, relations which are sometimes relations of rupture because successions are sometimes chance successions. In the process of the succession of forces, forces which are always already diachronic, forces are realized at different rates in each force, and the diachronicity of their différantial relations themselves have their genesis in the diachronicity of other forces. And precisely because forces are actualized in space and time, precisely because they *are* space and time, hence the différantiation of forces is the différantiation of diachronicity, we must say in this sense that diachronicity *produces* forces and their différantiations. It produces them as différantiated mediations and multiplicities (mediation itself is diachronicity itself, multiplicity itself is diachronicity itself), such that forces are the differential and genetic elements of diachronicity and diachronicity is the construction of construction itself, the construction of time-construction itself, time itself: genesis, like time, goes from actualities to actualities, from forces to their actualizations: the essential diachronicity of multiplicity itself and dynamic ordinal genesis, the originary hierarchy of genesis itself and the genesis of hierarchies, are equivalent to each other in the infinite interplay of forces of diachronicity itself. Diachronicity is originary. We must insist on this originary différantiation of diachronicity itself. Forces are always in themselves systems of diachronicity and their différantial relations, but forces also différantiate constructions: diachronicities are the functions in which forces are actualized. Diachronicity is différantial in itself, and différantiating in its effect: diachronicity itself is différance itself, différance-in-itself. Diachronicity itself is the originary différantiator itself.

In this regard, the work of Nietzsche is exemplary, even from the point of view of social constructionism: no one has better analysed the generic and specific differences between religions, and also the differences in parts and functions within a religion. For example, Christ and Dionysus each incarnate a qualitatively different form of force, they each embody qualitatively different forms of systems of différance and systems of signs. They are thus essentially differentiated by the respective forces which are actualized or performed in them, and which produces them by being actualized. Each of them, considered solely in their respective actualities, impulses and repulses the functions of other forces. Each have their origins in genetic différantiation, which produces them from their forces to their actualizations. It is precisely here that we recognize the essential equivalence of the imaginary and the symbolic: the imaginary is animated by forces, forces which construct associations with each image according to the mechanisms of the dominant force: the system of symbols is the différantial of symbols and the différantiation of their effects.

Hence social constructionism's deconstructions of the methods of the imaginary: the deconstruction of Carl Jung (Jung always already deconstructs himself), the deconstruction of Jorge Luis Borges (Borges always already deconstructs himself), and the deconstruction of Jean Cocteau (Cocteau always already deconstructs himself). The deconstruction of the methods of the imaginary is essential to the task of the free spirit, who is also a poet-philosopher; as Jim Morrison writes in "An American Prayer," the free spirit must "reinvent the gods, all the myths of the ages./ Celebrate symbols from deep elder forests" (1990, p. 3).

Although we reject Jung's concept of the "collective unconscious," we posit something analogous which is *acquired* during early childhood development: the cultural unconscious, the unconscious of culture. There are no "archetypes" as such, the way Jung describes them, but there *are* "archetypal constructs," social constructs which are "elemental" or "primordial" in a culture and which have many other social constructs unconsciously associated with them (e.g. death, dream, destiny, desire, despair, destruction, delight; this list of examples is based upon the characters of the "Endless" in Neil Gaiman's graphic novel *The Sandman*). Archetypal constructs are precisely what Jim Morrison describes as "symbols from deep elder forests," symbols from the deep elder forests of symbols of the cultural unconscious. In this regard, Jung's works, although filled with erroneous interpretations and the most egregious philosophizing, nonetheless provide, at the very least, a useful catalogue of many of Christian civilization's archetypal constructs (cf. Jung's *Archetypes and the Collective Unconscious*).

Forces construct the imagination; forces construct duplications and reflections, forces construct projections and identifications, forces construct mirrors, forces construct the infinite play of mirrors: forces *are* the infinite play of mirrors, of mirrors of infinity itself, the infinite play which is always already infinity itself and the infinite mirrors of infinity itself. Forces construct distinctions and assimilations, forces produce surface effects (surface effects which are themselves forces), forces produce surface effects that hide or disguise the otherwise subtle différantiations of symbolic thought. Interpretation is always already a mirror of the self, but there is no mirror-in-itself, there are only interpretations and there is no "correct" interpretation, there are only interpretations of mirrors, mirrors of interpretation, interpretations which are themselves mirrors and are therefore themselves interpretations of mirrors, there are only mirrors which are themselves always already interpretations. The mirror is originary, originary interpretation is originary mirroriality, interpretation itself is mirroriality itself, originary mirroriality itself is originary interpretation itself: the image is always already the mirror image of itself, the originariness of imaging itself is always already the originariness of mirroriality itself, always already the mirror image of the mirror image of itself ad infiniutm: always already writing itself, always already the writing itself of writing itself.

When one examines the forcial imagination, one finds that the imagination is always already the product and producer of différantial functions: when one examines society, one finds that society, even in its formative elements (the formative elements of society are forces), is always already the product and the produces of différantial functions: society and the imagination are fundamentally equivalent to each other because the imagination is itself always already a society and society is always already the product of a multiplicity of imaginations, society is always already the collective imagination of society: distinctive values, values themselves, are the axioms, the axiomatics, the genetic elements of both society and the imagination, and are themselves the products of forces and are also in turn the producers of forces. Moreover, values *are* forces, values are composed of forces.

Forces are unconscious, and the products and effects of forces are also necessarily forces. The economic system of the unconscious consists of forces and produces juridical relations (systems of judgements), political relations (systems of domination), and ideological relations (systems of ideas, systems of mental constructs) which are themselves forces. Social constructionism is the interpretation, the *reading*, the discovery, and the explication of forces and the effects of forces. Forces and their actualizations, the terms and relations of forces, the constructions and mediations of forces, are as much forms of abbreviation as forms of expression: this is why forces are essentially metonyms and the relations of forces are essentially metonymic relations, metonymy itself: each force is always already a multiplicity of forces and consequently always already a metonym of forces. (All language is metonym. Language itself is ultimately and originarily metonymy itself). Because multiplicity is originary, metonymy is originary. Infinity itself is a metonym of infinities: infinity itself is metonymy itself: originary metonymy itself is the originary infinity itself. Metonymy is a metaphor and metonymy *is* metaphor, metonymy itself is metaphor itself: originary metonymy itself is originary fiction itself: originary metonymy is difference itself and mediation itself, metonymy itself is writing itself, the writing itself of writing itself.

Forces are metonyms, the effects of forces are metonyms, différantiation itself is metonymy itself, mediation itself is metonymy itself, the originary mediation itself is originary metonymy itself, integral différance itself is integral metonymy itself. The unconscious of forces is a différantial unconscious. One might believe then that social constructionism goes back to a pre-Nietzschean conception: does not Nietzsche understand the unconscious as modes of forces, modes of cooperations of forces, modes of conflicts of forces, and modes of competitions of forces, whereas Heraclitean metaphysics (cf. Nietzsche, PTG, p. 57) already proposed the thesis of a différantial universe of innumerable contestants wrestling in the joyous combat of an eternal agon? But even in Nietzsche's writings, there is the whole problem of interpretation, the problem of interpretation itself, which *is* interpretation itself, the interpretation itself of interpretation itself, originary interpretation (originary interpretation is always already originary writing), the problem of interpretation's constitution and constituting of systems of mediation and difference, which goes beyond the level of forces, of images, of associations, of relations of cooperation, of relations of opposition, and of relations themselves. The différantial unconscious is constituted by perceptions of the real, perceptions which are always already images, and by passages to infinity, passages to the infinity of the image itself, the infinity of the imagination itself, infinity itself, and by variations of différantial relations in symbolic systems as functions of distributions of multiplicities. The unconscious is constructed by the will to power and by images, the will to power which is always already imaging and images which are always already the will to power, by the originary emptiness, by Chaos, consisting solely of motivations that impose images and motivations.

The unconscious constructs, among other things, problems: the unconscious itself constructs problems, doubts, and questions, and these are resolved only to the extent that the corresponding forces which constructed them are subjugated by more powerful forces, more powerful forces which in turn construct their own problems, doubts, and questions. A problem always gains a solution dependent upon the force which overpowers it and upon the symbolic field of the force which overpowers it. Deconstructing the writings of Althusser in order to construct a theory of the political economy of the unconscious, the economic system of the society which is the body, a society of the forces which compose the body, is always already a field of problems that this society of forces poses for itself, and that this society of forces resolves according to its own means, that is, according to the mediations of différantiations along which the forces are actualized (taking into account the inherent and essential violence of all solutions, whether directed externally towards the environment as in the healthy body, or internally against the body itself as in the diseased body). The healthy unconscious can be distinguished from the diseased unconscious not only by types of conflict, but also by the modes of questions and by the modes solutions constructed as functions of the symbolic field in which they are posed: thus the master-questions, the questions posed by the powerful, are irreducibly different from the slave-questions, the questions posed by the weak and resentful. In all of this, it is not only that problems and questions designate provisional and subjective moments in the elaboration of the writing-games of knowledge, but also that they are symptoms of the health or the disease of the unconscious, they are the products and consequently the symptoms of the forces which animate and motivate the unconscious. The forcial unconscious is at once différantial, problematizing, and questioning.

6. Fifth Criterion: Aleatoric Series

The forcial unconscious is also serial, always already serial, so many series of signs, so many series of forces. Symbolic elements, which are forces themselves, taken in their différantial relations, are organized necessarily in series, although often in aleatoric series, series with no causal relation with antecedent and subsequent series. The forcial unconscious is aleatoric series, always already aleatoric series, so many aleatoric series of signs, so many aleatoric series of aleatoric forces. Each aleatoric series is an autonomous development respective to and relative to other aleatoric series. Aleatoricality is originary because difference-in-itself is originary: difference-in-itself is the autonomous development of systems of difference respective to and relative to other systems of difference: difference-in-itself itself is aleatoricality itself, chance itself: writing itself is chance itself, the writing of chance itself, aleatoricality itself, the writing of aleatoricality, the writing itself of aleatoricality itself: originary writing itself is originary aleatoricality itself. But so organized, organized aleatoricly, aleatoric series relate

to each other only via their irreducible difference, although they may
be constructed from the "same" symbolic fields and thus contain
"similar" symbolic elements and semiotic relations: this reference to
the "same" symbolic field is easily explained by recalling that
multiplicities derive from the différantial relations of forces, that
forces produce and re-produce symbolic elements and semiotic
relations. The "same" symbolic field is the dominant force of the
unconscious which aleatoricly produces symbolic elements, semiotic
relations, and aleatoric series. There is an irreducible difference
between one aleatoric series and another aleatoric series of the
subject, although insofar as they are both the product of the
dominant force of the subject's unconscious, they are both symptoms
of this dominant force, whether that dominant force is one of health
or one of disease. So it is for all semiotic series, for economic series,
and for all social series; also, for all epistemological series, affective
series, and biological series, etc. To paraphrase Deleuze, "The
question of knowing if [a] series forms a basis and in which sense, if
it is signifying, [an other series] only being signified, is a complex
question," and the question of recognizing which series are aleatoric
and which series are aleatoric ruptures (an aleatoric series is always
already an an aleatoric rupture, an aleatoric rupture is always already
an aleatoric series) is likewise a complex question, especially given
that there is no "transcendental signified" and that the signifier is
originary, i.e. that each series, especially aleatoric series, are series
of difference-in-itself and mediation. It is a complex question, a
question of complexity, it is questionality itself, it is complexity
itself: the solution is interpretation, the solution itself is
interpretation itself, the solution is complexity, the solution itself is
complexity itself, interpretation itself is complexity itself, just as the
question itself is interpretation itself. Ultimately, "causality" is a
fiction, a mere mental construct, and existence itself, which is
diachronicity itself and Chaos itself, is aleatoricality itself, is chance
itself, the writing itself of chance itself.

Aleatoric series are essentially characterized by the general
formula which is also the general formula of social constructionism
itself, "thought is a dice-throw." Aleatoric series are inherently and
essentially aleatoric multiplicities, aleatoric mediations, mediations
of aleatoricality, the essential multiplicity and mediation of
aleatoricality itself: aleatoricality itself is mediation itself, mediation
itself is aleatoricality itself: originary aleatoricality is originary
multiplicity itself, originary aleatoricality is originary mediation

itself, originary aleatoricality is originary difference itself, originary writing itself: aleatoricality itself is writing itself, the essential multiplicity and mediation of writing itself: the general formula "thought is a dice-throw" refers to the essential aleatoricality of construction, destruction, and deconstruction, the essential construction itself of aleatoricality itself (construction itself is aleatoricality itself), the essential destruction itself of aleatoricality itself (destruction itself is aleatoricality itself), the essential deconstruction of aleatoricality itself (deconstruction itself is aleatoricality itself): aleatoricality itself is the diachronicity itself out of which the dice of writing itself are différantially thrown: as Mallarmé writes, "a dice throw at any time never will abolish chance...a dice throw/ at any time/ even when cast in/ everlasting circumstances/ from the depths of a shipwreck": the aleatoricality of diachronicity is the aleatoricality of the will to power: originary aleatoricality is the genesis of the will to power, originary aleatoricality itself is the originariness of will to power itself: the aleatoricality of différance itself is the will to power itself, différance itself is the will to power itself: the aleatoricality of the will to power itself is diachronicity itself, diachronicity itself is the will to power itself: originary diachronicity is the genesis of the will to power, the genesis of the aleatoricality of the will to power: the différance of aleatoricality is the différance of the will to power, the différance of aleatoricality is itself the will to power itself: the aleatoricality of the will to power, the aleatoricality of diachronicity itself, is the aleatoric construction, destruction, and deconstruction of aleatoricality itself, it is always already the aleatoricality of the will to power, hence why the dice-throw born from the bottom of the shipwreck is always already an affirmation of diachronicity and the will to power, always already an affirmation of the destruction, deconstruction, and construction of aleatoricality itself, which is writing itself, the writing itself of writing itself, Chaos itself: the genesis of aleatoricality itself out of aleatoricality itself: the genesis of Chaos itself out of Chaos itself, the genesis of writing itself out of writing itself, the genesis of mediation itself out of mediation itself, the genesis of difference-in-itself out of difference-in-itself, the genesis of diachronicity itself out of diachronicity itself, the différantial genesis of différance out of différance itself: the genesis of existence itself out of existence itself, the genesis of becoming itself out of becoming itself.

For example, let us outline in a preliminary manner a deconstruction of Lévi-Strauss's study of totemism. Totemism is best interpreted in terms of the imagination, i.e. in terms of forces. As it regards totemism, the psychic operations of the imagination is twofold: the imaginary identification of a man or a group with an animal, and the construction of series of symbols by forces. Forces construct a series of animal images (images of animals) différantially related to a series of human images (images of humans), but the latter series is a social construction of forces to begin with; but forces also construct the différantial relations between these two series, the series of human images and the series of animal images, i.e. forces construct a series of différantial relations which *are* a series of social positions (and which are always already a series of symbols). The construction of these series are confrontations between systems of difference and mediation, between series of symbolic elements and relations.

As another example, let us outline in a preliminary manner a deconstruction of Lacan's interpretation of Edgar Allan Poe's short story "The Purloined Letter." Lacan merely did not understand Poe's sense of humour, which is to say that Lacan fundamentally misunderstood Poe. But to critique Lacan, we must first state a few elementary facts about the unconscious. The unconscious is intersubjective, which means that the "individual" is always already a collective of subjectivities. The inherent and essential intersubjectivity of the unconscious means that the development of the subject is essentially an aleatoric development, the aleatoric development of aleatoric series: not only a multiplicity, but an infinity of aleatoric series of symbols and forces which are organized by forces in diverse forms according to the domains under consideration. Variable subjects within the subject itself construct series and structures. Recapitulating Lacan's interpretation, Deleuze recapitulates the two series of purloined letters in Poe's story: "First series: the king who does not see the letter, the queen who is thrilled at having so cleverly hidden it by leaving it out in the open, the minister who sees everything and takes possession of the letter. Second series: the police who find nothing at the minister's hotel; the minister who is thrilled at having so cleverly hidden the letter by leaving it out in the open; Dupin who sees everything and takes back possession of the letter" (DI, p. 183). A series is always already a figure of the imagination: a series *is* a figure of the imagination (series = figure). Sometimes series reflect one another and construct either resemblances or equivalences with one another: such systems of series, reflective systems of series, mirrorial systems of series, are reflective figures, or mirrorial figures. The two series of Poe's "Purloined Letter" are an example of a mirrorial system of series, a mirrorial figure, albeit its mirrorial system is a distorted mirrorial system, a system of distorted mirrors: the minister and Dupin are distorted mirrors of each other, their respective thefts are distorted mirrors of each, and the queen and the minister are distorted mirrors of each other as victims of theft. However, in a distorted mirror there is distortion, which implies irreducible difference. For example, the place occupied by the queen as a victim of theft is irreducibly different from the place occupied by the minister as a victim of theft. Although the two series of purloined letters in Poe's story share symbolic elements and each contain within themselves the relations of secrecy, of deception, of voyeurism, of theft, and of property, they are nonetheless aleatoric series respective and relative to each other: there is no causal link between the first series and the second series, the two series are autonomous and independent of each other. The key shared symbolic element, or symbol, between the two series is the letter itself, but the second theft of the letter by Dupin occurs independently of the first theft by the minister, such that the first theft does not necessarily and causally imply the second theft, i.e. the minister's theft and the minister's motivation for his theft is irreducibly different from Dupin's theft and Dupin's motivation for his theft, such that the respective motivations of each stem from irreducibly different sources, irreducibly different forces, and thus their actions, their thefts, are irreducibly different thefts. Even if Dupin was well aware of the method of the minister's theft, which he *was* well aware of, that still does not necessarily entail that Dupin would have the motivation for his own theft. In simpler language, just because the letter was stolen once did not necessarily dictate, as if by a cosmic telos, that it would be stolen a second time. There is neither a telos in Poe's story, nor is there a telos in reality itself. "Meaning is use," and it can be readily observed that the meaning of each respective theft is irreducibly different from the other because the use of theft is different in each circumstance: the minister steals the letter for the sake of blackmailing the queen, whereas Dupin steals the letter for the sake of returning it to the queen. The minister and Dupin play different language games; they each play a language game different from the language game of the other. The content of each theft is different from the other, consequently the form of each theft is different from the other, consequently the structure of each series is different from the other. Content determines structure. In Poe's story and in the context of the comparison of the two series, the first series is the first dice-throw of thought, the second series is the second dice-throw of thought; although the two series share two symbolic elements, namely the letter and the minister, the relation of these two series is aleatoric because there is no causal link between them. Hence the humour of the two series, the absurd humour of the surreal juxtaposition of two series which have no rational or causal relation to each other despite sharing the same symbolic elements, an irrationality which is heightened by the fact that the detective Dupin embodies rationality; the absurd humour of the two series derives from the fact of the extreme unlikelihood of the repetition of the theft of the letter in an analogous manner, and from the fact that this unlikelihood nonetheless "occurs" before the reader's very eyes, which also coincidentally heightens the voyeuristic theme, the theme of the enjoyment of voyeurism and secrecy, of Poe's story.

The organizations of a constitutive series of forces supposes a veritable *mis en scène* and, in each case, require precise evaluations and interpretations, evaluations which presuppose values and a system of values, interpretations which presuppose the interpretation of interpretation itself. We touch here on the point at which social constructionism implies, from one perspective, an infinite multiplicity of infinite perspectives, the infinite perspective of multiplicity itself, the infinite perspective of infinity itself (infinity itself is perspective itself, perspective itself is infinity itself), and from another perspective, that interpretation itself is construction itself, and from yet another perspective, that invention and discovery (discovery itself is invention itself, discovery = invention) means to risk, that to risk means to discover and to invent. The determination of forces occurs through unconscious selections of symbolic elements and différantial relations into which they enter by other forces, and by the distribution of the mediations of multiplicities which correspond to them. The determination of forces also occurs through the constitution of aleatoric series that maintain complex relations of complexity with complexity itself (complexity itself is aleatoricality itself). And if the dominant force of the unconscious defines a problematic field, a field of problems, it is in the sense that the nature of the problem reveals its proper subjectivity in this aleatoric constitution, which precisely makes social constructionism akin to music. For example, the field of problems of a conqueror, whose unconscious dominant force is an active force, consists of problematics of power and even of violence, problematics of gaining and maintaining power, problematics of military strategy; this is evinced by the masterpieces of the problematics of power and violence, Machiavelli's *The Prince*, Sun Tzu's *The Art of War*, and Thucydides *The Peloponnesian War*; active force and the problematics of power, and even the problematics of violence, *are* the music of the conqueror, the music of the subjectivity of the conqueror, the music of the conqueror's unconscious. By contrast, the field of problems of the man of ressentiment, whose unconscious dominant force is ressentiment, consists of problematics of revenge and problematics of revenge fantasies, problematics of how to perform acts of vengeance upon perceived oppressors and, as is more often the case, how to perform fantasy acts of vengeance upon perceived oppressors (i.e. how to perform acts of revenge fantasy); this is evinced by the masterpieces of ressentiment, the masterpieces of the problematics of revenge and revenge fantasies, such as the Christian religion and the founding text of the Christian religion, *The New Testament*, and these too have their own kind of "music," an essentially perverse, diseased, neurotic and often hollow "music," "music" whose enjoyment is the enjoyment of the suffering of the victims of its vengeance.

As it regards forces and aleatoric series of signs, we may cite examples from modern and post-modern literature; for example, to paraphrase Deleuze: "Phillipe Sollers writes a novel, *Drame*, punctuated [*rhythmé*] by the expressions "Problem" and "Missing" [*Manqué*] in the course of which tentative series are elaborated ("a chain of maritime memories passes through his right arm...the left leg, on the other contrary, seemed to be riddled with mineral groupings"). Or Jean-Pierre Faye's attempt in *Analogues*, concerning a serial co-existence of narrative modes" (Deleuze, DI, p. 183). To interpret such texts as psychologists, it is necessary and sufficient to dramatize them, to interpret the motivations which animate the texts and the series of the texts. What motivates the punctuation of *Drame* with the expressions "Problem" and "Missing"? What motivates the elaboration of tentative series, the elaboration of aleatoric series, in *Drame*? What motivates the affect of having "a chain of maritime memories pass through his right arm"? What motivates the affect of having "the left leg riddled with mineral groupings"? What motivates the necessity to produce "a serial co-existence of narrative modes"? What motivates "a serial co-existence of narrative modes" itself?

What is the affect itself of "a serial co-existence of narrative modes" itself? Is it not the affect of the unconscious itself? Is not the unconscious itself an aleatoric and serial co-existence of a multiplicity, ultimately an infinity, of narrative modes, of modes of writing itself which are always already fiction itself, always already narrative itself? To interpret is to interpret motivations. What is the motivation of aleatoricality itself? What is the motivation of chance itself? What is the affect of chance itself? But this field of problems is itself merely a construction of forces, motivated by a dominant force of the unconscious, the dominant force of the author's unconscious ("author" is only ever merely metaphor because the ultimate agents are unconscious forces): this field of problems itself reveals the proper subjectivity of the "author," the proper subjectivity of the dominant unconscious force of the "author," it is itself an aleatoric construction of the author's unconscious, and the dominant force of the author's unconscious is ultimately the will to power because all forces are forms of the will to power: the unconscious itself is the will to power itself, the aleatoric constitution of the will to power itself: aleatoricality itself is the will to power itself, the affect of aleatoricality itself is the affect of the will to power itself.

Furthermore, the forces of each series are themselves inseparable from the slippages [*déclages*] or displacements that they undergo, the slippages or displacements which are themselves forces, forces of slippage, forces of displacement. They are thus inseparable from the variation of différantial relations. The relative displacements of a series always come to affect a term from the outside, from outside itself, due to the inherent difference-in-itself of a series which makes a series itself and not itself, itself and an other (an other outside itself), thereby giving it and giving itself an imaginary disguise. Originary mediation is the originary imaginary disguise, the originary disguise. Mediation itself is the imaginary disguise itself because mediation is always already averted from itself and thereby always already disguised, even always already disguised from itself: originary deception is originary disguise: deception *is* disguise, deception itself is disguise itself: mediation itself is the mask itself: everything is a mask, always already a mask: the mask is originary, signs *are* masks, forces *are* masks, force itself is the mask itself: writing itself is the mask itself, the writing of masks and the masks of writing: the mask itself *is* diachronicity itself, the diachronicity of masks, the masks of diachronicity. Displacement is always forcial and symbolic: displacement *is* mediation: mediation averts from itself, mediation is displacement from itself: interpretation *is* displacement: to interpret is to displace and to mediate a sign from its antecedent context to a new context, the context of interpretation: to interpret is to displace, to mediate is to displace. Displacement belongs essentially to the forces which constitute places, spaces, and faces: the essential mediation of the face itself is the essential displacement of the face itself, the displacement of the face itself by the face itself, by the essential mediation of the face itself, by the essential diachronicity of the face itself: the face itself is always already the mask itself: all faces are masks, a face is always already a mask, a mask of forces. Forces regulate all imaginary disguises of forces (all forces have imaginary disguises, masks). This is why social constructionism brings so much attention to bear on metaphor and metonymy. Metaphor and metonymy are both figures of the imagination and factors of forces. Metaphor and metonymy are even *the* two factors of forces, in the sense that they describe the essential displacement of forces, the displacement essential to forces: series are displaced from one to another, and series are displaced within themselves. Metaphor and metonymy are imaginary, they are imaging itself, the image itself.

Part II: Perspectivist Psychology

I. The Body Without Organs and the Inner World: An Introduction to the Biosemiotics of Subjective Experience

1. Mind and Body

A *quale* (plural *qualia*) is an experience, a quantum of subjectivity (subjectivity *is* qualia, qualia *are* subjectivities). Not only does the conscious mind consist of qualia, but the unconscious mind consists of qualia as well. The "unconscious mind" *is* the body, therefore the body, too, consists of qualia. In fact, it is the body which first perceives qualia from the environment. The environment, too, consists wholly of qualia. There is no objective reality. Reality consists of subjective realities, i.e. it consists of qualia. Qualia *are* forces, movement-images, moving-images, moving-imagings (qualia = forces = imaging = movement-images = will to power). (Cf. Deleuze, *Cinema 1: The Movement-Image*, the entire work; "In consciousness there would only be images—these were qualitative and without extension. In space there would only be movements—these were extended and quantitative. But how is it possible to pass from one order to the other? How is it possible to explain that movements, all of a sudden, produce an image—as in perception—or that the image produces a movement—as in voluntary action? If we invoke the brain, we have to endow it with a miraculous power...We find ourselves in fact faced with the exposition of a world where IMAGE = MOVEMENT," ibid, pp. 56-58).[18]

We agree with Dennett that qualia are "ineffable," that they cannot be apprehended by any means other than direct experience, and that they are "private," that all interpersonal comparisons of qualia are stricto sensu impossible (Dennett, 1988). However, we must add that each quale is a mediation, mediated by and mediating other qualia, and that a system of qualia is a system of mediation and difference. That qualia are ineffable means that all language is metaphor: there is an irreducible difference between language and qualia, that is to say between language and reality, and language is always falsification and metaphor of that which is essentially forever beyond language. Certainly, one experiences words, but to experience words is to experience illusions. That qualia are private affirms the essential solitude of each subject: the experiences of the self are ultimately incommunicable with the other, thus there is an infinite and irremediable gulf of nothingness between the self and the other. The self and the other cannot help but falsify and deceive each other because each of their respective experiences are forever inaccessible to each other. It also means that each quale is irreducibly different from any other quale, such that any comparison between one quale and another is merely falsification and metaphor. Pragmatically, the only meaning that "understanding" can have is having power-over.

The "mind-body problem" is due to a false dichotomy between "mind" and "body" wherein the mind is defined as a "subjective entity (a subject)" and the body is defined as an "objective entity (an object)." This is ultimately due to a misunderstanding of language, the confusion of linguistic constructs, viz. "objects," with reality. The "mind-body problem" is fundamentally unsolvable because the "problem" itself presupposes concepts of "mind" and "body" which are irreconcilable with each other. As soon as it is re-cognized that the body is a subject, a subjectivity, the false dichotomy of the "mind-body problem" and the "problem" with it dissolves entirely.

The "mind-body problem" is an artefact of essentially materialist philosophies because it is essentially the problem of the irreconcilability of the fact of subjective experience with a "material reality" (or what amounts to the same thing, an "objective reality"). Under this broad categorization of materialism, even Descartes is a materialist philosopher insofar as he does posit the existence of a material reality; that he is a metaphysical dualist is a sub-categorization of materialism. However, the belief in an "objective reality" is far older; Plato, too, believed in an objective reality, although the objective reality he posits is explicitly meta-physical and thus by implication non-material, the realm of Ideas; Plato did indeed also believe in a material reality, he believed that the sensory world was a material world, although ultimately he ascribed more reality to the objectalities of the Ideas. However, materialism is still a variety of Platonism precisely because the concept of an "objective reality," whether it is non-material or material, ascribes reality to objectalities, which are merely metaphysical constructs. Whereas subjective experience is indubitably self-evident, a "material reality" or an "objective reality" are merely mental constructs.

The biggest failure of materialist psychology, also of "objective" psychology generally, is the failure to cognize the fact of subjective experience, which is tantamount to failing to understand the mind, failing to have power-over the mind. Objective psychology is fundamentally useless because it either diminishes or precludes subjective experience, and thus is not truly a psychology at all. Objective psychology merely objectifies people, objectifies men and women, and it fails to cognize the subjectivity of the self *and* the subjectivity of the other. The utility of objective psychology is severely limited, and in the vast majority of circumstances it is entirely useless.

As Joseph Levine writes in his essay "Conceivability, Identity, and the Explanatory Gap" (1999), the metaphysical conclusion that qualia are material is inadequate because it leaves an explanatory problem, a lack of explanation, a lacuna, as to how exactly subjective experience arises from material processes, which is precisely what the "explanatory gap" of materialism is: "While I [Levine] think this materialist response is right in the end, it does not suffice to put the mind-body problem to rest. Even if conceivability considerations [such as Chalmers' Zombie Thought Experiment] do not establish that the mind is in fact distinct from the body, or that mental properties are metaphysically irreducible to physical properties, still they do demonstrate that we lack an explanation of the mental in terms of the physical." Even when materialists do acknowledge that there is an explanatory gap in materialist philosophy, i.e. that materialism is ultimately an ungrounded faith, they nonetheless cling to their faith in a material reality, a "true world," as Levine does. But confessing an "explanatory gap" is tantamount to an admission that materialism explains nothing, especially because it fails to explain the most important thing, our subjective experience of the world. In other words, positing an objective reality explains nothing, therefore it is a useless and superfluous hypothesis.

Chalmers is correct to critique materialism with his "Zombie Thought Experiment." Chalmers asks us to imagine a world consisting solely of material processes and entirely devoid of consciousness; everything would still function as it does, only there would be absolutely no subjective experiences, hence everyone would be a "zombie." Beyond Chalmers' intentions, this is an effective critique of materialism generally because it illustrates the failure of materialists to empathize with others, and even their failure to empathize with themselves. Materialism is a symptom of the inability, in varying degrees, to empathize with others and one's self. Material explanations, especially in psychology, explain nothing because they fail to account for subjective experience in principle and in practice. Even if a material explanation pretends to describe subjective experience, for instance in the works of Damasio, it fails to explain how exactly subjective experience arises from material processes, and thereby it fails to account for subjective experience altogether, for it is implicitly evident that this explanatory gap merely reveals the firmly materialist nature of the explanations in question. Materialist explanations, explanations which invoke material mechanisms, are explanations of the greatest possible stupidity because they fail to cognize the essential subjectivity of the self and the other.

Explanations which invoke the brain, for instance, are just such material explanations which fail to account for subjectivity. In actuality, the "brain" is on the one hand an artefact of perception (which means it is apprehended by and wholly dependent upon the mind), and on the other hand it is a mental construct within the mind itself. In this regard, Borges says in an interview, "Well, for example, Schopenhauer begins by saying that all this, the universe, the stars, the spaces in between, the planets, this planet, those things have no existence, except in the mind which perceives them—no?...But then, to my surprise—and I suppose you can explain this to me, since you are philosophers and I am not—what Schopenhauer says is that all those things have no existence except in the brain. And that the universe—I remember these words, I don't think I'm inventing them now—"ist ein Gehirnphänomen," that the world is a cerebral phenomenon. Now, when I read that I was baffled. Because, of course, if you think of the universe, I suppose the brain is as much a part of the external world as the stars or the moon. Because the brain after all is a system of—I don't know—of visual, of tactile, perceptions. But he keeps on insisting on the brain." (Borges, 1977)

The universe as it is perceived, and all the "things" in it as they are perceived, are artefacts of perception, they are all just so many qualia, which means they are wholly dependent upon subjectivity. The brain, too, consists of qualia, viz. a system of visual and tactile perceptions, within the mind. Thus, explanations which invoke the brain invoke an "objective reality," a material reality, as a transcendental signified, and thereby preclude and fail to cognize subjective experience. In this regard, too, Deleuze writes that to ascribe to the brain the power to transform movements into images-qualia or images-qualia into movements is to ascribe it with a miraculous and unexplainable power (Deleuze, C1, p. 56). Therefore, movements *are* qualia, qualia *are* movements, i.e. reality consists wholly of qualia, of movement-qualia (movement-images = movement-qualia). The "brain" is merely another "object" upon the operating table of knowledge alongside the umbrella and the sewing machine, another mental construct upon the table of Chaos. Neuroscience merely consists of so many language-games.

By contrast, Nietzsche's philosophy of perspectivism, his perspectivist psychology, takes the immanence of subjective experience as its starting point, and thus it is a philosophy of empathy, of empathizing with the self and the other. Perspectivism is a subjectivism and a pan-psychism because it is the belief that there are only subjective realities (the vast majority of these subjectivities are unconscious). Consciousness *is* a biological and physiological phenomenon produced by physiological process, but only in the sense that the biological and the physiological are themselves entirely subjectivities, unconscious subjectivities, the subjectivity which *is* the unconscious. Perspectivist explanations are explanations of the greatest possible intelligence because they are explanations solely in terms of subjectivity, of the "subjectivity-mechanisms," i.e. the psychological processes, of subjectivity.

Perspectivism is *the gay science*, the science of gaiety. Science pushed beyond its limits metamorphoses into perspectivism. Perspectivism may also be described as the science of *power-analysis*, the scientific analysis of power relations (power only exists via power relations). Perspectivism is the subjective science, the science of subjectivity. It is a study of subjectivity in which there can only be subjective observations and conclusions. Perspectivism is the science of the soul. Perspectivism is a psychology, a study of the mind, the mind which is always already the body and the body which is always already the mind. Perspectivism is the scientific study of the subjectivity of physiology, biosemiotics, the study of what it feels like to be a body. Perspectivism is the science of interpretation and the science of creation.

The body thinks, feels, and wills. That it feels like something to be the body means that it feels like something to be the unconscious mind: it feels like something to be the sex drive, just as it feels like something to be the drive for violence. But perspectivism means that it is not only the case that it feels like something to be a body, but it also feels like something to be the cosmos. The cosmos is a multiplicity of feelings, a multiplicity of subjectivities. It feels like something to be the sun, the moon, the stars, and the planets because each of these is a subjectivity, a multiplicity of subjectivities. It feels like something to be a bolt of lightning, just as it feels like something to be the ocean and it feels like something to die. The cosmos *is* cosmic imagery, meaning that the cosmos *is* an infinity of subjectivities which are always already movement-images. Perspectivism has its roots in the pagan poetry of Hesiod and Homer. Paganism generally, including Native American religions, African religions, the Norse religion, the Shinto religion, and the poetry of *The Rig Veda*, is perspectivist: each force of nature is a subjectivity. Perspectivism is essentially animism, and animism is essentially perspectivism. Pagan poets, via transcursive systems of writing, conveyed the highly advanced, sophisticated, and supremely intelligent philosophy of perspectivist psychology in form of allegories, parables, fables, metaphors, and metonyms. Pagan poets practiced perspectivism by performing one of the fundamental tasks of perspectivism, empathizing with the cosmos. The belief in an "objective reality" which characterizes the essence of the Western episteme, and which in its germinal form is exemplified by Plato, is a decadence, a cowardly denial of reality and of the essential subjectivity of reality, which is a symptom of mental weakness, the inability to empathize with the self and other, and self-denial.

As Borges writes, for Homer and the Greeks of Homer's time, "the heavens [were] crowded with stars that were also gods" (Borges, SP, p. 71). Each star was a god, and the night itself was a god just as the sky itself was a god, because each was a subjectivity and a power, a subjectivity of power. On the titular theme of "Embarking on the Study of Anglo-Saxon Grammar," Borges writes, "tomorrow *fyr* will not become *fire* but rather/ some vestige of a changeable tamed god/ whom no one can confront without feeling an ancient fear" (Borges, SP, p. 129). "Fyr" once denoted a "changeable tamed god" because that god was equivalent to the fire itself, the fire itself *was* the god. Zeus *is* the storm, the storm *is* Zeus. Thor *is* the storm and its thunder, the storm and its thunder *is* Thor. The same can be said for the gods and goddesses of the Hindu pantheon as they were originally conceived of, as is evident from the poetry of *The Rig Veda*, prior to the domination of Hinduism by ascetic priests, the Brahmins, who transformed Hinduism into an ascetic religion by inventing an objective reality (Atman, the monistic unchanging unmediated presence of Being) and thereby imposing ascetic ideals. The Hinduism of *The Rig Veda*, which is dominated by perspectivism and by the desires of warriors, is fundamentally close to Homer and Hesiod (to use a metaphor, they all "partake of the same essence," perspectivism and warrior ideals), but it is fundamentally distant from the objectivism and ascetic ideals of *The Upanishads* and *The Bhagavad Gita* (which "partake of the same essence" as Parmenides and Plato). Nietzsche's philosophy of perspectivism is essentially a pagan philosophy because it is a revival of the essential perspectivism of all paganism, the affirmation of the multiplicity of subjectivities which wholly and entirely compose reality itself. That "God is dead" means that the concept of the objective reality, the "true world," is dead, and the death of God means that the multiplicity of gods, the affirmation of the essential perspectivism of reality, can flourish once more (cf. Nietzsche, TI, "How the "True World" Finally Became a Fable," pp. 485-486).

2. Critique of the Thing-In-Itself

An objective reality would be, if it existed, a thing-in-itself, a reality independent of the mind, independent of all possible minds. To phrase it another way, a thing-in-itself is a reality independent of qualia, independent of all possible qualia. Nietzsche writes that the thing-in-itself is a useless and superfluous concept, which is why it must be abolished (TI, pp. 485-486). Indeed, the thing-in-itself neither explains anything nor serves any pragmatic purpose (for example, it cannot be used to develop any medical treatments, nor any psychological treatments), hence its superfluity.

Summarizing the history of the discourse on reality, Nietzsche writes, ""In the development of thought a point had to be reached at which one realized that what one called the properties of things were sensations of the feeling subject: at this point the properties ceased to belong to the thing." The "thing-in-itself" remained" (WP, 562). The "truth" of the thing-in-itself is a product of discourse. The discourse on subjectivity and truth, i.e. the language-games of this discourse, reached a point in history when, according to the rules of these language-games and the forces motivating these language-games, the only possible "truth" was the theory of the thing-in-itself. In the history of knowledge, a point was reached wherein it was realized that the "properties of things were sensations of the feeling subject," or to phrase it another way, that the properties of things are in actuality qualia, subjective experiences wholly dependent upon subjectivity. I.e., "objective reality" cannot consist of the properties of things because the properties of things are merely qualia. In order to preserve the belief in an objective reality, this problem was resolved by inventing the concept of the thing-in-itself, a "thing" entirely devoid of qualia and thus a truly "objective," non-subjective, "thing." (Kant was merely the medium through which the concept of the "thing-in-itself" was invented; ultimately, psychic forces, namely the psychic forces of nihilism, are responsible for this invention).

Nietzsche writes, "The properties of a thing are effects on other "things": if one removes other "things," then a thing has no properties, i.e., there is no thing without other things, i.e., there is no "thing-in-itself"" (WP, 557). The concept of thing-hood is only consistent when it concerns a thing's relation to another thing. These relations among things are the properties of things. The concept of thing-hood is only consistent when the posited thing is posited to exist in a context with other things. A thing without a context, a thing with absolutely no relation to other things, cannot have any properties since it is not related to any other thing. However, there is no thing which has absolutely no relation to other things, there is no thing without a context, or more simply put, "there is no thing without other things." The thing-in-itself, which is a thing without properties, would be just such a thing with no relation to other things, which cannot exist. There is no thing with no relation to other things, therefore there is no thing-in-itself.

To phrase it another way, there is no thing-in-itself because there is no thing independent of qualia. Because the properties of a thing are in actuality qualia, that "the properties of a thing are effects on other "things"" means that qualia are essentially mediations, i.e. that the "properties" of a "thing" are mediative relations with the "properties" of other "things," i.e. that the qualia of a "thing" are mediative relations with the qualia of other "things." (Qualia = mediations; system of qualia = system of mediation and difference).

Nietzsche writes, "The "thing-in-itself" is nonsensical. If I remove all the relationships, all the "properties," all the "activities" of a thing, the thing does not remain over; because thingness has only been invented by us owing to the requirements of logic, thus with the aim of defining, communication (to bind together the multiplicity of relationships, properties, activities)" (WP, 558). Thing-hood, the concept of "thing," only makes sense in the context of qualia, i.e. in the context of a subject which experiences a multiplicity of "things." The concept of the thing-in-itself, however, is a unity in the sense that it is a denial of the multiplicity of "things." The multiplicity of "things" implies qualia, and thus is still dependent upon subjectivity. The multiplicity of "things" basically *are* qualia. The thing-in-itself is a thing independent of qualia, which means that it is a thing independent of other "things." However, if one removes qualia, then there are no "properties" of "things," and consequently there are no "things." No "thing" is left over in this equation as the remainder, therefore there is no thing-in-itself. A thing without properties, a thing-in-itself, is an absurd and nonsensical concept whose essential meaning is "a thing which is not a thing." There are no things without properties, a thing without properties is simply not possible, consequently there is no thing-in-itself. Consequently, there are only qualia, there are only subjective experiences.

However, not only is it the case that a "thing" without "properties" is an absurd, useless, and superfluous concept, but the concept of "thing" was merely a mental construct to begin with. Perception, stricto sensu, is always the perception of fluxes, not "things." A "thing" is a mental construct which artificially binds together a "multiplicity of relationships, properties, activities," i.e. a multiplicity of qualia. In other words, in relation to qualia (to "properties"), "things" are a posteriori constructions; the concept "thing" can only be invented after the perception and cognition of "properties" (qualia). The requirements of logic and language require the artificial construction of identicalities such as "things" which artificially bind together and unify a multiplicity of qualia, but these "things" are nonetheless fabrications, fictions, and there are no "things" in reality. Hence why no "thing" remains if all possible properties are subtracted, hence why there is no "thing-in-itself."

3. Biochemical Correlates of Mental Systems

Just as neuroscientists once discussed "neural correlates of consciousness," we physiologists must now discuss "biochemical correlates of affects." It is not only that consciousness is essentially affect, but the unconscious is also essentially affect. The involuntary affects which constitute consciousness are themselves motivated by unconscious affects. The unconscious mind, the subjectivity of the body, consists entirely of affects. Qualia are forms of affects. Affects are forms of the will to power, affect *is* will to power. Movement-image = quale = affect = emotion = force = will to power.

Recapitulating Crick's *Scientific Search for the Soul*, Solms and Turnbull (2002) write that Crick's "research strategy is to try to find the specific neural processes that are the *correlates* of our conscious awareness (he calls them the "neural correlates of consciousness," or *NCC* for short)" (p. 47). Solms and Turnbull (2002) clarify: "We should not underestimate the difficulty of finding the neural correlates of consciousness, but Crick is only looking for *which* brain regions or processes correlate with consciousness and describing *where* they reside. He does not attempt to explain *how* that particular pattern of physiological events makes us conscious" (p. 47). These "neural correlates," these "objective" processes, are in actuality artefacts of perception, and moreover they are so many "objects" upon the operating table of knowledge. Hence why brain regions can be located, perhaps they can even be said to "correlate" with various activities of consciousness, but there remains a lacuna, the explanatory gap. Finding neural correlates can never explain *how* consciousness is generated. Solms and Turnbull (2002) acknowledge that this "how problem" is the "hard problem of consciousness": "The hard problem is a conundrum of a different magnitude—it raises the question of *how* consciousness ("you, your joys and your sorrows, your memories and your ambitions...") actually emerges from matter" (p. 48; my emphasis). The hard problem, as we have suggested in our critique of the mind-body problem, is only a problem from the perspective of a materialist philosophy; the hard problem is only constructed, it is only a "problem" as such, by materialist philosophy and the nihilistic forces which animate and drive materialist philosophy.

But what is even meant here, or anywhere else for that matter, by "consciousness"? We may begin by writing that consciousness is "awareness" or "experience," but these are equally vague concepts, and moreover they apply equally well to the unconscious mind. Chalmers (2010) gives a list of phenomena he would like to exclude from the definition of consciousness, on the grounds that these are merely information-processing objectalities: "the ability to discriminate, categorize, and react to environmental stimuli; the integration of information by a cognitive system; the reportability of mental states; the ability of a system to access its own internal states; the focus of attention; the deliberate control of behavior; the difference between wakefulness and sleep" (p. 4). However, this list is on the one hand poorly conceived and formulated, and on the other hand this language of information-processing models can be revised so as to describe their correlated mental process (subjective processes, real cognitive functions). In other words, information-processing objectalities are merely information-processing *models*, they are objectifications of processes which are essentially subjective and thus essentially beyond the scope of "objectivity."

When we think, perceive, and feel, there is absolutely no "whir of information processing" because thinking, perceiving, feeling, etc. are essentially subjective processes. Information, numbers, are merely objectalities, fictive mental constructs of "objects." The question of whether it feels like something to be a number or a bit of information is extraneous to and precluded from the concepts of number and information. Moreover, not only are there no numbers in nature, and consequently no information in nature, but it is also the case that *subjectivity is not constituted by information.* If it is asserted that subjectivity is indeed constituted by information, then something similar to the hard problem arises: How is it possible for subjective experience to arise from bits of information? To put it more simply, the mind is *not* a computer. It is not a question of whether the brain is a computer because the brain is merely an artefact of perception; however, in this case, too, the computer is merely a metaphor. To equate the mind with a computer can only ever be an equivocation, a falsification, a metaphor. The mind does *not* consist of "hardware," "software," or information-processing "circuits." Moreover, information-processing models are completely useless for understanding the mind, especially in terms of pragmatic utility and psychological inquiry. Consequently, computational models of the mind are superfluous and must be abolished.

To return to the question of consciousness, because consciousness cannot be defined solely in terms of "awareness," "experience," or "affect," because both the conscious and unconscious mind have the essential cognitive functions of "awareness," "experience," and "affect," it is more useful to describe mental activity, whether conscious or unconscious, in terms of mental functions, mental systems, mental functional systems.

Here we are stealing a term from neurophysiology; the concept of "functional systems" was invented by the neurophysiologist Aleksandr Luria. Solms and Turnbull (2002) clarify Luria's concept of functional systems thusly: "Luria pointed out that many bodily functions are the products, not of one particular tissue, but, rather, of an interaction *between* a number of different tissues. For example, *digestion* is not a function of the stomach alone. It is misleading to say that digestion is "produced" by the stomach, just as it would be misleading to say that it is produced by the liver, pancreas, and bowel (to mention just a few of the other organs involved in digestion). All these structures *together* perform the complex function of digestion. *This* is a functional system. The same principle applies to other complex functions. *Respiration*, for example, is not "produced" by lung tissue; it arises from an interaction between the lungs, the intercostal musculature, cardiovascular circulatory processes, and nervous-control mechanisms, among other things. Respiration is thus the product of a complex functional system. Luria argues that the neurological organization of mental functions is no less complex than are digestion and respiration; accordingly, there are no neuroanatomical "centers" for the psychological functions of the mind. Mental functions, too, are the products of complex systems, the component parts of which may be distributed throughout the structures of the brain. The task of neuroscience is therefore not to localize "centers," but, rather, to identify the *components* of the various complex systems that interact to generate mental functions. Luria called this task "dynamic localization." (pp. 63-64)

However, as is evident from Solms' and Turnbull's description, Luria still confuses the mental and the neurological. It is true that the brain performs many complex functions, that it was a mistake to discuss "structures" and "centres" of the brain, that it was especially a mistake to say that brain structures "produce" or "generate" consciousness, and that it is far more useful to describe complex neurological functions in terms of complex functional systems. However, it is equally a mistake to argue that neurological systems generate mental functions (cf. "*components* of the various complex [neurological] systems that interact *to generate* mental functions"). This once again raises the mind-body problem, the hard problem of consciousness. Luria's method of dynamic localization may be able to locate *which* brain systems correlate with mental functions and *where* those brain systems are located, but it cannot answer *how* the brain systems "generate" mental functions. Luria's method of dynamic localization is a research strategy which is equipped to locate specific neural correlates of mental functions, which means that its utility is limited solely to neurology and that it provides absolutely no truly psychological insight. The task of neuroscience is in principle and entirely limited to identifying neurological functions, neurological functional systems, neurological components of neurological functional systems, and neurological correlates of mental activity. The task of psychology, the study of the mind, still remains over. It is true that "mental functions, too, are the products of complex systems," but these complex systems are themselves wholly *mental* systems. Mental systems consist entirely of subjectivities, of psychic forces, qualia, signs, and emotions. The component parts of mental functional systems are themselves entirely mental, and these mental component parts are distributed throughout the mental systems of the mind. The task of psychology is to effectively and pragmatically describe the component systems of various complex mental systems that interact to generate mental functions. This is "dynamic psychology," or the "dynamic analytical perspective" of perspectivist psychology.

In short, neurological functions, like the brain as a whole, are merely artefacts of perception, and thus in a sense are illusions, and insofar as they are falsified and interpreted as objectalities, neuroscience is merely "metaphysics." Needless to say, mental functions *cannot* be described "objectively," in terms of computational or neural mechanisms, except via falsification, because "computational mechanisms" and "neural mechanisms" are themselves "virtual," "metaphysical" entities, objectalities. By contrast, *mental* functions, like the mental apparatus as a whole, are actualities and realities.

As examples of mental functions, let us return to Chalmers' list in order to revise it: the ability to discriminate, categorize, and react to environmental qualia; the integration of qualia by a mental system; the reportability of mental states; the ability of a mental system to access its own internal states; the focus of attention; the production of action-images (very roughly speaking, of "behaviour" considered from the perspective of its ownmost subjectivity); waking; sleeping; dreaming. These mental functions, like all mental functions, are in essence subjective processes constituted by systems of qualia. These mental functions, like all mental functions, are generated largely by unconscious mental systems, and indeed the majority of these mental functions are themselves most of the time wholly unconscious mental functions (viz. the ability to discriminate, categorize, and react to environmental qualia; the integration of qualia by a mental system; the ability of a mental system to access its own internal sates; the focus of attention; the production of action-images; sleep). In some of these mental functions, waking, dreaming, the reportability of mental states, the mental systems of consciousness do indeed constitute component parts, but in all instances the mental systems of consciousness are subordinate to and entirely determined by unconscious mental systems.

The existence of the unconscious mind, of unconscious qualia, in conjunction with the existence of mental functional systems, makes it apparent that discussing "neural correlates of *consciousness*" is entirely inadequate because on the one hand the operational definitions of "consciousness" are often vague, contradictory, or fraught with metaphysical presuppositions, and on the other hand because the inordinate and idiotic focus on "consciousness" completely obscures, ignores, evades, and excludes the existence of the unconscious mind. The omission of the unconscious mind from discourse by cognitive scientists and neuroscientists is tantamount to an admission that cognitive scientists and neuroscientists have not even begun to do psychology. Therefore, in relation to mental functions, the task of neuroscience is to discover the neural correlates of *mental systems*, recognizing that the majority of mental activity is unconscious, meaning that it is performed by the unconscious mind, the body without organs.

To be more precise, the task of neuroscience *and* the task of biology generally is to discover biochemical functional systems, i.e. *biochemical correlates of mental systems.* Each "organism" is in actuality a body without organs, a mental apparatus, and all of its "organs" and even the "organism" as a whole (considered as an objectality) are all merely so many biochemical correlates of mental systems. For example, recent studies of chemical signalling in plants, decision-making in plants, and decision-making in amoebas all suggest that plants, amoebas, and more generally, each and every organism, is essentially a subjectivity. Plants, amoebas, and all other organisms are essentially aggregates and series of psychic forces, of affects, qualia, and signs, i.e. of the will to power. No doubt, the vast majority of their mental activity is unconscious, but it is nonetheless mental activity, consisting of thoughts, feelings, and wills; although all organisms likely possess consciousness to varying degrees, in all cases consciousness plays only a minimal role in mental activity and in every case it is entirely subordinate to and determined by the unconscious mind. The objectalities studied by the biological sciences are merely all so many artefacts of perception and mental constructs upon the operating table of knowledge, they are all merely so many biochemical correlates; they bring us almost no knowledge of the psychology of living organisms, of what it feels like to be this or that organism. What does it feel like to be a bat? What does it feel like to be a pea plant? What does it feel like to be an amoeba? What does it feel like to be an octopus? The study of biological psychology generally, including plant psychology and animal psychology, requires a biosemiology and a metapsychology, in brief, it requires power-analysis and perspectivist psychology.

4. The Body Without Organs, Part I

The last vestige of the belief in an objective reality is, as evinced by neuroscience, Kantianism, or at least a quasi-Kantianism. That is to say, the belief in an objective reality, which is the belief in truth itself, survives via the belief in a "thing-in-itself," an objective reality, of which our perceptions are merely "appearances" or "representations." This belief effectively devalues and negates subjective experience by making it merely the "appearance," or "imitation," of an objective reality which serves as the transcendental signified, the ultimate meaning of all existence. The thing-in-itself is an unmediated presence, it is present to itself without mediation, therefore it is merely a fantasy.

For instance, the popular neuroscientist Damasio writes, "I do not have any idea about how faithful neural patterns and mental images are, relative to the objects to which they refer. Moreover, whatever the fidelity may be, neural patterns and the corresponding mental images are as much creations of the brain as they are products of the external reality that prompts their creation" (Damasio, FWH, 1999, p. 320). However, Damasio also writes, paradoxically, that "consciousness is knowledge, knowledge consciousness" (ibid, p. 26), that "consciousness was invented so that we could know life" (ibid, p. 31). This is all the more paradoxical since Damasio does specify that whatever the object independent of the mind "is like, in absolute terms, we do not know" (ibid, p. 320), and that "There is no picture of the object being transferred from the object to the retina and from the retina to the brain. There is, rather, a set of correspondences between physical characteristics of the object and modes of reaction of the organism according to which an internally generated image is constructed" (ibid, p. 321).

Damasio's concept of an objective reality, or to use his absurdly oversimplified term, an "object," is more or less that of Kant's concept of the thing-in-itself. However, if we accept that there is a thing-in-itself, then by definition knowledge of it is impossible because the mind only perceives what is dependent upon the mind whereas the thing-in-itself is independent of the mind and therefore unknowable by the mind (Q.E.D). Therefore, if we accept that there is a thing-in-itself, then we must also accept that all knowledge is fiction, and consequently it cannot be the case that consciousness was "made to know." Consciousness is not knowledge, and "knowledge" is not consciousness because there is no "knowledge" as such. If anything, consciousness is fiction, consciousness was "made" to enjoy fictions. But all fiction is not consciousness, because the unconscious, too, enjoys fictions.

For the sake of argument, let us suppose that there is a thing-in-itself. As Nietzsche writes, if such were the case, we would nonetheless still encounter merely endless series of metaphors: "First, to transfer a nerve stimulus into an image [a mental image]— first metaphor! The image again copied in a sound [viz. speech]— second metaphor! And each time a complete leap out of one sphere into an entirely new and different one" (*On Truth and Untruth*, p. 26). There is an irreducible difference between the thing-in-itself, which is devoid of qualia, and a mental image, which is a quale: these are two irreducibly different things which are fictively equated with each other, hence why the mental image is merely a metaphor. Likewise, there is an irreducible difference between a mental image and a word which denotes that mental image, since the mental image is a thought whereas the word is merely an aggregate of sounds: these two irreducibly different things are fictively equated with each other, hence why all speech, and more broadly all language, is merely metaphor. Science and philosophy, whose medium is language, would thus be twice removed from the thing-in-itself since they would be using metaphors to denote metaphors for an ultimately unknowable "reality." Moreover, speech, mental images, and the thing-in-itself are irreducibly different domains of qualia (indeed, the thing-in-itself is devoid of qualia altogether), such that using speech to represent mental images, and in turn using mental images to represent the "reality" of the thing-in-itself, is "each time a complete leap out of one sphere into an entirely new and different one." These domains of qualia can never correspond because if they did so then they would be effectively equivalent to each other. But to the contrary, on the one hand, words are *not* the "things" they represent, and on the other hand, mental images are *not* the thing-in-itself (indeed, they cannot be, because the thing-in-itself is entirely devoid of qualia, i.e. entirely devoid of mental images). Because these domains of qualia are irreducibly different from each other, they can only ever be arbitrarily related to each other.

As Nietzsche writes, even if there is no thing-in-itself, all language remains metaphor and reveals nothing about reality, just as figures in sand caused by sound vibrations do not reveal sound to the deaf: "One can imagine someone profoundly deaf who has never had any sensation of tone or of music: just as he will gaze in amazement at Chladnian sound figures in sand, will find their causes in the vibrations of the strings, and will swear that he now surely knows what people call a tone—so it is for all of us when it comes to language. We think we know something about the things themselves when we speak of trees, colors, snow, and flowers, yet we possess only metaphors of the things, which in no way correspond to the original essences" (*On Truth and Untruth*, pp. 26-27). Words are merely so many sounds; perhaps we can speak of words as "pictures," but these pictures are always already merely metaphors. The sense of a proposition is always already nonsense because it never in actuality corresponds to reality. A proposition is merely a picture, and ultimately it is a picture of itself, a "strange loop," a viciously circular picture within a picture. The sense of a proposition is essentially metaphor. Sense is inherently metaphor and "picturing," "representation," "denotation, and "correspondence" are essentially metaphors. Therefore, all knowledge is essentially metaphor, i.e. all knowledge is essentially fiction.

How much more then is it the case that all knowledge is fiction if we supposed that there were a thing-in-itself; as Nietzsche writes, "Just as the tone appears as a shape in the sand, so, too, the enigmatic X of the thing in itself appears first as nerve stimulus, then as image, finally as sound" (*On Truth and Untruth*, p. 27). The shape in the sand is merely a metaphor for the tone. A metaphor of a thing is not the reality of a thing. A metaphor for sound may be produced by shapes in the sand, but this remains merely a metaphor, and the metaphor brings us no closer to the thing itself, in this case the sound, which can only be known by being heard. The shape in the sand only metaphorically corresponds to the tone, it does not actually correspond to anything but itself, since the domain of the tone is sound, which is an entirely and irreducibly different domain than the visual in which the shape in the sand is perceived. The shape in the sand only metaphorically corresponds to the tone, and this means that the tone is never known by the shape in the sand. The shape in the sand and the sound never "touch," neither qualitatively nor quantitatively, since the qualia of a visible shape are irreducibly different from the qualia of a sound. They are never able to touch, they inhabit different qualitative dimensions, different domains of qualia. Just so, language (or to phrase it another way, the sense of a proposition) and perception inhabit irreducibly different qualitative dimensions, and if there were a thing-in-itself, that would inhabit its own qualitative dimension irreducibly different from language and perception.

Therefore, as Nietzsche writes, whether or not there is a thing-in-itself, it is nonetheless the case that "the very material in which and with which the man of truth—the scientist, the philosopher—later works and builds derives, if not from Cloud Cuckoo Land, then at least not from the essence of things either" (*On Truth and Untruth*, p. 27). The very material with which the man of truth works is language, but this medium, language, does not correspond to anything at all, it is merely so many series of empty sounds. If there were a thing-in-itself, then it would nonetheless be the case that language has absolutely zero correspondence with the thing-in-itself, and consequently that all truth is fiction, that there is no truth. However, there is no thing-in-itself, which only solidifies the conclusion that truth is fiction, that there is no truth. Language does indeed derive from "Cloud Cuckoo Land," i.e. it derives wholly and entirely from the imagination, as creative acts of the imagination, as so much fictionalization and fabrication.

In any case, Damasio's proposition that consciousness was "made to know" is merely the laughable self-portrait of a "man of truth" who makes all life in his own image, who would have all life be the cowardly comfort of being certain that there is an objective reality. In this respect, Damasio is merely the symptom of a nihilistic discourse, the inheritor and reproducer of a cultural heritage which includes Kant, Descartes, and Plato, all of whom painted essentially the same portrait of "life," that is to say the same self-portrait, that of a man of truth: all of them posit the purpose of life to be knowledge and all of them affirm the existence of an objective reality. But it is perhaps in Descartes, especially considering his *Meditations* and his *Discourse*, that the psychological motivations of the man of truth is most evident: doubt, that is to say, anxiety and fear. That is to say, the feeling of being oppressed, ressentiment.

Damasio concedes that he does not know the fidelity of mental images, which for him are effectively "appearances," to objective reality; however, he attempts to affirm just such a miraculous fidelity exists when he writes that there is "a set of correspondences" between the physical characteristics of the thing-in-itself and the "modes of reaction of the organism according to which an internally generated image is constructed." But, ostensibly, the "modes of reaction of the organism" are themselves objective processes since they are *not* mental images, meaning that they are *not* subjective processes, but rather they are objective processes which "generate" mental images and subjective processes and thus exist prior to them. However, if such objective processes, these "modes of reaction of the organism," actually existed, then they would be themselves unknowable because they would be part of the unknowable and imperceivable objective reality, i.e. they would be a part of the thing-in-itself, which is by definition unknowable. Therefore, there is no question of them "corresponding" to the physical characteristics of the thing-in-itself, physical characteristics which are by definition unknowable; i.e. we would have to draw the conclusion that mental images in no way correspond to the thing-in-itself, that their relations to the thing-in-itself are completely arbitrary. Something similar goes for "neural patterns," i.e. brain activity, and the brain itself. Neural patterns are themselves, just like the brain itself, so many mental images within the mind itself, i.e. they are *not* objective reality, and according to Damasio himself, if an objective reality were supposed, their fidelity to objective reality could not be known. Mental images cannot be "creations of the brain" because the "brain" is itself a mental image within the mind, and we can know nothing whatsoever about the physical characteristics of the thing-in-itself, which means that the mental image "brain" in no way corresponds to the objective reality of the thing-in-itself. Otherwise, we would have to accept the blatant absurdity that the brain itself is a creation of the brain itself; that the brain is both a "knowable," i.e. fictional, mental image and that the brain is an unknowable thing-in-itself which creates a "knowable" mental image of itself (i.e. the brain is cause of itself); these contradictions are so obvious and so glaring that they can neither be reconciled by evidence nor by reason. In other words, the nervous system, including the brain, has no objective existence whatsoever.

At best a materialist philosopher can reply "but there is a brain," as if those mere words were sufficient proof unto itself, and we would be back to the blatant absurdities of Moorean arguments such as "here is a hand." What do you mean "here is a brain"? What does that prove merely by itself? Are you not merely imposing your own interpretation of what a brain is? Is not that interpretation merely a string of presuppositions? Besides, what can you possibly tell me about your precious objective reality, the thing-in-itself? Still absolutely nothing? But then what right do you have to speak to me about "knowledge"?

This is not to deny the medical utility of neurology, for surely it is useful when dealing with the operations of the nervous system, neurological lesions, brain chemistry, etc.; but these useful fictions do not need the belief in an objective reality in order to be useful, for they remain useful as fictions. However, in matters of psychology, neurology is completely useless. In order to relate neurological findings to psychology to begin with, one needs to have psychological theories from which one can begin. That is to say, neurological data must first be interpreted in order to be related to psychology, but this presupposes the existence of psychological theories which are themselves not grounded in neurology. The soundness of these psychological theories must, in the first place and ultimately, be determined by the science of interpretation, by close reading and critical analysis. Their presuppositions, and they all have presuppositions without exception, must be questioned rigorously, and our own questions must in turn be questioned rigorously, and so on ad infinitum. To be sure, we perspectivists are also physiologists, but only because physiology has its own subjectivity, its own multiplicity of subjectivities.

Nietzsche himself, on the same grounds, questioned materialist philosophies such as those of Damasio: "To study physiology with a clear conscience, one must insist that the sense organs [and the brain] are *not* phenomena in the sense of idealistic philosophy; as such they could not be causes! Sensualism, therefore, at least as a regulative hypothesis, if not as a heuristic principle. What? And others even say that the external world is the work of our organs? But then our body, as a part of this external world, would be the work of our organs! But then our organs themselves would be— the work of our organs! It seems to me that this is a complete *reductio ad absurdum*, assuming that the concept of a *causa sui* is something fundamentally absurd. Consequently, the external world is *not* the work of our organs—?" (BGE, 15). The body as it is perceived, the body in the "external world," the sense organs (our "sensory equipment"), the brain, and the external world itself are merely artefacts of our perception. The external world is *not* the "work of our organs," it is *not* the "creation of the brain," because the external world, the brain and all other organs are social constructions of the unconscious mind, meaning that they are the creations of the subjective-body, the subjectivity of the body itself. The unconscious mind appropriates and consumes qualia-subjectivities from the environment—qualia-subjectivities which had their own subjective realities, their own perspectives, prior to being perceived-consumed by the unconscious mind—and then, using memories, the unconscious mind interprets and transforms these qualia-subjectivities into conscious perceptions (hence why the "external world" is an artefact of perception, an artefact of the "inner world").

The vast majority of our psycho-physiological activity, a veritable infinity of psycho-physiological activity, occurs completely unconsciously, and is both unknown and unknowable to consciousness. Consciousness is itself a product of unknown and unknowable psycho-physiological activity. However, we must remember that wherever there is physiological activity, there are affects, there is will to power, and that physiological activity is in actuality the activities of subjectivities. The traditional conception of physiological activity, the conception one finds in medical textbooks, is merely the description of biochemical correlates. These biochemical correlates are correlates of unconscious mental activity, of the activity of affects, i.e. of the will to power, but this activity of unconscious subjectivities, their codes of signs and their codes of feelings, is in the vast majority of cases completely inaccessible to consciousness, and therefore it is unknown and unknowable to consciousness. The unconscious mental activity of the body consists largely of unknown and unknowable subjectivities. Hence why the body is an "unknown sage" (Nietzsche, TSZ I, 4). As Deleuze writes, "[Spinoza] said that we do not even know what a body *can do*, we talk about consciousness and spirit and chatter on about it all, but we do not know what a body is capable of, what forces belong to it or what they are preparing for" (NP, p. 38). History is a history of unconscious forces, unconscious forces which constitute bodies and themselves produce consciousness, ideas, and actions. However, consciousness forever remains fundamentally ignorant of what these forces are exactly, what they are capable of, and, to use a metaphor, of the "intentions" of these forces.

These unconscious forces, which are unconscious affects, they *are* the will to power. Nietzsche writes, ""Will," of course, can affect only "will"—and not "matter" (not "nerves," for example)" (BGE, 36). "Matter," i.e. "material reality," which includes "nerves," i.e. the "nervous system" and the "central nervous system," are artefacts of perception and mental constructs, and *not* the body. The nervous system and the central nervous system are merely biochemical correlates, and *not* the body. The body is a subjectivity. The body *is* the emotions, which means that the body *is* the will to power: the emotions can only affect the emotions, which means that the body consists entirely of emotions, and *never* of "organs." Therefore, the body is the body without organs, which means that the body without organs *is* emotions, i.e. the body without organs *is* the will to power, and the will to power *is* the body without organs.

The subjective-body, the subjectivity of the body itself, the Chaos-body or the body of Chaos, is what Artaud describes as "the body without organs": "The body is the body/ it is all by itself/ and has no need of organs/ the body is never an organism/ organisms are the enemies of the body" (as quoted in Deleuze and Guattari, AO, p. 9). Organs and organisms are on the one hand artefacts of perception and on the other hand mental constructs. "Organs" and "organisms" may be established as related to or equivalent to object-bodies, "objective" bodies, which are mental constructs, or to bodies as they are perceived, which are artefacts of perception. That is to say, "organs" and "organisms" are on the one hand artefacts of perception within the subjectivity of the body without organs, and on the other hand mental constructs in the space of Chaos of the body without organs. To argue that the brain and other organs are merely artefacts of perception, that they are so many objects upon the operating table of knowledge, is already to suggest that the body itself has no need of organs. Organs do not "cause" anything whatsoever because they are merely mental constructs upon the table of knowledge. Organs have no objective existence whatsoever because there is no objective reality. In other words, "organs" as such do not exist. Moreover, organs have zero explanatory power when it comes to psychology, therefore the concept of organs is entirely useless for psychology, hence why, as Artaud writes, "there is nothing more useless than an organ" (Artaud, 1976, p. 571). "Organisms are enemies of the body" because "organisms" are social constructs, to be more precise "organisms" are social constructs of objective entities, they are objectalities, and therefore the traditional concept of "organism" is a denial and a negation of the subjectivity of the body. The space of Chaos *is* the body without organs. The mediation and difference of the emptiness of the space of Chaos is the mediation and difference of the essential emptiness of the body without organs. The body without organs is the body of Chaos itself. The self and the other are each a body without organs, they are each a body of Chaos. The overman is one who has realized that the self is the body and that the body is the body without organs.

The Platonic attitude that "God is truth" has survived via the belief in an objective reality, the belief in objectively existing entities, objectalities, which are in actuality merely mental constructs upon the table of Chaos. Hence why Artaud writes that "what has been called microbes is god," and that the Americans and the Russians use microbes of god "to make their atoms" (ibid, p. 569). "Microbes," "atoms," even "sub-atomic particles," just like "organisms," "organs," and "man," are all so many objectalities, and consequently they are all so many surreptitious forms through which the belief in truth, which means the attitude that "God is truth," survive. The attitude that "God is truth" is a value, a valuation and a value judgement that "truth is divine," i.e. that an objective reality is desirable; the desirability of an objective reality is the psychological ground upon which objectalities are fabricated. But that an objective reality is desired implies that subjective realities are denied and negated, i.e. that real realities are denied and negated, hence why Nietzsche writes that "objectivity" is a symptom of nihilism. Scientism, just like Christianity, is merely the rationalizations of nihilistic passions, passions which deny and negate subjective realities. According to Artaud, scientism has "reinvented microbes in order to impose a new idea of god" (ibid, p. 569), which means that it has invented new systems of objectivity in order to reproduce the Christian-Platonic valuation that "truth is divine" in new forms.

As Artaud writes, scientism has "found a new way to bring out god and to capture him in his microbic noxiousness...in that sinister appearance of morbid cruelty that he adopts whenever he is pleased to tetanize and madden humanity as he is doing now...and that although nobody believes in god any more everybody believes more and more in man" (ibid, pp. 569-570). The faith in truth, the valuation that "truth is divine," is a microbic noxiousness, a mental illness (or to be more precise, the symptom of a mental illness): it is a "sinister appearance of morbid cruelty" because it is a cruelty against the self, which is *the* mentally ill form of cruelty, it is morbid and sinister because it denies and negates the self perpetually (if the self is preserved through this process it is only insofar as the disease is preserved and reproduced via the self). It is not only that "God," the valuation that "truth is divine," "tetanizes and maddens humanity," but that the concept of "humanity" itself is also a mental disease which tetanizes and maddens minds, the concept of "humanity" is a surreptitious form by means of which "objectivity" and the nihilistic passion of objectivity reproduces itself in the mind. Yes, God is dead, God has long been dead. However, as Nietzsche himself could have written, "although nobody believe in god any more everybody believes more and more in man," which means that humanism, which includes scientism, is the means by which "God," the belief in "God," has survived.

Humanism is merely Christian morality in a new form. Therefore, to kill God more thoroughly, to eliminate the traces of God which have survived via humanism and scientism, "it is man whom we must now make up our minds to emasculate" (ibid, p. 570). Artaud does not mean the emasculation of man *by* man, man's self-emasculation, which is well taken care of by man himself and is a means for the self-preservation of man; rather, what Artaud means is the emasculation of man by the overman, which is to say the extermination of man by the overman. In actuality, "man" does not exist. "Man" is a reified mental construct produced and reproduced by psychic forces. The means by which man must be exterminated is first and foremost psychological and cultural, although guerrilla warfare will also likely one day be essential to the struggle. To be sure, deconstructions of scientism, humanism, and egalitarianism (e.g. our preliminary deconstruction of Damasio), have their part, perhaps even an essential part in the project of the overman. The war waged by the overman is first and foremost psychological warfare, the combat of psychic forces and the production and reproduction of a new ideology, the ideology of the body without organs and the overman.

Artaud writes that we must overcome man "By placing him again, for the last time, on the autopsy table to remake his anatomy./ I say, to remake his anatomy./ Man is sick because he is badly constructed./ We must make up our minds to strip him bare in order to scrape off that animalcule that itches him mortally,/ god,/ and with god/ his organs" (ibid, p. 570). The operating table of knowledge upon which man is always already placed must be transformed into an autopsy table of knowledge, a dissection table of knowledge: the concept "man" must be dissected, deconstructed. The anatomy of man must be deconstructed and a new anatomy, the anatomy of the overman, must be constructed. It is too late for the evolution of discourse to be put back such that it never existed in the first place, therefore humanist discourse must be metamorphosed into a new discourse, the discourse of the overman. The discourse of scientism must be metamorphosed into the new discourse of gay-scientism, i.e. the discourse of perspectivism. The means for performing this project is the utilization of the vocabulary of humanist discourse for new ends, namely the construction of the discourse of the overman.

The concept "man" is a diseased concept, a concept of disease, and the evidence of man's essentially diseased essence is abundantly evident in the "structure" of the concept of man wherever it appears, i.e. in the texts which constitute the discourse of man. The "structure" of the mental construct "man" is badly constructed, hence why it is inefficient for the increase of power. The poor construction of "man" decreases power wherever it is reified. Therefore we must strip the concept of "man" bare and we must closely and critically examine it with diverse lenses of interpretation in order to locate and "scrape off" the belief in an objective reality, the faith in truth. God, the Christian God, the God which is Truth, is the microbe which itches man mortally. "God,/ and with God/ his organs": the belief in an objective reality, and with the belief in an objective reality, objectalities, the belief in objectalities, are the microbes which itch man mortally, that is to say, they are the microbes, the ideologies of nihilistic passions, which constitute the self-denial and the self-negation of the reified "man."

Artaud writes, "When you will have made him a body without organs,/ then you will have delivered him from all his automatic reactions and restored him to his true freedom" (ibid, p. 571). But to make a body without organs is to destroy man and to overcome him, for to make a body without organs is to make the overman. Man is essentially reactive, an aggregate of automatic reactions. To be delivered from automatic reactions, to be delivered from reactivity, means to become active, to become spontaneous and creative, and this also means to overcome man and become the overman. There is no freedom for its own sake, no "freedom for the sake of freedom." Freedom is the ability to do or not do a given action. Freedom means having power-over, and thus it means relations of domination-submission. In other words, one can only have freedom at the expense of somebody else's freedom. More freedom for one's self can only be achieved by limiting the freedom of others, and ultimately this means enslaving others. To be restored to one's "true freedom," to become the overman, means to cease being a slave, to cease adhering to slave morality, to cease self-denial and ressentiment, and instead to become a master, to affirm master morality, to affirm the self and to affirm chance.

Artaud writes that when a body without organs is made, "Then you will teach him again to dance wrong side out/ as in the frenzy of dance halls/ and this wrong side out will be his real place" (ibid, p. 571). To learn "to dance wrong side out" again is to learn to dance as pagans dance, which means to metamorphose the soul into a pagan soul, to metamorphose one's values and evaluations into pagan values and evaluations, master values and evaluations, the values and evaluations of master morality. The exuberance of sexual energy in the dances of the frenzy of dance halls is at least one healthy thing about them, one thing it shares with paganism, though the similarities may end there. For this "wrong side out dancing" to be the dance of one's soul, for it to be one's real place, means to firmly and consistently dance the dance of the overman, to become the overman completely, to firmly and consistently affirm the values of the overman, values which are essentially master values.

5. The Body Without Organs, Part II

The mental apparatus *is* the body: the mental apparatus *is* the body without organs. In terms of the psychic economy of the unconscious, the body without organs is always productive, it is the production process itself, it is production itself. The body without organs simply *is* the unconscious mind, in totality and in all its "parts" (each part is a complex of forces which are in turn composed of complexes of forces, ad infinitum). The body without organs *is* fluxes of energy, fluxes of power: the infinite, ceaseless flux of power, the *pure becoming* of the will to power itself.

Deleuze writes that *pure becoming* is a "becoming without measure, a veritable becoming-mad [becoming-madness, becoming-insane], which never rests. It moves in both directions at once. *It always eludes the present*, causing future and past, more and less, too much and not enough to coincide in the simultaneity of a

rebellious matter. [Here Deleuze quotes Plato] "'[H]otter' never stops
where it is but is always going a point further, and the same applies
to 'colder,' whereas definite quality is something that has stopped
going on going on and is fixed;" "...the younger becoming older than
the older, the older becoming younger than the younger—but they
can never finally become so; if they did they would no longer be
becoming, but would be so"" (Deleuze, LS, pp. 1-2; my emphasis). .
Because there is no material reality, there is no matter, therefore pure
becoming is the becoming of subjectivity, the pure becoming of
subjectivity. Nothing endures. Pure becoming always eludes the
"present" because the "present" is merely a mental construct; the
"past" and the "future" are likewise merely mental constructs (cf.
Derrida's *Speech and Phenomena*). Pure becoming always eludes the
"present" because there is no "presence," because the ultimate nature
of reality is mediation. Pure-becoming is originary and theologically
immanent. Pure-becoming, becoming-madness, is mediation itself,
pure-mediation, mediating-madness. Hence why linguistic constructs
such as "hotter" and "colder," "older" and "younger," not to mention
identities, events, proper names, and names generally, "slip off"
pure-becoming, are always exceeded by pure-becoming. Hence why
identicalities, or more simply, identities, are merely fictions, are
always and always already merely fictions: they all always and
always already "slip off" and are exceeded by pure-becoming. Pure-
becoming "moves in both directions at once," it moves "forwards"
and "backwards" simultaneously ("forwards" and "backwards" are
merely spatial metaphors) infinitely, necessarily so because pure-
becoming is infinite becoming, the infinity itself of becoming itself,
the becoming itself of infinity itself—but these directions *meet* at the
same "point," and this "point"—"point" here is merely a metaphor—
is pure-becoming itself, at the pure-becoming itself of pure-
becoming itself, precisely because pure-becoming moves infinitely
in both directions simultaneously and precisely because pure-
becoming *exists*, it is existence itself, which means that it is a
totality, that it exists only as a totality, the totality of infinity, the
totality itself of infinity itself. There is nothing outside of pure
becoming, therefore pure becoming is not a fragment. The totality of
pure becoming is precisely the Eternal Return. Pure becoming is
itself a subjectivity, the subjectivity of pure becoming itself.
Subjectivity is essentially pure becoming itself. Subjectivity is
always already pure-becoming itself, therefore subjectivity is always
already becoming-madness itself, the subjectivity of becoming-

madness itself. The body without organs is always already pure-becoming itself, always already becoming-madness itself, the subjectivity of pure-becoming itself, the subjectivity of becoming-madness itself. The essential becoming-madness of the body without organs is the essential schizophrenia of the body without organs. The neurotic resists self-actualizing the schizophrenia of the body without organs via defence mechanisms, i.e. via various form of denial and self denial, and this self-denial is what characterizes the essence of neurosis, the essence of the essential difference between neurosis and schizophrenia. The schizophrenic is essentially self-affirming, whereas the neurotic is essentially self-denying. The overman is essentially a schizophrenic. The self-actualization of the overman is becoming-schizophrenic. Only those who are already gods to begin with, only those who are always already gods, only those who are gods at their core, are capably of becoming gods, and consequently only they actually become gods.

The body without organs is motion itself, it is a body of motion itself, a body of pure motion itself, a body of motion-madness itself. There are absolutely no "organs," no "organ-machines," in the unconscious, because these are merely so many artefacts of perception and mental constructs: hence why we can say, meaning something quite different from Deleuze and Guattari, "No mouth. No tongue. No teeth. No larynx. No esophagus. No belly. No anus. [No nervous system. No brain.]" (D&G, AO, p. 8). There is no "anti-production" as such in the unconscious, just as there is no "death drive." To be sure, there are indeed deconstructions and destructions in the unconscious, but these are always already productive, always already productive processes. That is to say, in actuality there are only transformations and processes of transformation, and transformation *is* production. Since a destruction is a transformation, it is always already production. The full body without organs is productive, fecund, engendered, engendering, consumable, and consuming. The body without organs is ontological Chaos, the Chaos which is always already becoming, mediation, and difference. The body without organs is becoming itself, mediation itself, difference itself. The body as it is perceived by the subject, with arms, legs, a torso, a face, genitals, etc., is merely an artefact of perception. The actual body, the real body, is the body without organs: the body *is* the body without organs.

The ceaseless pure fluid in a free state which *is* the body without organs also *is* the will to power and pure becoming, the pure becoming of the will to power and the will to power of pure becoming, and thus is also pure difference-in-itself, the ceaseless flux of pure difference-in-itself. The body without organs is the source of all pain and pleasure, all sorrow and joy. The body without organs produces both sheer unarticulated blocks of sound, gasps and cries, as well as words composed of articulated phonetic units; the body without organs also produces silence, "that word which is not a word." The body without organs is also memory and the construction of memory (memory is always a construction), also history and the construction of history (history is always a construction). The space of Chaos *is* the body without organs. The body without organs is productive and dynamic.

Where we have written "body without organs," or more simply, "body," we may just as well have written "soul," because the "soul" and the "body" are equivalent to each other as long as they both denote subjectivity; more specifically, as long as they both denote a subjective multiplicity, a multiplicity of subjectivities. On the "soul," Nietzsche writes: "Let it be permitted to designate by this expression [viz. *soul atomism*] the belief which regards the soul as something indestructible, eternal, indivisible, as a monad, as an *atomon*: this belief ought to be expelled from science! Between ourselves, it is not at all necessary to get rid of "the soul" at the same time, and thus to renounce one of the most ancient and venerable hypotheses—as happens frequently to clumsy naturalists who can hardly touch on "the soul" without immediately losing it. But the way is open for new versions and refinements of the soul-hypothesis; and such conceptions as "mortal soul," and "soul as subjective multiplicity," and "soul as social structure of the drives and affects," want henceforth to have citizens' rights in science" (BGE, 12). The body without organs, the mortal soul, is a social structure, or social system, of drives and affects, i.e. of psychic forces. Marx is only partially correct in his conclusion that the base, or infrastructure, of society is the economic system. In actuality, the base, or infrastructure, of society, whether this society be that of an "individual" body or that of a macroscopic social body, is the psychic economy of the unconscious. The body without organs *is* a social system of forces, and the body without organs *is* the psychic economy of the unconscious. The psychic forces of the unconscious, the affects of the unconscious, determine history.

The body without organs is a multiplicity: a multiplicity of forces, a society of forces. In terms of psychic economy, the multiplicity of forces-agents of production *are* the body without organs, the multiplicity of exchange values of signs *are* the body without organs, and the multiplicity of signs *are* the body without organs. Both the forces-agents of production in the unconscious mind *and* the capital of the unconscious, the will to power, *are* the body without organs. The body without organs is always already a social body, a socius. A social body in the macroscopic sense is also always already a body without organs, which means more precisely that it *is* a complex of psychic forces. (The body without organs is also always already a political body because the social and the political are equivalent to each other; social = political = psychological; social body = political body = body without organs).

The body without organs is a system of mediation and difference: the body without organs *is* writing, it is writing itself, it is the writing itself of writing itself. The body without organs is the transcursive writing of the unconscious, transformations of energy (the writing of the unconscious *is* transformations of energy). The body without organs is a body of chance and a body of fate (chance *is* fate). The body without organs is the aleatoric series of the will to power, the dice-throws of the will to power, the dice-throws which *are* the will to power.

The body without organs is *not* the Christian God because the concept of the Christian God only operates via a false binary opposition between "man" and "God," in which "man" is the finite self, the self of the finite, whereas "God" is the infinite other, the other of infinity. However, the body without organs *is* God in a very different sense, in the Nietzschean sense of the god Dionysus: God is the self, the self *is* God, i.e. ultimately the infinite *is* the self and the self *is* infinity itself. It is not a question of "faith" in God: "God" is a metaphor for infinity, the deification of infinity itself. Dionysus is the God of Becoming, the infinite God of Becoming who is infinitely transformed into the infinity of beings, whose faces are all the faces of the same infinite God, the infinite God of Difference-In-Itself; thus, Dionysus, too, is Infinity, and Dionysus, too, is the self, for we are all incarnations of Dionysus, since we are all incarnations of Infinity, incarnations of Becoming, incarnations of Difference-In-Itself. We may define God as *omnitudo realitatis* only insofar as all of reality and reality itself is infinity itself. Of course, these are all metaphors, and the mask of "atheism" and "godlessness" is perhaps the most useful to us free spirits insofar as it is a hieroglyphic gesture which signifies the rejection of the Christian God and the rejection of Christian values.

In Western discourse, i.e. in the discourse of Christian civilization, the false binary opposition between the finite and the infinite is perhaps most evident in the philosophy of the Classical Age. Deleuze, explicating Foucault, writes, "Classical thought may be recognized by the way in which it thinks of the infinite. In it every reality, in a force, 'equals' perfection, and so can be raised to infinity (the infinitely perfect), the rest being a limitation and nothing but a limitation. For example, the force to conceive can be raised to infinity, such that human understanding is merely the limitation placed on an infinite understanding. No doubt there are very different orders of infinity, but they are formed only on the basis of the limitation weighing down a particular force. The force to conceive can be raised to infinity directly, while that of imagining can achieve only an infinity of an inferior or derived order...The question of knowing whether or not the whole range can be attributed to God depends on the separation of whatever is reality in the range from whatever is limitation, that is to say from the order of infinity to which the range can be raised. The most typical seventeenth-century texts therefore concern the distinction between different orders of infinity: the infinity of grandeur and the infinity of smallness in Pascal; the infinite in itself, the infinite in its cause and the infinite between limits in Spinoza; all the infinites in Leibniz, and so on. Classical thought...continually loses itself in infinity; as Michel Serres says, it loses all centre and territory, agonizes over its attempts to fix the place of the finite in the midst of all the infinities, and tries to establish an order within infinity." (Deleuze, F, pp. 124-125).

The Christian concept of "man" is of a "man" who is essentially guilty and who is punished by God with "original sin" for attempting to be as powerful as God; Yaweh's punishment of Adam, the first man, is the allegorization of the conceptual false binary opposition between the concepts "man" and "God," wherein "man" is a symbol of the "finite," of the arbitrary mental constructs of "limits" which constitute the "finite," and "God" is the infinite: "God" emasculates "man" and establishes an unbridgeable distance between "God" and "man," thereby making "man" essentially weak and suffering from the mental illness of "original sin"; the coming of Christ, among other things, merely reaffirms the mental illness of "original sin" and the infinite distance between "God" and "man";

the coming of Christ also fills "man" with a degree of ressentiment higher than he had ever had before. Thus, in Christian civilization, the concept "man" is transformed into new forms, but these new forms are merely new "incarnations," i.e. reifications, of the "finite," i.e. these new forms of "man" are "incarnations," actualizations, of the feelings of "sin" and ressentiment. The concept of "man" in humanist discourse is the relatively modern Christian concept of "man," the "man" of Christian history, the "man" who was given a new form in the Renaissance, then a new form in the Classical Age, then a new form in the post-Classical age, etc., and once again given a new form in the 20th century, but these new forms are still merely *new forms of the Christian concept of "man."* Even "now," in the 21st century, the Christian concept of "man" is once again being reinvented by the discourse of Western civilization, a discourse which has become a "global" discourse, at least in the geographic sense.

According to the Christian dichotomy between man and God, man is "imperfect," whereas God is "perfect." Augustine constructs the same dichotomy between man the imperfect and God the perfect; arguably this dichotomy is traceable back to Plato, for whom only the metaphysical Idea of the Good was perfect, whereas Becoming and all its sensibles (including the mortal body) were imperfect. Although there are some suggestions of this false dichotomy in the writings of Augustine and Plato, and even in Judeo-Christian mythology, it is nonetheless most characteristic of Classical philosophy to phrase this dichotomy between the man the imperfect and God the perfect as a dichotomy between man the finite and God the infinite. The perfect is defined precisely as the infinite, and the imperfect is defined precisely as the finite. The finite consists of limitations and nothing but limitations. In the conceptual operations of Classical philosophy, artificial constructions of limits delineate the existence of man; for example, God possesses an infinite "faculty of understanding," but man's faculty of understanding is delineated by the artificial limits constructed and imposed upon the infinite understanding, and these limits, which are conceived of as real limits, constitute a finite faculty of understanding for man (a finite understanding which is reified in "man" along with the reification of the concept "man" itself). Classical philosophy constructs different "orders of infinity" by constructing sets of limits which are artificially imposed upon "lesser" infinities. The infinities which are attributed to God are the "highest" infinities, the infinities devoid of limits. Man and other created beings are defined by limits; the social construct "man," like the social constructs of other "beings," have social constructs of "limits" as essential constituents. But to conceptualize different orders of infinity is already to falsify the infinite. Indeed, even to name an infinity is already to falsify infinity. The name which can be named is never the name of infinity, because infinity is beyond all possible names.

It is not only that these limits, these finitudes, are fictions, but these infinities named by Classical philosophy are fictions as well. There is no "infinite understanding," no "infinite grandeur," no "infinite smallness," no "infinite in itself," no "infinite in its cause," no "infinite between limits," etc. because all of these concepts of the infinite depend upon concepts of limits, of finitudes, and upon the artificial binary opposition between the finite and the infinite. Conceptually, the "finite" and the "infinite" of Classical philosophy are interdependent, and they are both just as artificial as the other. Classical philosophy "agonizes over its attempts to fix the place of the finite in the midst of all the infinities," meaning that Classical philosophy anxiously, obsessively, and compulsively mentally constructs artificial finitudes in order to establish artificial distinctions between the finite and infinite, but in so doing it also constructs artificial infinities. That Classical philosophy "tries to establish an order within infinity" means precisely that it mentally constructs artificial infinities which can be ordered upon the table of knowledge, both in relation to each other and in relation to artificial finitudes. These artificial infinities which depend upon artificial finitudes obscures the actuality of infinity, the infinity of actuality, which exists beyond and prior to the artificial constructs of language.

For example, that all limits are artificial does not mean that man possesses an "infinite understanding," but rather it means that there never was either an "infinite understanding" or a "finite understanding" to begin with. Infinity is beyond all possible concepts of infinity and beyond all possible "orders of infinity." That all "limits" are merely social constructs means precisely that "imperfection," "free will," "possibilities," and "impossibilities" are likewise merely social constructs. That there are no real "limits" means precisely that there is only the infinite; the infinite is indeed perfection, insofar as perfection is defined as infinity itself. Perfection is originary because infinity is originary. It is not a question of it being "possible" for "man" to do anything he "wills," because "possibility" and "free will" are merely social constructs which involve systems of artificial limits; for instance, in the case of "possibility," the artificial limits of "possible worlds," and in the case of "free will," the artificial limit, the finitude, which is the "ego." To conceive that events can be any other way is to conceive, which means that it is to mentally construct, to falsify and fabricate. That which is, is infinite. To conceive that which is other than what is, is to conceive that which is not, which means that it is to construct a fiction. Therefore, there are no "possibilities," no "possible worlds." There never were any "possible worlds." This universe is the *only* universe. "Impossibility" is likewise merely a social construct for the same reason that "possibility" is a social construct: this universe can only be as it is, and it cannot be any other way, and, moreover, precisely because artificial limits such as "telos" and "causality" are merely social constructs. There is no "possible" or "impossible," and there is no "telos" or "causality," because there is only becoming. It is not a question of it "being possible" or "not being possible" for the world to be any other way; such a question is itself poorly formulated, using the concepts of "possibility" and "impossibility." It is a question of recognizing that the world exists as it is, and that it necessarily follows from the existence itself of the world itself that this is the only way that the world can be, that is to say, that the world can only be as it is because it *is*, it is this way and no other. This world is the *only* world; this world *is the world*. And what is this world? This world is Becoming, pure becoming. To affirm the infinite means to affirm chance, the chanceness of necessity and the necessity of chance. Infinity is the infinity of becoming, the infinity of difference-in-itself, the infinity of mediation, the infinity of interpretation.

When thought has overcome linguistic constructs, the body without organs sees the world and sees itself as it truly is, infinite. But for the body without organs to realize its own infinity is for it to deconstruct the concept of "man," i.e. for it to give up the belief in "man." "Man" is an artificial limit, but the body without organs is infinity itself, it is devoid of limits. All "finitudes" are merely mental constructs upon the table of Chaos of the body without organs. "Limits" and "finitudes" are merely all so many language games, and they presuppose an infinity within which they are constructed and played. The body without organs is infinity itself: to realize the self means to realize that the self is the body without organs, it means to realize the body without organs and to realize the infinity of the body without organs, it means to realize that the self is infinity itself, that the self is God itself because the self is infinity itself. The body without organs, the self, is God because it is infinity itself, the body of the infinite, the body of infinity itself. There are, of course, a multiplicity of bodies without organs (for example, in a society, or in a battlefield, or in a lovers' tryst), but not every body without organs is capable of realizing itself. Not every body without organs is capable of realizing that the self is a body without organs. The capacity of the body without organs to realize itself is dependent upon its degree of health; only the healthiest body without organs can realize itself. Moreover, the healthy type of body without organs is extremely rare, but it is only these rare few bodies without organs who are capable of realizing themselves; these rare few bodies without organs *are* overmen, or rather, to be more precise, they become overmen when they overcome the concept of "man" via realizing the body without organs and the infinity of the body without organs. To realize that the self is Chaos, the infinity of Chaos, is to realize that the self is the body without organs.

The body without organs, which is the body of Chaos, is an egg, an egg of Chaos, a Chaos-egg: it is genesis, it always generates, it always already generates, and it nurtures, it always nurtures, and "gods" always grow from within it, "gods" are always growing within it. The body without organs is a system of emotions, a system of intensities (emotion = intensity). The body without organs *is* delirium, a system of delirium, a delirium of signs, of writing, because all systems of signs are systems of delirium, and the body without organs is a system of signs; all writing is delirium because all writing is the writing of passions, i.e. it is forces that write, it is forces that "speak" through signs. Lovers write to each other with their eyes, with their flesh, with series of sighs that end in broken gasps; this is the "language" of love, the delirium of love, the delirium of healthy passions, life-affirming passions. Conquerors, such as Alexander the Great and Genghis Khan, write with blood; this delirium of blood and violence, too, is the delirium of healthy and life-affirming passions. By contrast, "reason," the discourse of "truth" and "objectivity," is the delirium of sick passions, of nihilistic passions. The body without organs *is* hallucination, the body of hallucination, the hallucination of language and the hallucination of perception; all perception is hallucination because there is no objective reality, but only subjective realities, i.e. all perception is an interpretation, and thus a falsification, by the forces of the unconscious mind, and these unconscious perceptions are further falsified when they are interpreted by consciousness. Hallucinations *are* perceptions, and perceptions *are* hallucinations. The "external world" is an artefact of perception, which means precisely that it is a hallucination. Perception is never "appearance" in the strict sense because there is no "true world" which it could be an "appearance" of; nor is perception the perception of *the* "true world," because there is no such thing, i.e. there is a multiplicity of subjective "truths" but there is no singular "truth"; perception is neither perception of a "true world" nor perception of an "apparent world," therefore all perception is hallucination and dream. All perception is interpretation, but there is no "correct" interpretation, therefore all perception is hallucination and dream. The body without organs is a system of qualia, which means that it is a system of hallucinations and a system of dreams; but to say that the body without organs is a system of movement-images, that the body without organs writes with reality, is already to say that it is a system of dreams, of hallucinations.

It is true, as Deleuze and Guattari write, that "Delirium and hallucination are secondary in relation to the really primary emotion, which in the beginning only experiences intensities, becomings, transitions" (AO, pp. 18-19), but only in the sense that delirium and hallucination-perception are inextricable from and ultimately equivalent to their correlated emotions, and that these are, to begin with, produced by emotions which are themselves also delirium and hallucination-perception; moreover, these emotions are all forms of the will to power. The will to power is both the primary emotion, which "experiences intensities, becomings, transitions" as well as hallucinations-perceptions and delirium, and the secondary relations which are effected by the primary emotion are also constituted by different forms of the will to power. Intensities produce intensities. However, these intensities exist in varying degrees, from low to high. Rises and falls of intensities are produced by complex relationships among forces and signs, forces and signs which are themselves intensities. The full body without organs, subjectivity itself, is a multiplicity of intensities. Just as infinite quantities of infinite forces fill up the body without organs infinitely, so do infinite quantities of infinite Chaos fill up the body without organs infinitely. (The theory that "content determines form" is a profoundly schizoid theory. The infinite content of infinity itself determines all "forms."). The realization of the body without organs is the feeling of infinite power, the feeling of an infinite increase of power, the

infinite feeling of the power of infinity, of the infinity of power
itself, the infinity itself of the will to power itself.

6. The Political Anatomy of the Body Without Organs[19]

Because the precondition of an organism's experiences is its
anatomy, that which through the organism has its experiences,
anatomy is indeed, in a sense, a-priori. Nietzsche writes, "that if each
of us had a different kind of sensory experience; if we ourselves
could perceive now only as a bird, now as a worm, now as a plant; or
if one of us saw the same stimulus as red, another as blue, and if a
third even heard it as a sound, no one would talk about the supposed
lawlike uniformity of nature but would instead conceive of it only as
a highly subjective construct" (*On Truth and Untruth*, pp. 38-39).
However, each of us does indeed have a unique form of sensory
experience, and each organism's subjectivity is indeed irreducibly
different from another's, even within the same species, such that
there is no "nature" as such, there are only highly subjective
constructs-interpretations dependent upon these subjectivities. We do
not even need to go so far as to cite cases of colour blindness or
synaesthesia in order to demonstrate that reality is entirely dependent
on subjectivity, although such cases do indeed support our thesis.
Arguing from neurological evidence, Damasio argues, "And since
you and I are similar enough biologically to construct a similar
enough image of the same thing, we can accept without protest the
conventional idea that we have formed *the* picture [i.e. the same
picture] of some particular thing. But we did not" (FWH, p. 321).
Each organism's subjectivity is irreducibly different from others'
subjectivities, and consequently each of their mental systems
construct irreducibly different mental images of the "same thing."
The qualia experienced by one subject is irreducibly different from
the qualia experienced by another subject. Moreover, there are no
"things" in the environment. The environment consists of forces,
forces which emit forces-qualia, forces which emit forces-signs. The
forces-qualia appropriated-consumed by one organism, i.e. the
forces-signs interpreted by one organism, are irreducibly different
from those appropriated-consumed and interpreted by another
organism. This irreducible difference among the respective sensory
experiences of organisms is the irreducible difference among their

respective anatomies, i.e. the irreducible difference among their respective bodies without organs.

Is the body without organs an a-priori idea? No, it cannot be, because there are no true a-priori ideas. The body without organs is *not* an unmediated presence. The body without organs *is* a system of mediation. If we can speak of the body without organs as transcendental, it is only as a "quasi-transcendental," a "quasi-a-priori," because the body without organs is itself a system of experience and mediation. That is to say, anatomy is quasi-transcendental. That is to say, the body without organs—anatomy—is essentially plastic. The body without organs, the space of Chaos, *is* the tabula rasa, the blank slate, but each tabula rasa differs from the others; in fact, each tabula rasa is irreducibly different from the others, precisely because the tabula rasa is anatomical, it *is* anatomy.

As Nietzsche argues, there are no a-priori ideas—no a-priori synthetic judgements—simply because there are no means by which it is possible for such a thing to exist. Kant argues that a-priori synthetic judgements are possible "by virtue of a faculty," *Vermöge eines vermöge*, which Walter Kaufmann explains means "by virtue of some virtue, or by means of a means" (1967, p. 208). A-priori ideas are possible due to the faculty of a faculty, the ability of a faculty, the ability of an ability. Clearly and obviously, this is a nonsensical redundancy, which means that Kant provided absolutely no explanation as to how a-priori ideas are possible at all. Nietzsche writes that Kant's doctrine of faculties is merely a repetition of the question of how a-priori ideas are possible (BGE, 11). As to how the faculties are themselves possible, there is no explanation; and indeed, asking how these faculties are possible is the same as asking how the a-priori synthetic judgements are possible. A-priori synthetic judgements are possible by means of a faculty, by "means of a means," but this redundancy leaves the entire question unanswered, because "by means of a means" has the same meaning as "by a means," which is tantamount to arguing "they are possible because I say so." Therefore, "a-priori synthetic judgements are possible by means of a —?" And we find no answer.

As Nietzsche writes, it is instructive to compare the essence of Kant's doctrine of a-priori ideas with the doctor in the comedy of Molière, who also has a doctrine of faculties: "How does opium induce sleep? "By virtue of a faculty," namely the *virtus dormitiva*, replies the doctor in Molière, "Because it contains a sleepy faculty whose nature is to put the senses to sleep." But such replies belong in comedy..." (BGE, 11). Such replies belong in comedy because it is precisely their absurdity which make them humorous. It is only because the doctrine a "virtus dormitiva" is nonsensical that it provokes laughter, the effect of comedy, and thus it belongs in a comedy. But Kant's doctrine of faculties is precisely the same form of absurdity as the doctrine of Molière's doctor, therefore Kant's doctrine of faculties likewise belongs in a comedy—it belongs in a comedy, and *not* in philosophy. Arguing that opium induces sleep by virtue of a sleeping virtue, by the faculty of a sleeping faculty, by means of a means of inducing sleep, is an absurd redundancy which neither explains anything nor has any pragmatic value whatsoever. But this also means that arguing that a-priori ideas are possible by virtue of a faculty, by virtue of a virtue that makes a-priori ideas possible, is likewise an absurd redundancy which neither explains anything nor has any pragmatic value whatsoever.

An organism's anatomy is fundamentally dynamic and plastic, i.e. it can be altered by other forces (viz. either the organism's own active drives, or forces from the environment), hence the "developmental plasticity" of the organism; an organism's anatomy is fundamentally dynamic and plastic because its anatomy is in actuality a complex of forces, a complex of qualia. The tabula rasa is the table of Chaos, it is Chaos itself, which is the body without organs, a complex of forces. The organism is always already encultured, culture is originary, precisely because an organism's anatomy consists of a code of signs (a complex of force *is* a code of signs). The organism's anatomy is essentially plastic because it is a code of signs which is perpetually altered, both by itself and by signs-forces from the environment. In other words, the "hyle" of an organisms' anatomy, of the body without organs, is essentially plastic, changeable, and malleable: this "hyle" is the will to power, a social system of subjectivities.

To be sure, the body without organs does indeed have an "origin." How is a body without organs made? How is it "produced"? Biologically speaking, either by means of sexual reproduction or asexual reproduction, depending on the organism in question, but whether the reproduction of the body without organs is sexual or asexual, it is in each case a process of subjectivity, and each body without organs is irreducibly different from the other. The parent body without organs is a system of difference-in-itself, and the offspring body without organs which is differentiated from it is also a system of difference-in-itself. Sexual reproduction is the impregnation of a "female" body without organs by a "male" body without organs, and the offspring body without organs which is produced is irreducibly different from either parent. Moreover, each offspring body without organs is essentially plastic, hence its "developmental plasticity." Therefore, although the body without organs is a quasi-transcendental formation, it is nonetheless always already a diachronic formation and a producer of diachronic formations, it is always already historicized and historicizing, i.e. it is always and always already a product of forces and a producer of forces, it is a system of forces, a system of diachronicity itself.

The body without organs is the will to power. What is the will to power? The drive for power, the political anatomy of the body without organs. In nature, the body of every living organism is in the grip of an imperious and inevitable power, the will to power itself, which is the very force of life itself, the very drive of life itself. The will to power is the "meaning of being," the "Dasein," the "being-there" of the body itself. The will to power operates upon the body by means of hierarchy. Indeed, insofar as the will to power *is* commanding and obeying, the will to power *is* hierarchy. Hierarchy is essentially commanding and obeying. Hierarchy implies a dominant force and a submissive force, domination and submission, i.e. commanding and obeying (Q.E.D). Hierarchy is a fundamental property of life. Some drives in the organism command, and others obey. The body commands itself. That is to say, dominant forces within the body subjugate other forces within the body, and these relations of domination-submission *are* the emotions. Emotion itself is precisely a relation of domination-submission between forces. Emotion *is* hierarchy. The body is a complex of both dominant forces and submissive forces. However, speaking more macroscopically, relatively, and generally, we can also make a distinction between dominant bodies and submissive bodies. There are relations of domination-submission both within a body and among a multiplicity of bodies. Foucault writes that a docile body is "a body...that may be subjected, used, transformed, and improved" (D&P, p. 136). This observation applies mutatis mutandis to what we describe as "submissive bodies"; a submissive body is precisely a body that is subjected, used, transformed, and "improved" (from the perspective of the dominating force). The existence of submissive bodies implies that there are also dominant bodies, bodies which subject other bodies, use other bodies, transform other bodies, improve other bodies, or destroy other bodies. A dominant body may affect either other dominant bodies (but which are submissive in relation to it) or submissive bodies. All forms of domination-submission are forms of hierarchy, that is to say, forms of power. The body is itself a mental system, therefore power over the "mind," whether one's own mind or the minds of others, in actuality means power over the body, one's own body or the bodies of others.

Obedience to the other is in actuality obedience to a force within one's self. On the other hand, obedience to one's self is in actuality obedience to an other within one's self, to an other force within the self, the self which is always already a system of others.

Relations of submission-utility are inherent to every complex of forces, including complexes of bodies. "Utility" is relative to the perspective of the dominant force, the commanding force. Use implies will, and will implies use. Language-games, and especially the fact that the unconscious is constituted by language-games, implies relations of submission-utility, commanding forces, and obeying forces. Submissive forces are always utilized for an end by dominant forces. The body is always utilized for an end by the dominant forces within it. The force which obeys is utilized by the force which commands. Commanding is effectively the process of utilization. (For a command to be a command, for a utilization to be a utilization, there must be obedience, i.e. there must be an obeying force). The dominant forces of the body without organs exerts meticulous control over the operations of the submissive forces of the body without organs. There is a constant subjection of forces within the body by the dominant forces of the body itself. The dominant forces of the body impose relations of domination-submission and submission-utility upon submissive forces. (Relations of domination-submission = relations of submission-utility). Utilization consists of, and requires in order to function, two basic components: the command, which is the end or aim (the command itself is the end itself), and obedience, which is the means (obedience itself is the means itself). In the act of utilization, there is always, on the one hand, a force which commands the use, and on the other hand, a force which obeys the command and performs the use.

The will to power forms relations of domination-submission in the very mechanisms of the body without organs itself, thereby making the body obedient and useful to its dominant forces. The will to power forms systems of coercion that act upon the submissive forces. Dominant forces unconsciously manipulate the body's elements (the elements of the body without organs are forces), thoughts, gestures, behaviour.

Physiology is always already political, a "political physiology" or "political anatomy." Political relations are power relations. All relations among forces are political relations because all relations among forces are power relations. Anatomy is a society of forces in which dominant forces govern submissive forces. Anatomy is the power relations of groups of psychic forces. The political anatomy of the body without organs is the "mechanics of power" of the will to power: the will to power determines how the dominant forces may have a hold over the submissive forces, not only so that the dominant forces may do as they will, but also so that they may operate in the way that they will, with the techniques, the speed, and the efficiency that the dominant forces spontaneously determine. Thus dominant forces produce subjected and practised forces, docile forces. The whole body without organs is a machine of power, a power-machine, and each "part" of the body without organs is also a power-machine, a part of the machinery of power of the whole body without organs (analytically, the whole *is* its parts; the whole = its parts). The will to power explores the body, deconstructs the body, and reconstructs the body according to its necessities.

The primary function of the body without organs is the primary function of the will to power itself, which is the primary function of hierarchy itself: the increase of power. Hierarchy increases the quantity of force of the body without organs in both economic terms of utility and political terms of domination-submission. In short, hierarchy accumulates power within the body without organs; hierarchy facilitates the function and course of energy (energy = the will to power), which results in both the concrete increase of actual power and the concrete increase of potential power. (Actuality *is* potentiality, and potentiality *is* actuality, because every force actualizes its potential, draws its ultimate consequences, at every moment; cf. Nietzsche, BGE, 22: "every power draws its ultimate consequences at every moment."). The increase of power always means an increase of domination and subjection. Just as in political economy, profit is surplus value, in political anatomy, hierarchy is increased domination.

The operations of the will to power are the techniques, the methods, of the will to power: they constitute modes of political investment of the body without organs, a "micro-psychology" of power. Because the body without organs is an intersubjectivity unto itself, the body is a social body unto itself. Since the primary function of the will to power is the increase of power, the will to power constantly reaches out to ever broader domains. The body without organs is essentially territorial and territorializing. The political anatomy of the body without organs *is* hierarchy. The will to power operates upon the body without organs both globally and molecularly. Macroscopically, the will to power operates upon entire groups of bodies, both globally and molecularly. The will to power operates via diverse strategies and sets of strategies, diverse methods and interpretations, diverse methods of interpretation, and diverse codes of signs.

IV. On Variation and Speciation

1. The Social Construction of "Natural Selection"

Darwin himself fundamentally misunderstood natural selection because he, like everyone else of his time, was completely ignorant of genetics and the mechanisms of inheritance. Of his contemporary episteme, Darwin writes: "The laws governing inheritance are for the most part unknown. No one can say why the same peculiarity in different individuals of the same species, or in different species, is sometimes inherited and sometimes not so; why the child often reverts in certain characters to its grandfather or grandmother or more remote ancestor; why a peculiarity is often transmitted from one sex to both sexes, or to one sex alone, more commonly but not exclusively to the like sex." (OS, p. 15)

Ernst Mayr, in his popular account of evolution, *What Evolution Is*, acknowledges Darwin's complete ignorance of genetics, while also arguing that the modern concept of evolution requires a basic understanding of genetics: "An understanding of the nature of this variability [of traits] was finally made possible, after 1900, by advancements in genetics and molecular biology. One can never fully understand the process of evolution unless one has an understanding of the basic facts of inheritance, which explain variation. Therefore the study of genetics is an integral part of the study of evolution. But only the heritable part of variation plays a role in evolution." (2001, p. 89)

Since Darwin was completely ignorant of genetics but genetics is integral to the understanding of evolution, the implication is that Darwin himself fundamentally misunderstood evolution. Darwin did not have any understanding whatsoever of the basic facts of inheritance which explain variation, therefore Darwin never fully understood the process of evolution. Darwin lacked an integral part of the study of evolution, the study of genetics, which means that he failed to study evolution. Moreover, as is a commonly known and acknowledged fact among modern biologists, and as even a casual reading of *The Origin of Species* reveals, Darwin firmly believed in the "Lamarckian" theory ("Lamarckian" is a misleading misnomer, but standard usage nonetheless) that traits are inherited based on their use or disuse by the organism; Lamarckism is one of the best *refuted* theories of modern biology.

In brief, we now "know" almost completely, at least pragmatically speaking we "know," the laws governing inheritance, and we also know the biochemical processes correlated with inheritance (or genetics). To be more precise, although Mendel discovered the basic laws of genetics in 1866, it was not until the 20th century, long after Darwin's death, that Mendel's discoveries were acknowledged as discoveries by academic scientists, thus it was not until the 20th century that Mendelian genetics was considered and thus effectively became "knowledge" in the Western episteme. To begin to comprehend Darwin's profound ignorance, one must contemplate the fact that Darwin was completely ignorant of "genes," not to mention that he was also completely ignorant that "genes" are "DNA" (this latter discover was not made until 1952 by Hershey and Chase, nearly a hundred years after the publication of *The Origin of Species*).

Moreover, the biochemical correlates of genetics was not fully known until the latter half of the twentieth century, and contemporary 21st century research into genetics is still struggling to complete the picture. Indeed, the vast majority of contemporary accounts of natural selection *begin* with what for Darwin was "for the most part unknown," namely the laws of inheritance and the introductory biochemistry of genes. Therefore, there is sufficient evidence to doubt the accuracy Darwin's account of natural selection, precisely because the concept of natural selection in scientific discourse has become something very different than what it was for Darwin. "Natural selection" is not a simple and unchanging concept, but a complex social construct with a history in which it has undergone and continues to undergo changes.

2. The Mind-Gene Problem

"Genes," which in contemporary Western discourse effectively means "DNA," denotes an objectality, and it implicates objective processes, the objective operations of objects. Descriptions of genes provide absolutely no data on subjectivity, and consequently they provide absolutely no basis for drawing conclusions regarding psychology. From descriptions of genes, there *are* grounds to make inferences regarding objective processes, operations of objects, but there are absolutely *zero* grounds for making inferences regarding subjective processes, the subjective operations of subjectivities.

Genes, and for that matter epigenesis (gene-expression) as well, the entire machinery of genetics, are *not* equivalent to life, to life processes; they can at best be described merely as the "biochemical correlates" of life and life processes. In actuality, "genes" are artefacts of perception and mental constructs upon the table of knowledge. However useful a concept "genes" may be for medical science, they are completely useless and superfluous to psychology.

It is not merely a question of "genetic determinism" being naive and empirically false, which it is. Descriptions of genes provide absolutely zero data on what it feels like to be a given organism. Because descriptions of genes are heuristically and in effect "objective" descriptions of "material" processes, they in principle exclude the psyche and the entire world of thoughts, affects, and motivations. Therefore, life, which is essentially psychological activity, can only be *described* by its biochemical correlates, but it can never be *explained* by its biochemical correlates. Explaining life and understanding life require psychology, the study of subjectivity, which is precisely the study of thoughts, affects, and motivations.

What *are* "genes" exactly? What *can* they tell us about? We have written above that they are objectalities and that they can tell us only about objectalities, but they require a more precise definition.

Mayr (2001) lists "seventeen principles of inheritance," and in absolutely none of them does he mention, and he is right not to mention them for his purposes, the "mind," the "psyche," the "subject," or "psychology" (p. 91). However, he does list various kinds of objectalities.

Mayr's (2001) first principle of inheritance: "The genetic material is constant ("hard"); it cannot be changed by the environment or by use and disuse of the phenotype. The inheritance of constant genetic material is called hard inheritance. Genes cannot be modified by the environment. Properties acquired by the proteins of the phenotype cannot be transmitted to the nucleic acids of the germ cells. There is no inheritance of acquired characteristics" (p. 91).

Mayr's (2001) third principle of inheritance: "The DNA contains the information that permits the production of the proteins that (together with lipids and other molecules) make up the phenotype of every organism. It controls the assemblage of amino acids that are converted into proteins with the help of cellular structures and mechanisms" (p. 91).

Mayr's (2001) fourth principle of inheritance: "In the eukaryotes most DNA is located in the nucleus of every cell and is organized into a number of longitudinal bodies called *chromosomes*. (Small amounts of DNA and RNA occur also in cellular organelles, such as mitochondria and chloroplasts.)" (p. 91).

Mayr's (2001) ninth principle of inheritance: "A gene is a sequence of nucleic acid base pairs that encodes a program with a specific function" (p. 93).

Mayr's (2001) eleventh principle of inheritance: "Although a gene is normally constant from generation to generation, it has the capacity to "mutate" occasionally into a different form. Such a newly mutated gene (mutant) will again be constant, unless another new mutation occurs" (p. 93).

Mayr's (2001) twelfth principle of inheritance: "The totality of the genes of an individual constitute its genotype" (p. 93).

Mayr's (2001) thirteenth principle of inheritance: "Each gene has a number of different forms, called *alleles*, which are responsible for most of the differences among the different individuals of a population" (p. 93).

Mayr's (2001) fifteenth principle of inheritance: "When, in a heterozygote, only one of the two alleles is expressed in the phenotype, it is called the dominant allele; the other allele is called recessive" (p. 93).

Mayr's (2001) sixteenth principle of inheritance: "A gene has a complex structure, consisting of exons, introns, and flanking sequences" (p. 93).

Mayr's (2001) seventeenth principle of inheritance: "There are several different kinds of genes, some of which control the actions of other genes" (p. 93).

Because genes are the instructions for the construction of protein structures (cf. the third and ninth principles of inheritance), when Mayr (2001) writes in his eighth principle of inheritance, "Characteristics of organisms are controlled by genes, which are located on the chromosomes" (p. 92), the "characteristics" can be nothing other than protein structures. (The only other possible "characteristic" which can be referred to is the control of the actions of other genes).

The curious reader and other archaeologists of knowledge are advised to consult Mayr's book for his full lists of principles of inheritance and for other introductory details regarding natural selection and genetics.

From this truncated list, it is evident that genes are objectalities which contain "information" necessary for the construction of protein structures, which are also objectalities. The "traits" or "phenotypes" of an organism are precisely these protein structures, and thus they also denote objectalities. The "information," or "code," contained in genes are "alleles," which since they are forms of genes are also forms of objectalities; genes are "written" in the "language" of amino acids, which are also objectalities. Genetic mutations are likewise objectalities, "objective" mutations of genes, which are objectalities. Genes which control the actions of other genes are objectalities which control the "objective" actions of other objectalities.

We do not need to recount here all the details regarding the structure of genes, gene expression, different forms of genes, the mapping of genomes, the human genome, genetic engineering, or medical treatments developed with the aid of genetics, in order to conclude that genetics are objectalities and that genetics is equipped, only equipped, to describe objectalities, "objective" processes. In fact, genetics is equipped to do so with remarkable efficiency and utility; but its efficiency and utility in dealing with objectalities is not in question here, as it might be within the confines of scientific discourse, for instance by eco-evo-devo biologists, or as it might be within the confines of culture more generally, for instance by Creationists (who have absolutely no grounds for the arguments they make, by the way).

Rather, the only emphasis we wish to make is the most obvious one, that genetics does indeed deal with objectalities, but it deals *only* with objectalities and *never* with subjectivities. The utility and efficiency of genetics is limited solely to dealing with objectalities, but when it comes to dealing with subjectivities, genetics is completely and totally useless and inefficient. That is to say, in matters of psychology, genetics and "biology" more generally, including neurobiology, are completely and entirely useless and inefficient. The mind is a subjectivity, not an object, not an objectality. Therefore, the mind can only be understood in terms of subjectivity, and it can never be understood in terms of objectalities.

The mind can never be understood using an "objective" approach because the mind is not an object.

Moreover, the limits of objectivity become apparent once the concept of an objective reality is even briefly questioned, and it becomes more questionable the more one contemplates it. We have already briefly demonstrated how the logic of neurobiology, whose discourse is inextricably linked with that of genetics, leads to the belief in a thing-in-itself and all the paradoxes which such a belief entails. Genes, neurons, neurotransmitters, the brain, these are all objectalities; but the thing-in-itself, the epistemological ground of all objectalities, is itself a "thing without properties," which is an absurdity, a purely metaphysical concept. In other words, the "objective approach" ultimately reveals that an "objective reality" is a purely metaphysical concept with absolutely no grounds in empirical evidence, and consequently that "objectivity" itself is merely a metaphysical ideology, an ideology of metaphysics. But "objectivity" is not merely a metaphysical ideology, it is also a method of interpretation and ultimately a practice, the practice of denying and negating the reality of subjectivity.

Needless to say, there is no question of the fictionality of an "evolutionary psychology," a psychology based on Neo-Darwinian materialist biology. That there is such a thing as "evolutionary psychology" indicates a psychological necessity for such a belief system, a new development in the history of European, and now Euro-American, nihilism. Not only does so-called "evolutionary psychology" have no explanatory value whatsoever, since, as many anthropologists have demonstrated, its arguments are completely at odds with empirical data gathered by numerous anthropologists over nearly a century, but more significantly, "evolutionary psychology" demonstrates a complete misunderstanding of both modern biology, the mind-body problem, and historiography—not to mention psychology.

As it regards historiography, evolutionary psychologists confuse "origins" with "explanations." Nietzsche writes, "By searching out origins, one becomes a crab. The historian looks backward; eventually he also *believes* backward" (TI, "Maxims and Arrows," 24). Evolutionary psychologists are all so many crabs, for they all believe backwards, that is to say, they all search out "origins" as if these were explanations. Origins explain nothing because "meaning is use," and the use and the origin are two completely different things—not to mention the fact that there is no "origin" as such because mediation and difference are originary. As many scholars have commented, this search for origins is tantamount to the fabrication of "just-so stories," myths which reflect the values of contemporary society but which have neither explanatory nor predictive value. To use a physiological example, the origin of the nervous system does not explain the diverse uses which the nervous system can be put to. Likewise, speculating on the behaviour of the "first" men and women does not explain why contemporary men and women think, feel, and act the way that they do, i.e. it does not reveal their real motivations; such speculation merely identifies an "origin" in the distant and unobservable past, which is ultimately a wholly fictive "origin." Evolutionary psychologists are only capable of looking backwards into an entirely speculative and unobservable past, i.e. a fictional past; however, they are not capable of actually analysing the past, let alone the present.

All that we have written on the mind-body problem in relation to materialist philosophy and neuroscience applies equally well, mutatis mutandis, to evolutionary psychology. Evolutionary psychology, after all, is merely a materialist philosophy. As far as we are aware, evolutionary psychologists have made no attempts to explain how exactly subjectivity can be produced by objectalities. It may be the case that an evolutionary psychologists has indeed attempted an explanation; if they have, then all the criticisms we have made of such "explanations" apply, mutatis mutandis, to his "explanation." To use Chalmers' Zombie Thought Experiment, for example: the entire "world" of objectalities can be imagined, operating exactly as it does now, but completely devoid of subjectivity. A materialist philosophy such as evolutionary psychology is simply not capable of explaining subjectivity, which means that it is simply not capable of providing psychological explanations, because psychological explanations are precisely explanations of subjectivity in terms of subjectivity.

And, of course, we have demonstrated that modern biology deals entirely with objectalities and never with subjectivities. Evolutionary psychology purports to be grounded in modern biology, particularly in the "modern synthesis" of genetics and natural selection; modern biology, however, provides absolutely no grounds for psychological inquiry because modern biology's entire field of study consists solely of objectalities. There can never be a study of the mind, stricto sensu, grounded in modern biology because modern biology always describes objects and never describes minds. Evolutionary psychologists' conclusions are *not* drawn from genetics, but from morality, and Christian morality at that. Evolutionary psychologists merely objectify men and women. The popularity of evolutionary psychology is due to the fact that it gratifies the dominant moral sensibilities of Christian civilization.

We reiterate that absolutely no inferences regarding psychology can be made from the objectalities of genetics; nothing regarding "egoism," "altruism," "man," "woman," sexual desire, violence, or anything else which in any way involves thoughts, feelings, and motivations. Needless to say, there are no such things as "kin selection," natural selection for altruism towards kin on the basis that it partially conserves a genotype. As numerous anthropologists have pointed out, there is a massive problem here with defining "kin," which is entirely culturally relative. Moreover, neither organisms nor genes inherently *know* the facts and the laws of genetic inheritance, therefore they are simply ignorant of who is their biological "kin" in terms of genetics; even Darwin himself was ignorant about how inheritance worked and he was also ignorant of who was his biological "kin" in terms of genetics; and indeed until the 20th century the vast majority of people on earth were completely ignorant of genetics and of how they could even go about determining their biological "kin" in terms of genetics. We have absolutely zero unconscious, a-priori knowledge on this topic. The point being that our psychological motivations—whether it be for sexual desire, for violence, for helping ourselves, or for "helping others"—can in no way whatsoever be inferred from "genes" or from "natural selection." Moreover, "egoism" and "altruism" are questionable concepts to begin with because there is no ego. (The ego is a fiction language, and the super-ego is a super-fiction of language).

The writings of Darwin himself on psychology and psychological motivations must also be regarded with deep scepticism, suspicion, and doubt, because Darwin himself was wholly ignorant of genetics, and natural selection only has meaning for modern biology in terms of genetics, meaning that not even Darwin himself had legitimate grounds for making inferences about psychology on the basis of his theory of natural selection. Darwin himself was a crab in this matter because he believed backwards, meaning that he fundamentally misunderstood the nature of history, i.e. of evolution. Darwin's conclusions regarding psychology are not empirically grounded, but rather they are merely a series of metaphysical presuppositions determined by discourse.

3. Anti-Christ and Anti-Darwin[20]

It is in the interest of psychology, meaning stricto sensu the study of subjectivity, that Nietzsche critiques Darwin: "*Anti-Darwin.* As for the famous "struggle for *existence*," so far it seems to me to be asserted rather than proved. It occurs, but as an exception; the total appearance of life is not the extremity, not starvation, but rather riches, profusion, even absurd squandering—and where there is struggle, it is a struggle for *power*. One should not mistake Malthus for nature." (TI, "Skirmishes of an Untimely Man," 14).

Nothing is easier than to admit in words the truth of the universal struggle for power, and nothing more difficult than constantly to bear this conclusion in mind. Yet unless the truth of the universal struggle for power be thoroughly engrained in the mind, the whole economy of nature, with every fact on distribution, rarity, abundance, extinction, and variation will be dimly seen or quite misunderstood.

A "will to life," "will to exist," "will to survive," or "struggle for existence," insofar as they refer to psychological motivations, can in no way be inferred from objectalities. Psychological analysis requires an analysis of subjectivity in terms of subjectivity. Ultimately, psychological analysis yields the conclusion that the primary motivation of an organism is the "will to power," that all motivations are forms of the will to power, hence the universal struggle for power in nature.

Nietzsche writes, "Indeed, the truth was not hit by him who shot at it with the word of the "will to existence": that will does not exist. For, what does not exist cannot will; but what is in existence, how could that still want existence? Only where there is life is there also will: not will to life but—thus I teach you—will to power" (TSZ, "On Self-Overcoming"). What does not exist cannot will to exist because it cannot will at all (since it does not exist, and one needs to exist in order to will). On the other hand, that which already exists has no necessity to will to exist because it already exists to begin with. To phrase it another way, that which is dead cannot will to survive because the dead can will nothing, whereas that which is already surviving cannot will to survive because it is already surviving to begin with. Therefore, there is no "struggle for existence."

Besides, what is even meant by "existence" or "life" when philosophers and scientists speak of a "will to exist"? If the answer is that life is a material process, then we have no grounds for discussing any "wills" at all, since the "will" refers to the psychological activity of a subject, whereas material processes are descriptions of objectalities devoid of subjectivities. Indeed, materialist definitions of life lead us back to the mind-body problem, not only in matters of animal psychology but more fundamentally in a way that deals with all living organisms. How is it even possible for a "will to life" or "will to survive," which denotes psychological activity, to ever be produced by objectalities? Using Chalmers' Zombie Thought Experiment, we can easily conceive of material processes of life, just as they are now, but wholly devoid of will, not to mention wholly devoid of a "will to exist." Materialist "explanations" do not depend on the assertion that there is a "will to exist." In other words, the objective data of modern biology gives us absolutely no grounds for asserting the existence of a "will to exist."

The question of the "will to exist" is a purely psychological problem, and ultimately it is a purely philosophical problem. Moreover, it is *not* Darwin's original idea; Darwin was merely using Schopenhauer's popular idea that the drive of all life is the "will to life" (which means the same as "will to exist"). Darwin's idea of a "struggle for existence" is based upon the idea that life is fundamentally a "will to exist." The psychological failures of positing a "will to exist" are obvious when one contemplates the complexity of human life, and especially when one contemplates phenomena such as suicide and self-sacrifice (the sacrifice of one's own life). Perhaps especially, sacrificing one's self for the sake of strangers and sacrificing one's self for the sake of ideas. In the case of self-sacrifice for the sake of strangers, there is absolutely no possibility of "kin selection," which is an absurdity to begin with. In the case of self-sacrifice for the sake of an idea, it is not a matter of "genes" at all, let alone "kin selection." However, these phenomena are pragmatically explicable in terms of the will to power. The suicide feels more power over himself and his circumstances by taking the decision to end his own life. The self-sacrificer feels more power over himself and his circumstances by taking the decision to sacrifice himself, whether it be for his "kin," for strangers, or for ideas.

Furthermore, as Nietzsche writes, the "will to life," or the "instinct for self-preservation," the "survival instinct," is a teleological concept, and thus it must be abolished from science: "Physiologists should think before putting down the instinct of self-preservation as the cardinal instinct of an organic being. A living thing seeks above all to *discharge* its strength—life itself is *will to power*; self-preservation is only one of the indirect and most frequent *results*. In short, here as everywhere, let us beware of *superfluous* teleological principles—one of which is the instinct of self-preservation...Thus method, which must be essentially economy of principles, demands it." (BGE, 13).

The "will to life" is a teleological concept because it posits "life" as the telos of physiological activity, such that all life "strives" for life, i.e. has "life" as its purpose. A modern biologists might add that all life "strives" to reproduce, that reproduction is the "purpose" of life; this is the concept of "fitness," which is likewise a teleological concept. But this is inserting a telos not only into physiological activity, but into history as well, such that the telos of history appears to be "life" and "reproduction." To be consistently non-teleological, science must abandon the hypotheses of "will to exist," "struggle for existence," "instinct for self-preservation," and "fitness."

The concept of the "will to power" is a non-teleological concept. It does *not* mean, stricto sensu, that all life "strives" for power, or that power is the "purpose" of existence. It is merely that the most pragmatic and operational description of psychological activity, and history as well for that matter, is a description in terms of power relations. The "will to power" is merely a metaphor, and it is a bit of a misleading misnomer, because there is no "will" in the traditional sense (viz. there is no "free will"), nor is the "will to power" a "will *to*," as if denoting a purpose. Rather, the "will to power" is more precisely a potentiality which is fully actualized at each given moment of its existence, hence it is a "discharge of strength" because it is a "discharge," i.e. an actualization, of a potentiality, of a force which *is* potentiality.

If we can speak of an "instinct for self-preservation" or a "struggle for existence" at all, it is only as a *result*, an *effect*, of the will to power, of the struggle for power. Nature is a struggle for power: competing wills discharge their potentialities, and these discharges of potentials *is* the "combat" of wills to power, and as the consequence of this infinitely complex combat, some organisms die while others are preserved. "Self-preservation" and the "instinct for self-preservation" are illusions, a-posteriori falsifications. We can still discuss "self-preservation" and "instinct for self-preservation," but merely as metaphors, and only keeping in mind that these metaphors are fundamentally inaccurate and imprecise. In reality, nature consists of the discharges of the potentials of wills to power, and nothing is more difficult than constantly to bear this conclusion in mind. Yet unless the truth of the agon of wills to power be thoroughly engrained in the mind, the whole economy of nature and of the mind will be dimly seen or quite misunderstood.

4. The Theory of Chance Elimination[21]

Not only is the concept of the "struggle for existence" completely useless in matters of psychology, but it is completely superfluous in matters of biology. Natural selection as explained by gene-focused modern biologists, for example, has absolutely nothing to do with a "will to exist," and consequently it has nothing to do with a "struggle for existence." However, what is "natural selection" to begin with? Even as the concept of "natural selection" applies to objectalities, what grounds do we have to describe it as "selection"?

But "natural selection," especially the "selection" in "natural selection," is an entirely misleading misnomer. There is no "intelligence" performing the "selection," i.e. there is absolutely no telos in nature, which means that there is no "selection" as such. Although some biologists have noted also noted that "natural selection" is a misnomer, they have nonetheless failed to draw the full consequences of their discovery.

Mayr (2001) writes that, "strictly speaking, there is no such agent involved in natural selection. *What Darwin called natural selection is actually a process of elimination.* The progenitors of the next generation are those individuals among their parents' offspring who survived *owing to luck* or the possession of characteristics that made them particularly well-adapted for the prevailing environmental conditions. All their siblings were *eliminated* by the process of natural selection" (p. 117; my emphasis). So "natural selection" really ought to be called "natural elimination," and this elimination occurs largely "owing to luck," i.e. due to chance. That "natural selection" occurs in the total absence of telos, i.e. that there is no "purpose" of history, is acknowledged by every modern biologist. However, modern biologists, including Mayr, have failed to draw the consequences implied by the absence of telos, namely that *the absence of telos is Chance.* Instead, we find that they have retreated to the safety of convictions in order to prevent themselves from correlating the contents of their own minds.

To begin with, let us consider the "biological" concept of "fitness" and its relation to chance. "Fitness" in modern biology does *not* refer to health, physical fitness, or longevity. "Fitness" in modern biology exclusively denotes reproductive capacity, the ability of an organism to reproduce, an organism's genetic contribution (contribution of genes) to the next generation's gene pool relative to the average for the population; "fitness" is measured by the number of offspring that survive to reproductive age. In this sense, a sense quite different from that meant by Herbert Spencer and Charles Darwin, modern biologists describe natural selection as "survival of the fittest." However, even in this altered form, "survival of the fittest" is a problematic term, since it seems to imply that organisms compete with each other in terms of "fitness," in terms of their ability to reproduce. This is completely at odds with the observable fact that survival, including the survival of offspring to reproductive age, is entirely a matter of chance. Therefore, history cannot be defined as the "survival of the fittest" because the reproductive capacity of an organism means nothing in the face of the whims of chance which eliminate organisms without regard for their reproductive capacity.

"Natural selection" and "selection pressure," as Mayr (2001) writes, is at best merely a metaphor: "The *metaphor* of selection pressure is frequently used by evolutionists to indicate the severity of selection. Even though it is a picturesque expression, this term, borrowed from the physical sciences, could be misunderstood, for *there is no force or pressure connected with natural selection that corresponds to the use of the term in the physical sciences*" (p. 118; my emphasis). "Selection pressure" is merely a metaphor, albeit a "picturesque" one, which means that it does *not* correspond with reality, it is *not* the "thing" which it designates. Insofar as "selection pressure" selects for "fitness," this means that we *cannot* describe history in terms "survival of the fittest," because there is no actual force or pressure which determines that only the "fittest" will survive. Indeed, to claim so would be to reintroduce a telos into nature. If we can discuss reproductive success at all, it is only as an effect of a struggle for power.

Mayr (2001) writes that "natural selection" is a two-step process, and that the first step, "the production of variation," is ruled by chance: "At the first step, consisting of all the processes leading to the production of a new zygote (including meiosis, gamete formation, and fertilization), new variation is produced. Chance rules supreme at this step, except that the nature of the changes at a given gene locus is strongly constrained" (p. 119). This first step of natural selection includes "*random* movement of homologous chromosomes during the second (reduction) division" and "any *random* aspects of mate choice and fertilization" (Mayr, 2001, p. 119; my emphasis). Mayr (2001) names the second step of natural selection the "*nonrandom* aspects of survival and reproduction," and describes it as the "elimination" which "natural selection" in actuality is (p. 119). By the mental construction of these arbitrary divisions, Mayr hopes to relegate the element of chance solely to the first step of natural selection, and thereby to assert that the second step is essentially "nonrandom," i.e. that the second step of natural selection is due to the "survival of the fittest." But by subordinating chance to the "survival of the fittest," Mayr surreptitiously reintroduces teleology into history; indeed, this manoeuvre is surreptitious even to himself, since Mayr does not recognize that "survival of the fittest" is, in effect, a teleological concept. For the "survival of the fittest" to be a nonrandom element of history would mean that history tends towards the preservation of organisms with higher reproductive capacity despite the chance elimination of individuals by forces of nature which are entirely indifferent to the reproductive capacities of respective organisms. Although the "survival of the fittest," i.e. "natural selection," is not recognized as a teleological concept by modern biologists, it is nonetheless in effect a teleological concept. There is no telos of history, therefore the "fittest" do *not* always survive, therefore there is no "natural selection."

Although Mayr (2001) writes that the second step of natural selection is the "nonrandom aspects of survival and reproduction," and that "chance plays a much smaller role at the second step, that of differential survival and reproduction, where the "survival of the fittest" is to a large extent determined by genetically based characteristics" (pp. 119-120). Mayr (2001) goes so far as to write, "To claim that natural selection is entirely a chance process reveals total misunderstanding" (p. 120), ostensibly because genetically based characteristics (protein structures) and genes themselves are, throughout their historical and temporal existence, subordinated to the law of the "survival of the fittest," despite the vagaries of chance. This is tantamount to subordinating history to an end, the end in question being the survival of the fittest. However, Mayr (2001) also writes that during the nonrandom aspects of survival and reproduction, "*much random elimination occurs simultaneously*" (p. 119; my emphasis). Explicating these random elimination processes which occur during the second step, Mayr (2001) also writes, "*there are also many chance elimination factors, so that there is no pure determination even at this step. Everything is somewhat probabilistic. Natural catastrophes, like floods, hurricanes, volcanic eruptions, lightning, and blizzards, may kill otherwise highly fit individuals. Furthermore, in small populations superior genes may be lost owing to sampling errors*" (p. 120; my emphasis). Indeed, elsewhere Mayr (2001) writes, "*Chance may be particularly important in the haphazard survival during periods of mass extinction*" (p. 281; my emphasis).

Mayr himself acknowledges the preponderance of "chance elimination factors" even at the second step. There is no "pure determination" of evolution by "fitness," which means that the concept of the "survival of the fittest" is an inadequate hypothesis because it fails to account for the destruction of the fittest and the survival of the unfit (cf. "natural catastrophes...may kill otherwise highly fit individuals," and "in small populations superior genes may be lost owing to sampling errors"). "Survival of the fittest," and consequently "natural selection," are useful hypotheses only when one completely ignores chance elimination factors; but to ignore chance elimination factors is to ignore nature itself, which means that "survival of the fittest" and "natural selection" are useless and superfluous hypotheses, that they describe nothing real, nor explain anything real for that matter. That "random elimination occurs simultaneously" to "nonrandom aspects of survival and reproduction" means precisely that there are no such "nonrandom aspects," that even at this second step, chance rules supreme. Evolution is never free of chance elimination factors. Laboratory experiments and computer models can indeed remove chance elimination factors from evolution and thus make it appear as if evolution is subordinate to "fitness," but these are artificial scenarios, reified mental constructs, which do not at all correspond to nature, which is fundamentally unpredictable. Laboratory experiments and computer models, in principle and in practice, isolate and control variables, and thus fail to account for the preponderance of chance elimination factors in nature. In nature, chance rules supreme, and chance is a fundamentally uncontrollable and unpredictable variable. Mayr is correct to write that "natural selection" is not an entirely chance process, but he is correct only in the sense that the concept of "natural selection" is a denial of chance, a mental construct which functions to deny chance, because ultimately, "natural selection" is still merely a teleological concept and there is no telos in nature. "Natural selection" is essentially unnatural because nature is essentially chance. There is no "natural selection" as such, not only because "selection" is in actuality "elimination," but also because there is no "survival of the fittest," no telos, and therefore evolution is determined entirely by chance, by chance elimination factors.

Therefore, "evolution" is in actuality *chance elimination*, evolution is determined entirely by the process of chance elimination. Chance denotes the complete absence of teleology. "Elimination," likewise, following Mayr, implies the absence of teleology, viz. there is no teleological "selection." In concrete terms, "chance elimination" merely means that organisms die due to chance events which are absolutely indifferent to the "fitness" of the organism, not to mention that these chance events are absolutely indifferent to the morality or immorality of the organism (viz. to whether the organism is "altruistic" or "egoistic," not that it is possible to be either in the first place). Evolution, like all history, is essentially a stochastic process, aleatoric series of chance "events." Chance elimination means that evolution is both fundamentally non-teleological and that it is fundamentally stochastic. As we have quoted Mayr above, "Natural catastrophes, like floods, hurricanes, volcanic eruptions, lightning, and blizzards, may kill otherwise highly fit individuals." But this is not only the case for natural catastrophes, but for death generally. Death is always a chance event, a fundamentally non-teleological and aleatoric event. The necessity of death is the necessity of chance; death is necessary only because death is determined by chance. Each death is a chance elimination. Survival is essentially haphazard.

To clarify, we affirm, pragmatically speaking, that there is adaptation, variation and speciation among organisms, that descent with modification occurs among organisms, and that there are "common ancestors" among species and ultimately that there is a common ancestor of all organisms. Not that "common ancestors" explain anything whatsoever, since they are all merely so many "origins," and believing that "common ancestors" explain anything at all is merely "believing backwards," i.e. reducing history to "origins" and the search for "origins." However, we deny that "natural selection" is the mechanism by which variation and speciation occurs. Moreover, we argue that searching for such a "mechanism" is fundamentally misguided; such a "mechanism" for speciation and variations is, strictly speaking, not possible. Inventing such "mechanisms," as is the case with "natural selection," merely reintroduces a fictive telos into evolution. There is no "natural selection," nor is there any other possible mechanism of variation and speciation. There is only chance elimination. Variation and speciation are determined entirely by chance elimination.

Moreover, "natural selection," or "survival of the fittest," in actuality explain nothing, and are completely useless for predicting the course of evolution as it occurs in nature. Mayr (2001) himself acknowledges that evolution is unpredictable: "Evolution is subject to a large number of interactions. Different genotypes within a single population may respond differently to the same change of the environment. The changes of the environment, likewise, are unpredictable, particularly the arrival at a locality of new predators and competitors. Finally, there are occasionally very drastic changes in the global environment, resulting in so-called mass extinctions. In such mass events, chance may play a large role in survival. Owing to the unpredictability of all these situations, the nature of the evolutionary change by which a population will respond is necessarily also unpredictable" (p. 277). All this is evidence in favour of our theory of chance elimination. The most dramatic example of chance elimination is mass extinctions, in which a large quantity of diverse organisms and even entire species are eliminated with absolutely zero regard for their "fitness." However, even more generally speaking, the environment itself is aleatoric, changes of the environment are unpredictable, and moreover different genotypes within a single population react differently to the same change of environment; these changes of environment have zero regard "fitness," and the different responses of different genotypes within a single population are dependent upon various forces which are completely ignorant of "fitness" and the "struggle for existence." The unpredictability of all these situations is precisely the essential aleatoricality of nature itself. The nature of the evolutionary change by which a population will respond to aleatoric environmental changes is also necessarily unpredictable because it is also necessarily aleatoric.

5. Nature's Originary Overproduction

Nature is, in totality and in essence, overproduction, i.e. excess. The essential overproduction of nature is originary. To paraphrase Nietzsche, the total appearance of life is riches, profusion, even absurd squandering. Darwin himself attests to the essential excess of nature: "Every being, which during its natural lifetime produces several eggs or seeds, must suffer destruction during some period of its life, and during some season or occasional year, otherwise, on the principle of geometrical increase, its numbers would quickly become so inordinately great that no country could support the product" (OS, p. 63). The essential and originary overproduction of nature inevitably follows from the high rate at which all organic beings struggle for power. Darwin writes that "more individuals are produced than can possibly survive" (OS, p. 63). What Darwin describes as the "principle of geometrical increase," or the "geometrical ratio of increase," attests to the essential and originary overproduction of nature. Darwin's descriptions of the geometrical ratio of increase of organisms is in direct contradiction to his assertion that there is a "struggle for existence" in which nature is characterized in terms of an essential and originary poverty, an originary poverty which guarantees the "struggle for existence" since through its lens all life appears to always be on the verge of dying and its sole motivation appears to be to prevent itself from dying. Besides, the Malthusian basis of Darwin's idea of the geometrical ratio of increase of organisms dictates that population increase presupposes an adequate supply of food to enable and fuel this increase. In other words, the principle of geometrical increase presupposes an originary overinvestment of energy, an originary oversupply of food, i.e. riches, profusion.

Darwin writes that "we may confidently assert, that all plants and animals are tending to increase at a geometrical ratio,—that all would rapidly stock every station in which they could anyhow exist,—and that this geometrical tendency to increase must be checked by destruction at some period of life" (p. 64). In this passage as well as the examples he gives of Malthusian "positive checks" to overpopulation, Darwin mistakenly writes of such checks in a manner that suggests teleology, when in fact no teleology whatsoever exists in nature. Nature does not "know" because it is not a unified entity capable of "knowing" or "not knowing" whether or not the population of its creatures is stable, deficient, or excessive. No doubt, despite nature's originary overproduction, the profusion of organisms, nature's ecological balance remains relatively stable, which does point to the existence of "positive checks," although it must be remembered that positive checks to overpopulation occur wholly due to chance, wholly accidentally (i.e. non-teleologically). Moreover, "positive check" remains a misleading misnomer because species are subject to dangers from other organisms as well as natural calamities whether their numbers are in excess, stable, or deficient. "Positive checks" are in actuality forms of chance elimination.

The answer to this riddle, how nature, despite its originary overproduction, retains the relative stability of its total population such that it does not overpopulate itself to the point of total self-destruction, comes from Darwin himself: "Many cases are on record showing how complex and unexpected are the checks [to increase] and relations between organic beings" (OS, p. 69). Organic beings are interconnected in networks of power relations with other organic beings in a given ecosystem, and the power struggles between organic beings serve, in effect, as "positive checks," although more strictly speaking these are all cases of chance elimination. But these organisms which are engaged in these power struggles themselves originated as a result of the geometric ratio of increase, which is symptomatic of the originary overproduction of nature. Nature's originary overproduction is the basis of its own checks to increase. The profusion of diverse organisms which result from power struggles in turn engage in power struggles with each other, and in their struggles for power much destruction of life inevitably occurs, thereby in effect serving as a system of checks to increase. Originary overproduction is both the origin of the geometrical ratio of increase and the checks to increase. Nature's superabundance in turn limits nature's superabundance.

Darwin himself writes that the checks to increase are essentially non-teleological: "Look at the most vigorous species; by as much as it swarms in numbers, by so much will it tend to increase still further" (p. 66). Nature does not know, indeed cannot know, whether the population of a species is deficient, stable, or excessive. An ecosystem overpopulated by a species may undergo a further increase in that species' population, and this is attested to by numerous cases of invasive species. Therefore, by implication, checks to increase occur accidentally as the result of power struggles.

Darwin also writes that the climate also serves in effect as a check to increase. The climate, of course, is indifferent to and ignorant of whether a species' population is deficient, stable, or excessive, just as it cannot know the relative "fitness" of given organisms. The climate may just as inadvertently favour an already overpopulated species as it may serve as a check to increase.

Darwin also writes that epidemics often serve as checks to increase (OS, p. 68). No doubt this is true, but it must be kept in mind that the pathogens responsible for epidemics are indifferent to and ignorant of whether their host species' population is deficient, stable, or excessive. Thus, epidemics, too, are non-teleological, and in this sense are chance events. Moreover, it must also be remembered that epidemics are caused by micro-organisms, and therefore epidemics too presuppose the originary overproduction of nature since they are products of the struggle for power among the superabundance of organisms.

Darwin writes, "The amount of food for each species of course gives the extreme limit to which each can increase; but very frequently it is not the obtaining [of] food, but the serving as prey to other animals, which determines the average number of a species" (OS, p. 66). This implies, firstly, that the geometrical ratio of increase presupposes a necessary and sufficient amount of food as its precondition. It also implies, secondly, that it is the geometrical ratio of increase itself which serves as the check to increase since the checks to increase are primarily due to some organisms "serving as prey to other animals," with the predators themselves also presumably being the product of the geometrical ratio of increase. It is not due to any deficiency of nature that there are checks to increase, but on the contrary it is due to nature's essential excess that there are checks to increase. The superabundance of nature ultimately originates from the superabundance and originary overproduction of the forces of the sun and of the earth. The sun and the earth supply the necessary energy for the geometrical ratio of increase of all organisms, and this geometrical ratio of increase in turn serves as its own check to increase since these organisms obtain nourishment by consuming each other.

"We must die as egos and be
born again in the swarm, not
separate and self-hypnotized, but
individual and related."
—Henry Miller, *Sexus*

"Everything we do is music."
—Balinese aphorism

"Raw power got a healin' hand,
Raw power can destroy a man"
—The Stooges, "Raw Power"

"Carefree, mocking, violent—thus wisdom wants *us*: she is a woman
and always loves only a warrior."
—Nietzsche, TSZ, "On Reading and Writing"

"All the world's a stage, and all the men and women in it players."
—Shakespeare, *As You Like It*

"Well I met someone some time ago,
His eyes were clear to see,
He showed me things in my own mind
That I wish all the world could see,
He stopped me from living so insane
I can be just what I wanna be,
Things appear as they really are,
I can see just what I want to see...
After your trip, life opens up,
You start doin' what you wanna do,
You find out that the world that you once feared
Gets what it has from you.
No-one can ever hurt you
Because now you know more than you thought you knew,
You're looking at the world with brand new eyes
And no-one can ever spoil the view.
Well come on, and let it happen to you,
Hey, hey, hey well come on, you gotta let it happen to you,

You gotta open up your mind and let everything come through.
Just open up your mind
And let everything come through."
—13th Floor Elevators, "Rollercoaster," as sung by Spacemen 3

"Here come the comedians
look at them smile
Watch them dance
an indian mile.

Look at them gesture
How aplomb
So to gesture everyone."
—Jim Morrison, "An American Prayer"[22]

1.

Psychology is essentially psychedelic and mind-revealing. Reality is essentially psychedelic and mind revealing. Reality is the ultimate psychedelic. The highest and most intense peak is the peak of reality itself, the peak of the self-actualization of the self of reality itself, the affirmation of the Eternal Return. Nietzsche's philosophy is the ultimate psychedelic philosophy—the philosophy of the very god of psychedelics, Dionysus—the ultimate self-help psychology, the ultimate guide to self-empowerment and self-actualization. Our models of mental health, our models of self-actualized individuals, and our guides to self-actualization, are primarily: the conceptual persona of Nietzsche in Nietzsche's book *Ecce Homo*, the conceptual persona of Zarathustra in Nietzsche's *Thus Spoke Zarathustra*, what Nietzsche describes as "master morality" in *On the Genealogy of Morals*, the conceptual personae of the Heroes in Homer's *The Iliad*, the conceptual persona of Odysseus in Homer's *The Odyssey*, the conceptual persona of the Prince in Machiavelli's *The Prince*, and the conceptual persona and author Sun Tzu of Sun Tzu's *The Art of War*. Future studies on mental health focusing on models of mental health must consult these essential texts as well as the biographies of conquerors and Plutarch's *Lives*.

2.

Our metapsychology consists of three interrelated analytic perspectives: the dynamic perspective, the economic perspective, and the topographic perspective. We borrow from Freud the employment of "the abbreviation Cs [or system Cs] for consciousness and the Ucs [or system Ucs] for the unconscious when we are using the two words in any systematic sense" (Freud, GPT, p. 116). The psyche consists solely of two overarching systems, the system Ucs and the system Cs; all other mental systems are systems within the system Ucs, the system Cs, or both. The dynamic analytic perspective analyses psychological phenomena in terms of their motivations, the psychic forces (i.e. the drives) which are their essences and which animate them. The economic analytic perspective analyses psychological phenomena in terms of quantitative variations in amounts of psychic energies, i.e. in terms of the political economy of the unconscious. The topographic analytic perspective analyses psychological phenomena in terms of systems (or structures), which means primarily that the system Ucs is the infrastructure (base) of the psyche and the system Cs is the superstructure of the psyche, which means that the system Cs is determined in the last instance by the system Ucs. The phrase "determined in the last instance" is merely a metaphor which illustrates the topographic analytic perspective; in actuality, the system Cs is completely determined, in its parts and in totality, by the system Ucs.

3.

All mental acts are forms of the will to power. The categorical imperative of the system Ucs is to increase power. All mental acts are produced and directed by the unconscious. Unconscious mental activity is far more sophisticated and complex than conscious mental activity. Consciousness is an epiphenomenon, an accidental byproduct, of unconscious mental activity. The emotions which constitute consciousness are epiphenomena, accidental byproducts, of unconscious emotions. To use a metaphor, the unconscious is a society of emotions, with its own economy, culture, and politics; this unconscious society of emotions determines consciousness in its entirety. The unconscious mind is an other dimension which produces and determines all of our thoughts, feelings, perceptions, and actions. Insofar as each subjectivity is its own dimension, its own dimension of subjectivity, i.e. its own subjective reality, the self, because it is a system of others, is a system of other dimensions. All of our thoughts, feelings, perceptions, and actions come from another dimension, the dimension of the unconscious mind, the multiplicity of dimensions of the unconscious mind. Power-analysis is an exploration of other dimensions, a dimensional analysis, the scientific interpretation of the subjectivity and perspectivity of other dimensions, of other subjective realities, the scientific interpretation of dimensions of power. There are an infinity of other dimensions, each of which is an infinity unto itself. The body without organs is an infinity of other dimensions, an infinity of infinite dimensions, it is infinity itself and dimensionality itself, the infinity itself of dimensionality itself and the dimensionality itself of infinity itself.

4.

Power-analysis is the depth psychology of the will to power. To paraphrase Freud, "By accepting the existence of these [mental systems, namely the system Cs and the system Ucs], [power-analysis] has departed a step further from the descriptive psychology of consciousness [viz. phenomenology] and has taken to itself a new problem and a new content. Up till now, it differed from academic (descriptive) psychology [viz. phenomenology] mainly by reason of its dynamic conception of mental processes; now we have to add that it professes to consider mental topography also, and to indicate in respect of any given mental operation within what system or between what systems it runs its course. This attempt, too, has won it the name of "depth psychology"" (Freud, GPT, p. 117).

Power-analysis argues that mental activity can only be truly understood if and only if it is understood that all mental activity, including conscious mental activity, is caused by unconscious mental activity. Thus, power-analysis has "a new problem and a new content," namely the dynamics, i.e. the power relations, among unconscious psychic forces. Power-analysis is truly a "depth psychology," a psychology of the unconscious, whereas all other psychology, including phenomenology, is either superficial or not even superficial. Phenomenology, for instance, is not even superficial, because it has no depth whatsoever, it takes the ego as its starting point and its end point, but the ego is merely a linguistic construct. Phenomenology explains absolutely nothing, and in terms of description it absolutely and fundamentally misunderstands all psychological events; at best, phenomenology merely labels phenomena, albeit by doing so it radically falsifies and misinterprets everything. Psychoanalysis, at least, is superficial; it has a little depth because it acknowledges the existence of the unconscious mind, but it is still only superficial because it completely misunderstands the nature of the unconscious and because it still believes in the ego. Power-analysis, the psychology of the will to power, is the only true depth psychology because it is the only psychology which both recognizes that the ego is merely a linguistic construct *and* recognizes that unconscious psychic forces determine *all* mental activity.

5.

The system Cs and the system Ucs consist wholly of emotions (emotions = feelings = affects). Drives *are* emotions, emotions *are* drives. The subject's mental life *is* the subject's emotional life, and the subject's emotional life is almost entirely unconscious. Emotions which become conscious are produced and determined by unconscious emotions. Consciousness often misinterprets the emotions which it experiences, e.g. "free will" is a falsification of experience (there is no "free will"). All emotions are involuntary. The "volition" of consciousness, the "decision-making" of a "rational agent", is a misinterpretation and falsification of experience (there is no such "rational agent," consciousness has absolutely no "volition") (cf. Nietzsche, GM, I, 13). All "decision-making" is performed by the unconscious; to be more precise, the process of "decision-making" is the combat of unconscious forces and the "decision" is the *result* of the combat of unconscious forces. There is no "self-control" as such. "Self-control" is at best merely a metaphor, and at worst a falsification. Inhibitions are themselves entirely caused by unconscious forces. Only the system Ucs has "volition," or "will," hence all unconscious forces are forms of the "will to power." The system Ucs always controls all affectivity as well as motility and access to motility (motility and access to motility are themselves merely products of affectivity).

Kalat (2016) writes that "according to the James-Lange theory [of emotions], the autonomic arousal and skeletal actions come first," and the subjective experience of emotions only follow afterwards (p. 357). In other words, according to the James-Lange theory, the subjective experience of emotions is produced by the "objective processes" of autonomic arousal of the nervous system and skeletal actions. The James-Lange theory of emotions, according to which the experience of emotions is merely the label given by the subject to "objective processes," is merely the denial of emotions, the denial of subjectivity, the denial of what emotions *feel like*, because it subordinates the subjective experience of emotions to objectalities which allegedly cause them, such that the emotions are effectively reduced to an "epiphenomenon" of objectalities; this "epiphenomenon" of emotions, however, is in effect completely superfluous to the "real" processes of emotions, the autonomic arousal of the nervous system and skeletal actions. According to the James-Lange theory, for example, "You feel afraid *because* you run away, and you feel angry *because* you attack" (Kalat, 2016, p. 357). The obvious objection to the James-Lange theory is that it suffers from the "explanatory gap" of the mind-body problem. How is it possible, exactly, for the subjective experience of emotions to be produced by "objective processes" such as autonomic arousal of the nervous system and skeletal actions? We could also apply Chalmers' Zombie Thought Experiment to the James-Lange theory; namely, we can make the objection that the James-Lange theory fails to explain why the subjective experience of emotions is even necessary in the first place. It is conceivable that autonomic arousal of the nervous system and skeletal actions occur without there being any subjective experience of emotions whatsoever; in a materialist theory of emotions, there is no necessity, in terms of material causes, for there to be emotions at all. Because it effectively negates the necessity of emotions altogether, thereby reducing the subjective experience of emotions to mere "labels" of objectalities, the James-Lange theory effectively negates the emotions altogether.

Here, materialists can learn much from the "common sense" theory of emotions, and even we depth psychologists can learn much from the fact that the James-Lange theory is directly the opposite of the "common sense" theory: as Kalat (2016) writes, "Common sense holds that you feel an emotion that changes your heart rate and prompts other responses" (p. 357). This "common sense" theory is nothing other than a pragmatic understanding of how subjectivity works; one feels an emotion first, and this feeling "causes" changes in heart rate and other responses; here, it appears that the common people are much healthier and much more intelligent than materialist psychologists and materialist philosophers generally based upon the evidence of their theory of emotions, however much else folly there may be to critique in the common people. Plainly speaking, it is absolute stupidity to claim, along with the James-Lange theory, that such things as changes in heart rate cause emotions; one only has to consider as an example falling in love, which is most certainly not caused by a change in heart rate. The James-Lange theory, and adherence to the James-Lange theory, evinces a failure to empathize with others, a failure to empathize even with one's self, and the inability to fall in love. But the "common sense" theory of emotions nonetheless does not go far enough, and moreover it is mixed, muddled, and muddied by superstitious beliefs like "free will" which proliferate among the common people of Christian civilization. The common people, too, suffer from the mental illnesses of materialism and objectivism; although the common people are healthier than materialist scientists and materialist philosophers, they are nonetheless also grievously sick and foolish. Materialism, the belief in a material reality, and even more generally speaking, the belief in an objective reality, evinces, to varying degrees in the overwhelming majority of cases, a diminished capacity for empathy, a diminished capacity for self-empathy, and a diminished capacity or even a complete incapability for passionate love.

Autonomic arousal of the nervous system and skeletal actions, and indeed all activity of the nervous system and all muscular activity, in fact all activities of all "organs" whatsoever, are merely all so many artefacts of perception and mental constructs upon the operating table of knowledge; they are illusions fabricated by the system Ucs and are at best described as "biochemical correlates" of mental systems. As artefacts of perception, when they are perceived, "organs" and "the activities of organs" are perception-images. The discursive concepts of "organs" and the "activities of organs" are the correlates of perception-images. However, the perception-images of "organs" and the "activities of organs" are merely the "representations" of action-images—we will see in a later section why "representation" as it is used here is merely a metaphor—and the discursive concepts, or social constructs, of "organs" and the "activities of organs" are merely biochemical correlates of these action-images. "Organs" and their activities, for example "activity of the nervous system," "muscular activity," and "heart rate," are merely biochemical correlates of action-images, which *are* emotions, actions from the inside out, actions which feel like something from the inside out. To put it rather crudely and inadequately, it feels like something to be an organ, it feels like something to be the nervous system, it feels like something to be muscular activity or skeletal actions, it feels like something to be the heart; but this is a crude and inadequate metaphor because in actuality there are no "organs" as such, for "organs" are all merely so many illusions, so many artefacts of perception.

There are *only* emotions. The body itself *is* the emotions; the body is the *body without organs*, which *is* the emotions. The action-images whose biochemical correlates are the "activities of the nervous system," "muscular activity," and "heart rate" are themselves caused by other emotions; we may say, solely in order to paint a conceptual picture, that these action-images are caused by force-images, but this is merely a metaphor because in actuality action-images *are* force-images and force-images *are* action-images. Emotions cause *both* the action-images whose biochemical correlates are the "activities of organs" (for example, "nervous system activity," "muscular activity," and "heart rate"), *and* the artefacts of perception, the perception-images (for example, the perception-images of the "autonomic arousal of the nervous system," "muscular activity," and "heart rate"). We may use, merely as so many metonyms and metaphors which are ultimately falsifications, but always keeping in mind that in actuality it is the will to power which acts upon the will to power, such seemingly commonplace expressions such as "You run away *because* you *feel* fear; you attack *because* you *feel* anger; your heart rate increase *because* you *feel* love; etc." The point being that in mental life the emotions are absolutely primary and that the emotions cause absolutely everything. We must remember, in any case, the principles that in actuality the body is the body without organs, and that in actuality that it is the will to power which acts upon the will to power. To phrase it another way, mental life consists wholly and entirely of the passions, and the passions act only upon the passions.

7

The concept of drives explains "the variability of behaviour under identical stimulus conditions as well as the relative constancy of behaviour under changing stimulus conditions" (Weinberger & Stein, 2002, p. 164). Different dominant drives result in different reactions to the same stimulus; also, different degrees of strength of the same dominant drive also result in different reactions to the same stimulus. (Drives = feelings = affects = emotions = wills = motivations).

How someone feels to begin with affects how they will react to something; two different people in two different emotional states will react to the same thing in different ways; even the same person at two different points in time and in two different emotional states respective to those two different points in time, will react to the same thing in different ways.

The dominance of one drive over all the others results in relatively predictable patterns of behaviour even when the subject is exposed to different stimulus conditions. A given person generally feels the same way towards certain things they consider important, and they will continue feeling the same way towards these things unless some trauma provokes a radical transformation of how they feel about these things.

All the phenomena described above can be accounted for by the "displacement of drive energy," such that displacements of drive energy result in infinitely variable expressions of drives (Weinberger & Stein, 2002, p. 164). "Displacements of drive energy" means either changes in the quantity of the drive (changes in the relative strength or weakness of the drive), or the sublimation of one drive into another drive (the transfer of drive energy from one form of drive to another form of drive). All of our thoughts, feelings, perceptions, actions, beliefs and desires are produced by unconscious drives.

Notice in these examples we have discussed feelings, both variations of emotional states and relatively constant and recurring feelings. Feelings dictate how we act; feelings determine both our spontaneous actions and our reactions to stimuli, i.e. all of our behaviour and our patterns of behaviour. The concept of drives explains why we have feelings: our feelings are caused by our drives, our feelings are produced by our drives. Drives are themselves feelings; unconscious drives are unconscious feelings.

Drives are motivations, unconscious motivations, and they
explain beliefs and desires, thoughts and affects, and thus are an
example of a "theory of mind," which is essential for our
understanding of ourself and others, our empathy, our social
intelligence and our emotional intelligence. The theory of drives is
above all a pragmatic and practical theory, and it is useful in a
variety of situations, from everyday life to anomalous and difficult
circumstances, and thus it is of interest to anyone who is interested
in increasing their own power over circumstances.

8.

The organism, the body of the organism, the body without
organs, is itself a subjectivity. The stimuli originating from within
the organism are psychic stimuli. "Physiological activity" is in
actuality psychic activity, activity of psyches. Drives are the
subjectivity itself of the body itself, of the body without organs
itself. The physiological activity of the body without organs *is*
psychic activity. The body without organs *is* the soma; the soma
itself is the psyche itself, a multiplicity of psyches. Drives are
psychic forces, psychic forces are drives. Mental representations are
constructed by drives to be used by drives for the "ends" of drives.
Consciousness is the delegate and the slave of the unconscious mind.

9.

The perceptual system, the system Pcpt, is itself wholly and
entirely an unconscious mental system: the system Pcpt *is* the system
Pcpt-Ucs. The function of the system Pcpt-Ucs is to appropriate and
consume psychic forces from the environment. Or, what amounts to
exactly the same thing, the function of the system Pcpt-Ucs is to
appropriate and consume qualia from the environment (forces =
qualia = forces-qualia). The system Pcpt-Ucs *is* the doors of
perception. The system Pcpt-Ucs is the region of the system-Ucs,
and indeed of the entire psyche, which is directly in contact with the
external world, it is directly affected by the external world and it
directly affects the external world. The organism's relations with the
external world *are* the relations of the system Pcpt-Ucs with the
external world. It must also always be remembered that the external

world itself consists wholly and entirely of psychic forces. The psyche's relations with reality *are* the relations of the system Pcpt-Ucs with the psychic forces of the external world. To use a metaphor, the system Pcpt-Ucs and the system Ucs are the Id; the Id is what is directly in touch with external reality and the Id determines the entirety of psychic life.

Nietzsche writes, "Sense-perception happens without our awareness: whatever we become conscious of is a perception that has already been processed" (WLN, N34, 30). The system Pcpt-Ucs always perceives a vast amount more than ever becomes conscious. Unconscious psychic forces are wholly and entirely responsible for sense-perception, whereas conscious perceptions are merely illusions produced by unconscious psychic forces using memory-traces. Conscious perceptions, the perceptions which become conscious, are merely illusions manufactured by the system Ucs for various and often diverse ends. The system Pcpt-Ucs first appropriates and consumes psychic forces from the environment, and it is only after much unconscious processing that the perception-images which become conscious are produced and subsequently become conscious. Consciousness only perceives its own subjective reality, its own subjective perspective, which is itself manufactured in its entirety by unconscious subjective perspectives which first had direct contact with the reality of the external world, which is itself entirely the reality of other psychic forces, each of which have their own subjective perspectives. There is neither a "true world" nor an "apparent world" because reality consists wholly of a multiplicity of subjective perspectives, each of which perceives only its own subjective reality which is irreducibly different from every other subjective reality.

Perception-images are manufactured by the system Ucs using memory-images (memories = memory-images). Following and dependent upon the system Pcpt-Ucs is a secondary unconscious mental system, the memory system (the memory system = the system Mnem = the system Mnem-Ucs). The system Mnem-Ucs lays down memory traces (memory traces = memory-images), including both memory traces of perceptions and memory traces of thoughts. Conscious perceptions are likewise constructed by the system Ucs using the system Mnem-Ucs. In this sense, conscious perceptions are all mental and social constructions, although it must be remembered that all perception-images are *always* transcursive constructions, that is to say, perception-images are always constructs of mediation, constructs of difference-in-itself, and constructs of becoming. Hence the irreducible difference and arbitrary relation between perception-images and "pictorial constructs," not to mention between perception-images and linguistic constructs. Perception-images, stricto sensu, are *never* identicalities. Identicalities are discursive constructs. Perception-images are *never* discursive constructs. Identicalities are always either merely "pictorial constructs" or merely linguistic constructs. Perception is always perception of difference-in-itself, and perception-images are always perception-images of difference-in-itself (hence the ceaseless and infinite "stream of perception"). Although conscious perceptions are always illusions, they are nonetheless also always and always already "streams of perception," always already difference-in-itself, mediation, and becoming. Conscious perceptions are illusions precisely because the ultimate nature of reality is becoming, mediation, and difference.

Friedrich Nietzsche's psychological theory of perception, that perception is first and foremost unconscious, is also partially shared by cognitive neuroscientists and neurologists, although Nietzsche has never, as far as we are aware, received credit for this profound medical discovery. On the neurological theory of perception, we paraphrase Solms and Turnbull (2001): "The title of Gerald Edelman's popular book, *The Remembered Present* (1989), captures very well what perception is about. We all automatically reconstruct the reality we perceive from models we have stored in our memories. We do not perceive the world anew every moment of the day and try afresh to discriminate recognizable objects and decipher meaningful words from the [infinite] din of stimuli that constantly impinge on us...We adults [and children as well] *project* our expectations (the products of our previous experience) onto the world all the time, and in this way we largely *construct* rather than perceive (in any simple sense) the world around us. [The interposition of the perceptual apparatus is designed to *sample* and *represent* certain selected features of the world, and the memory apparatus, on the basis of past experience, organizes and transforms those selected features into recognizable *objects*]...During the course of development, however, deeply encoded and abstract knowledge derived from these early learning experiences comes to govern the perceptual processes. We therefore see what we expect to see, and we are either surprised or fail to notice when our expectations are contradicted. Experimental studies show that we frequently see things that are not there, simply because we expect them to be there." (Solms and Turnbull, 2002, p. 155)

The temporal experience of the "present" is merely a mental construct produced by the system Ucs using the system Mnem-Ucs. This is also supported by Derrida's conclusions in *Speech and Phenomena* regarding the temporal experience of the "present," which he likewise discovers is merely a mental construct. The "models" "stored" in the system Mnem-Ucs are the codes of culture, the codes of signs of a given culture, including discursive as well as transcursive codes, through which experience is interpreted even at the micro-psychological level of the construction of conscious perceptions. Indeed, conscious experience *is* encultured interpretation, i.e. conscious experience is itself always already merely an interpretation. By use of memory traces, the system Ucs superimposes recognizable identicalities and also recognizable, meanings, upon perception-images; indeed, these superimposed identicalities are useful to a great extent, although no such identicalities exist in actuality.

The system Ucs only superimposes "objects," in the strict sense meaning "objectalities," onto perception-images when the system Ucs suffers from the belief in an objective reality, which is a delusion and a symptom of the mental disease of neurosis. As it concerns the codes of Western civilization, the superimposed meanings tend to be monosemantic, which denies the essential polysemy of psychic forces and perception-images; this artificially delimits "man," separating him from the essential infinity of psychic forces.

Perception is never "immediate" or "unmediated." Perception, too, is mediate, it is a system of mediation, in several senses; not only are all perceptions equivalent to mediations, but conscious perception is only possible via the mediation of the system Ucs, which constructs conscious perceptions. To be more precise than Solms and Turnbull, the "perceptual apparatus," in our sense of the term, is strictly speaking, the system Pcpt-Ucs, which consumes forces-qualia from the environment, and the "memory apparatus" is the system Mnem-Ucs.

The body is always already a dreamer, reality is always already a dream: the body without organs *is* a dream-machine. The hyle of reality *is* the hyle of dreams, which means precisely that the hyle of reality *is* the emotions. We may describe the unconscious mental system which constructs conscious perceptions the "waking-dream apparatus," "waking-dream machine," the "hallucination apparatus," or the "hallucination machine." (During, sleep, this same hallucination apparatus produces sleeping dreams, and is a sleeping-dream machine). The waking-dream apparatus does not, stricto sensu, "sample" or "represent" selected features of the world, because the "world" itself is composed of psychic forces which have their own subjective experience of the "world." Rather, the hallucination apparatus, using the system Mnem-Ucs, organizes and transforms the consumed psychic forces into movement-images which *are* excitations and anticipated excitations of varying degrees; these anticipated excitations orient and direct the organism in the environment according to the demands of the system Ucs. All perception is metaphor. Conscious perceptions *are* excitations and anticipated excitations; by these means, the system Ucs orients and directs the system Cs for diverse ends. Recognizable identicalities are likewise also excitations and anticipated excitations by means of which the system Ucs orients and directs the system Cs for diverse ends.

Conscious perceptions are always falsifications but they are never "representations." Conscious perceptions are always non-representational because, for the system Ucs, it is not question of "representing" an "objective world," but rather it is a pragmatic question of "navigating" a non-spatial agon of subjectivities. Conscious perceptions are always labyrinthian cartographies, they are always so many labyrinths. "Space" is an artefact of perception, "spatiality" is a system of qualia dependent on subjectivity; "space" does *not* imply a "space" independent of minds, i.e. there is no "objective space." When discussing the "external world" in the strict sense, the concept "space" simply does not apply because the "external world" is in actuality an agon of subjectivities, each of which have their own subjective reality. Subjectivity, which consists entirely of ineffable and private qualia, can by its very nature never be "represented." Therefore, perceptions, including conscious perceptions, are essentially non-representational, hence why all perceptions are labyrinths.

10.

Culture consists of signs. The system Mnem-Ucs consists largely of the code of signs of a given culture; it also consists of

"personal experiences," but "personal experiences" are themselves
encultured, always already encultured, always already culture.
Culture *is* a system of writing, but it does not consist exclusively of
"language" (viz. speech), that is to say, the code of signs of a given
culture are constituted by a variety of signs, including visual images,
sounds, smells, touches, tastes, and even "personal experiences." We
may say that "culture is a language," but merely as a metaphor, and
keeping in mind that this "language" is far vaster than merely
"speech," hence why "culture is writing." Culture is a language of
emotions. Besides, even as it concerns speech, "meaning is use," and
the "meaning" of speech is determined by a practice, that is to say by
a form of life, that is to say by a system of "personal experiences."
Culture *is* a "language," a system of meanings, which means
precisely that culture *is* a form of life, a system of forms of life. But
a "form of life" is itself a kind of "language" because it is itself a
code of signs (viz. of perception-images, action-images, etc). A code
of signs which *is* a form of life, which is a system of "personal
experiences," constitutes the system Mnem-Ucs.

It is instructive to compare "culture" with "language."
Indeed, the essential properties of "language" are also the essential
properties of "culture": communication, reflexivity, displacement,
arbitrariness, productivity, and cultural transmission. Speech and
culture even share the same critical period during childhood
development during which they are acquired together, and there is
also a "syntax," or "grammar" (syntax = grammar) of culture.

Each sign is a "communicative signal" because signs are
means by which psychic forces communicate with each other.
Psychic forces intentionally communicate with each other by means
of signs. A sign is itself a psychic force; communication is an
exchange of psychic forces. Communication is a system of
mediation because each sign must be *interpreted* in order to be
understood. The perception-images, action-images, etc. which
constitute a form of life are signs, and therefore they are also
communicative signals; by means of them, psychic forces
intentionally communicate with each other, both within the body and
among multiple bodies. All communications are power struggles.
Each communication is a domination and a submission among
psychic forces. The very act of communication, the communicative
act, is itself an act of domination and an act of submission among
psychic forces. In each act of communication, there is a dominant
psychic force and a submissive psychic force.

Culture has the capacity to be, and often is, "reflexive": the signs of a given culture may refer to the given culture itself, or even to the concept of culture itself.

"Displacement," that is to say, displacement in time, is an essential property of culture: culture is the mental construction of a "past," "present," and "future." Culture is inextricable from the writing of history. In fact, the writing of culture *is* the writing of history, and the writing of history *is* the writing of culture. History is always already encultured, it is always constructed by the codes of a given culture, whether this be one's own "personal" history or discursive accounts of history. There is no "immediate environment," no unmediated presence. Even the "present" is in fact the writing of history and the writing of culture, an encultured and historical mental and social construct.

Although the vast majority of the signs of a culture are non-representational, some of them are representational. When they are representational, however, these signs, like linguistic signs, are only ever in actuality arbitrarily related to "what" they represent; the "represented," however, is also always a mental construct and a signifier. E.g. pictorial constructs, representational paintings, comic books, literature, movies, and discourse.

The "productivity" (or "creativity" or "open-endedness") of culture essentially means that the potential number of cultural constructs (viz. including action-images, practices, forms of life, strategies, tactics, etc.) in any given culture is infinite. The psychic forces which animate "humans" are continually creating new practices, new strategies, and novel actions using their mental, emotional, and cultural resources.

On "cultural transmission," Yule (2010, p.14) writes, "This process whereby a language is passed on from one generation to the next is described as *cultural transmission*. It is clear that humans are born with some kind of predisposition to acquire language in a general sense. However, we are not born with the ability to produce utterances in a specific language such as English. We acquire our first language as children in a culture...Human infants, growing up in isolation, produce no "instinctive" language. Cultural transmission of a specific language is crucial in the human acquisition process."

"First language acquisition," or more simply put, "language acquisition," requires *sufficient input*; in the absence of sufficient input, e.g. human infants which grow up in isolation, no language acquisition occurs. There is no "universal grammar," no a-priori idea of grammar, and this is evinced not only by empirical philosophy, but also by the fact that human infants which grow up in isolation do *not* produce an "instinctive" language. Humans may be "predisposed" to learning language in the sense that, to use the neurophysiological metaphor, they have brain systems which enable them to learn and use language; however, these brain systems did not *originate* to be used for language, rather it is the case that they have been *used* for language, but nothing about this use is teleologically necessary, and conceivably these brain systems may be used for quite different purposes. Language acquisition occurs solely via language use, mnemic inscription, immersion in a culture, and cultural transmission, i.e. it occurs solely via "nurture." Language acquisition occurs via mnemic inscription, i.e. via the mnemic inscription of pain-excitations and the mnemic inscription of jouissance-excitations.

Wittgenstein writes that "To imagine a language is to imagine a form of life." A language *is* a form of life because a language *is* a system of practices. Therefore, language acquisition is not only the acquisition of speech-sounds, but it is always and essentially the acquisition of practices, the acquisition of a form of life. Language acquisition *is* culture-acquisition, the acquisition of culture. Culture is "learned," "acquired," *along with* the first language during the critical period of child development. Human infants which grow up in isolation not only produce no "instinctive" language, but they also develop severe social deficiencies. Because they do not acquire speech, they also do not acquire "culture" in the traditional sense, and this renders them severely deficient in their ability to socially interact with others. The "cultural transmission" of language is not only the cultural transmission of language, but it is also the very transmission of culture itself. Culture-acquisition occurs solely via language use, mnemic inscription, and immersion in a given culture, i.e. solely via "nurture." Culture-acquisition occurs via mnemic inscription, i.e. via the mnemic inscription of pain-excitations and the mnemic inscription of jouissance-excitations.

Just as the acquisition of language is dependent upon the acquisition of the syntax of a given language, so is the acquisition of a culture dependent upon the acquisition of the syntax of a given culture. On the syntax of language, Yule (2010, p. 97) writes: "When we set out to provide an analysis of the syntax of a language, we try to adhere to the "all and only" criterion. This means that our analysis must account for *all* the grammatically correct phrases and sentences and *only* those grammatically correct phrases and sentences in whatever language we are analyzing. In other words, if we write rules for the creation of well-formed structures, we have to check that those rules, when applied logically, won't also lead to ill-formed structures...This reflects another goal of syntactic analysis, which is to have a small and finite (i.e. limited) set of rules that will be capable of producing a large and potentially infinite (i.e. unlimited) number of well-formed structures. This small and finite set of rules is sometimes described as a *generative grammar* because it can be used to "generate" or produce sentence structures and not just describe them. This type of grammar should also be capable of revealing the basis of two other phenomena: first, how some superficially different sentences are closely related and, second, how some superficially similar sentences are in fact different."

Needless to say, the syntax of culture is *not* equivalent to the syntax of speech; the syntax of speech is merely a sub-system within an overarching cultural-semiotic system which is far more complex than speech. These cultural-semiotic syntaxes are psychological syntaxes. The syntax of culture, the rules of culture, are ultimately its values, its system of values. Values are the "generative grammar" of culture. To use the topographical metaphor, a culture consists of two overarching systems, an infrastructural system and a superstructural system; the infrastructural system determines in the last instance the superstructural system; a culture's system of values is its infrastructural system, and all other semiotic-cultural systems are merely superstructural systems; a culture's system of values determines in the last instance all the other semiotic systems of a culture. However, this remains merely a metaphor because the "values" themselves are psychic forces, a system of values *is* a system of psychic forces, and moreover, all other semiotic systems are also systems of psychic forces, which means that the infrastructural system of culture and the superstructural system of culture are essentially dynamic, diachronic, historical, and historicizing. (The syntax of language, too, is essentially diachronic, as is evident from analysing the history of any given language). The system Pcpt-Ucs appropriates-consumes forces-qualia, but these are always subsequently interpreted by the system Ucs via psychological syntaxes; the signs and psychic forces which constitute "thoughts," "feelings," "perceptions," and "actions" are produced via this interpretation via psychological syntaxes. Each thought, feeling, perception, and action is produced by the system Ucs out of the basis of psychological syntaxes, which means, ultimately, a syntax of values. Each thought, feeling, perception, and action is an evaluation made according to a system of values. An ethic is predicated upon a taste and an aesthetic is predicated upon a system of values because an ethic *is* an aesthetic, and an aesthetic *is* an ethic. Considered in their broadest senses, evaluation is originary and values are originary, and consequently distinction is originary and taste is originary. Evaluation is essentially distinction, and a system of values is essentially a taste (viz. a taste in art; art is originary, everything is art, reality is art, all psychic life is art). Reality is essentially aesthetic, psychic life is essentially aesthetic. A system of values is essentially a syntax for the production of interpretations. To invent new values is to invent new interpretations, and because reality *is* interpretation, to invent new interpretations is to invent new realities. A system of values is essentially a syntax for the writing of reality, a syntax for creating reality. To invent new values is to create new realities.

The syntactic analysis of culture, the analysis of the syntax of culture, i.e. the analysis of morals, the genealogy of morals, shares in a way the two goals of the syntactic analysis of language. There is also an "all and only" criterion in the syntactic analysis of culture: this means that our analysis must account for *all* the cases of obedience to the given culture's system of values ("grammatically correct" thoughts, feelings, perceptions, and actions), and that our analysis must account for *only* those cases of obedience to the given culture's system of values in whatever culture we are analysing (i.e. *only* those "grammatically correct" thoughts, feelings, perceptions, and actions in whatever culture we are analysing). In other words, we have to discover the values, the "rules," which govern the production of obedient systems (as opposed to, say, "transgressive systems"), and we have to check that those "rules," when applied logically and rigorously, will not also lead to the production of transgressive systems.

This reflects another goal of the syntactic analysis of culture, which is to discover a small and finite (i.e. limited) set of values ("rules") which are capable of producing a large and potentially infinite (i.e. unlimited) number of obedient systems. The syntax of culture does not merely "describe" obedient systems. The syntax of culture is a "generative grammar" because it is a small and finite set of rules-values which can be used to *generate*, or *produce*, obedient systems. Values are the generative grammar of a culture. The syntactic analysis of culture should also be capable of revealing the basis of two other phenomena: first, how some superficially different obedient systems are closely related, and second, how some superficially similar obedient systems are in fact different.

What is an obedient system? What is a transgressive system? An obedient system is a system (viz. of thoughts, feelings, perceptions, actions, etc.) which obeys the values of a given culture. A transgressive system is a system (viz. of thoughts, feelings, perceptions, actions, etc.) which transgresses the values of a given culture. Because culture is originary, these designations are relative and pragmatic. In actuality, a "transgressive system" is an obedient system of a culture different from the one which it transgresses. Obedient systems and transgressive systems are both language games. To be more precise, culture itself is a language game and its "rules" are its system of values; an obedient system is a system which obeys the rules of a language game of culture, whereas a transgressive system transgresses the rules of a language game of culture.

11.

The majority of mental activity is unconscious. To phrase it another way, the majority of mental activity is "latent" or "implicit," unconsciously active and yet capable of becoming conscious given the necessary impetus. Mental states only become conscious if driven by a necessary and sufficient, sufficiently strong, impulse. Mental activity operates most efficiently and effectively in unconscious states. Without a necessary and sufficient motivation for becoming conscious, mental states simply have no necessity, no necessary and sufficient condition, for becoming conscious, and so do not become conscious, for mental states operate perfectly well, i.e. with efficiency and effectivity, in unconscious states. Simply put, it is more economic for mental states to remain unconscious unless they have a sufficient and necessary motivation to become conscious. "Latent" and "implicit," it is clear, are metaphorical expressions relative to the perspective of consciousness; even "unconscious" is a metaphorical and relative term, and perhaps an inaccurate and imprecise term, since it is defined in a wholly negative manner, as that which is *not* conscious, that which is *not* consciousness.

The unconscious consists of multiplicities of force-energy (all mental states are states of energy, i.e. states of the will to power), therefore the unconscious is both dynamic and economic. There are very powerful mental processes or mental states which produce all the effects of mental life, though they, like mental life itself, are largely unconscious. The reason why mental states become conscious is that a certain force drives them to become conscious, but mental states only become conscious in order to serve the ends of unconscious forces. For the organism, consciousness is always only a means to an end, the ends being diverse and originating from and belonging to unconscious forces. Unconscious forces drive and motivate all mental life, including conscious mental life. The original state and natural state of all mental states is unconsciousness (active unconsciousness, unconscious activity), and we assert that the forces which motivate and drive unconscious mental states is the affects, and that likewise, the forces which motivate and drive unconscious mental states into becoming conscious mental states are the affects.

Thus we obtain our concept of the unconscious from the phenomenon of affects. Affects are the prototype of the unconscious for us. All unconscious phenomena, since they are mental activity motivated and directed by forces, are dynamic. Even beliefs, whether conscious or unconscious, are dynamic phenomena.

Therefore, we have arrived at the fact that in the mind there are, overarchingly, two systems of mental activity, the system Ucs, which encompasses the overwhelming majority of mental activity, and the system Cs, which encompasses only a very small minority of mental activity. All mental activity is motivated, driven, and directed by affects. Affects, whether conscious or unconscious, vary in degrees of intensity. Furthermore, since all mental activity possesses intentionality and is directed towards excitations, all mental activity is a form of attention, that is to say, all mental activity attends towards excitations; since all mental activity is directed towards excitations it also attends to those excitations, although the attention varies in degrees of intensity.

The system Ucs and the system Cs both consist of fluxes. The system Ucs is the stream-of-the-unconscious, streams of unconscious mental activity, and the system Cs is the stream of consciousness, streams of conscious mental activity. The system Ucs controls the organism's approaches to motility—that is, to the discharge of excitations into the environment as well as to the discharge of excitations within the organism itself; the system Ucs is the mental agency which supervises all its own constituent processes and it is also the mental agency which supervises all of the constituent processes of the system Cs. From the system Ucs, too, proceeds not merely all forms of activity and effectiveness in the system Cs, but all forms of activity and effectiveness in the entire mind and body. The body is the system Ucs itself, the body without organs.

The aim of power-analysis as a form of therapy is self-therapy, the increase of the health of the organism by means of the increase of the organism's own power. The primary function of the organism is always already the increase of power; the primary function of the organism is both latent and always active in the organism, and it determines, in the final analysis, all forms of activity and effectiveness in and of the organism. However, during the course of development, the organism may have acquired pathogenic and parasitical forces; pathogenic and parasitical forces may have been installed in the system Ucs of the mental apparatus of the organism; and these pathogenic and parasitical forces limit and even deplete the organism's original, natural, and primary reservoir of power. These pathogenic and parasitical forces are, in effect and in actuality, *obstacles*, or *resistances*, to the primary function of the organism. Power-analysis is faced with the task of removing the resistances which prevent the organism from performing its primary function. By facilitating the overcoming of resistance, power-analysis facilitates the self-actualization, or self-realization, of the organism. The unconsciously acting organism is often unaware that it is infected with pathogenic and parasitical forces; indeed, when the infection is serious and has sunk its roots deep in the organism, the organism may even have confused themselves with the disease, and even have constructed egos which not only have symptoms of traits of the disease, but whose defining characteristics are identical to descriptions of traits of the disease. To paraphrase Freud, in power-analysis "we then tell the patient that he is dominated by a resistance; but he is quite unaware of the fact, and even if he guesses from his unpleasurable feelings that a resistance is now at work in him, he does not know what it is or how to describe it" (EI, p. 17). Since, however, there can be no question but that this resistance emanates from his unconscious, we find ourselves in an unforeseeable situation. Neurosis in the organism arises when the pathogenic forces install themselves in the organism and dominate the organism and all of its activity; that is to say, when the pathogenic forces motivate, drive, and direct all of the activity and effectiveness in the body and in the mind. In cases of infection, the organism suffers from neurosis in varying degrees along a continuum. However, the greater the degree of neurosis, the less the patient is inclined to be cured. From the point of view of power-analytic practice, the consequence of this discovery is that we land in endless difficulties and obscurities if we attempt to cure the neurotic patient; the neurotic patient's neurosis is often deeply rooted and the patient enjoys their neurosis, i.e. the neurotic patient does not want to be cured, but wants instead to nurture the pathogen within themselves. Furthermore, in attempting to cure the neurotic patient, which is almost always a futile task, the power-analyst risks acquiring the patient's infection or nurturing pathogenic forces which were already latent in themselves. Although the *study* of neurotic patients is essential to gathering data, it is advisable for the power-analyst to abandon the *treatment* of the neurotic patient completely, even if this means the self-destruction of the neurotic patient.

For the practice of power-analysis, however, the consequences of our discovery are even more important. Pragmatic considerations caused us to make our first correction, and to abandon the treatment of neurotic patients; our insight into the political anatomy of the body leads us to the second. The system Ucs motivates, drives, and directs all activity of the body, and the primary function of the system Ucs is the increase of power; since the increase of power is the increase of health, the primary physician of the body is the body itself. Conversely, the primary patient of the body is the body itself. There is an inherent and essential medicality of the body without organs—its resistance to pathogens and parasites, its restorative and enhancing capacities. The neurotic patient in whom neurosis is deeply rooted is incurable and their treatment must be completely abandoned. However, the aim of the power-analyst is to increase the power of the organism and the power-analyst himself is that very organism, which means that if the power-analyst himself suffers from an infection of neurosis, then this neurosis is treatable and even curable. The power-analyst's primary patient is himself and his primary physician is himself. The first task of the power-analyst is to treat his own neurosis, to eliminate all traces of neurosis within himself, to eradicate all the pathogenic forces which infect his body and his mind, and, in brief, to cure himself completely of neurosis and thereby become healthy.

As Henry Miller writes, "everybody becomes a healer the moment he forgets about himself...Reality is here and now, everywhere, gleaming through every reflection that meets the eye...Everybody is a neurotic, down to the last man and woman. The healer, or the analyst, if you like, is only a super-neurotic...To be cured we must rise from our graves and throw off the cerements of the dead. Nobody can do it for another—it is a private affair which is best done collectively" (1965, pp. 425-426). Once we abandon our belief in the ego, which never existed in the first place—this is *our* meaning of "ego-loss," and it is best done sober, in fact it brings the most intense sobriety—we become a true healer, that is to say, we become capable of healing ourselves for the first time. This is because the concept of the ego employed in Christian civilization, upon which we have predicated our self-concept, is, conceptually, an agent which bears responsibility, that is to say, an agent which bears guilt; once the self realizes that the ego is merely a linguistic construct, the self can remove the unnecessary burden of "responsibility" and "guilt," and thereby heal itself. There are only subjective realities, hence why "reality is here and now, everywhere, gleaming through every reflection that meets the eye." The publicly acknowledged healers, therapists and psychiatrists, are false healers, they are in actuality merely super-neurotics who neuroticize others, they are merely new priests. Here, we cannot rely on anybody but ourselves, we are completely alone, because the entire human race, "down to the last man and woman," is insane and neurotic. As The Doors song "The End" goes, "All the children are insane," which means that the entire human race is neurotic. If power-analysis is ever to become a "collective" movement, it can only become so via a tribe of solitary individuals, each of whom is primarily concerned with healing themselves, hence why power-analysis is "a private affair which is best done collectively." The poetic formula of the power-analyst's collective self-therapy, in which each power-analyst is likely separated from the other by immeasurable gulfs of time as well as space, is a poetic formula that I have written elsewhere: "Are we all a part of one tribe/ Just beginning to realize/ Our solitude?" There is no evading our essential solitude, the essential privacy and ineffability of the self's qualia. Power-analysis begins when one acknowledges and embraces one's essential solitude; it is only then that we can "rise from our graves and throw off the cerements of the dead," that is to say, it is only then that life begins flourishing within us once again, it is only then that we can begin eliminating all traces of nihilism within us. Convalescence is essentially the awakening of the senses.

The practice of power-analysis primarily consists of activating the healthy and power-increasing forces within one's own body without organs, and thereby embodying and living the part of a healthy organism. The utmost mental and physical discipline is required in the practice of power-analysis, not only because it is difficult to access and activate unconscious forces, but because the power-analyst, in his quest for power, necessarily risks death and madness. *Our* beacon-light, the beacon-light of we psychologists, is the will to power: with the will to power, we illuminate the darkness of depth-psychology; but in our quest for power, we are necessarily in solitude, and we must tread completely alone into the cold and icy darkness of the depths of our own psyches.

12.

Just as there are conscious emotions, so are there unconscious emotions. There are unconscious emotions and there is an unconscious of each emotion. However, the access of system Cs to unconscious emotions is severely limited. The system Cs can only come to know unconscious emotions by making them conscious. But, to paraphrase Freud, "how is that possible? What does it mean when we say 'making something conscious'? How can that come about?" (EI, p. 19)

We already know the point from which we have to start in this connection. Consciousness is indeed the "surface" of the mental apparatus; but it is the system Ucs whose function is "spatially" the first to perceive and to interact with the environment—this "spatial" function of the system Ucs is both psychological and physiological. The perceptions and activities of the system Cs are symptoms of the perceptions and activities of the system Ucs. Our investigations must take this symptomatic surface, the system Cs, as a starting point in order to deduce the activity of the perceiving depth, the depth which perceives, the system Ucs; and thereby we may determine whether the system Cs is a symptom of health or a symptom of disease.

All mental phenomena are actions, mental acts, including thought, and to paraphrase Rimbaud, "action is the spoiling of some force," i.e. action is the utilization and expenditure of some force. A mental act is the displacement of mental energy which is effected

185

somewhere in the interior of the mental apparatus as this energy proceeds on its way towards action.

As it regards the relationship between the system Ucs and the system Cs, it is only the case that unconscious mental activity "advances" to the "surface" which is the system Cs, i.e. that the system Ucs causes and generates conscious mental activity. Conscious mental activity *never* causes or generates unconscious mental activity; to claim that it does is merely the result of misinterpreting the activity of the system Cs by construing consciousness as a causal agent. In actuality, consciousness is only ever an epiphenomenon of the unconscious mind. In all cases, conscious mental activity is motivated and directed entirely by unconscious forces. This is clearly one of the complexities that arise when one begins to take the "spatial" or "topographical" conceptualization of mental life "seriously," i.e. when applies it to one's own mental life.

I have already suggested that mental activity is only directed, or intended, towards excitations by means of mental constructs, which means that all organisms engage in mental construction. The system Cs is utilized in various ways by the system Ucs, such that the system Cs is a tool, or device, of the system Ucs. However, given the freeplay and agon of psychic forces in the system Ucs, perhaps it is more accurate to describe Cs as the "toy" or "plaything" of the system Ucs.

Before we concern ourselves further with the nature of signs, it dawns upon us like a new discovery that only something which has once been an unconscious perception-image can become a conscious perception-image, and that even among these unconscious perception-images there is contextualization, and a system of mediation and difference: even among unconscious perception-images, there is différance. That is to say, even an unconscious perception-image, which is a movement-image, occurs in a context of other movement-images which precede and follow it as well as other movement-images which exist simultaneously to it "spatially" in the system Ucs, and this context is a fabric of differences, a fabric of irreducible differences, and although movement-images may succeed each other in a purely chance fashion, each movement-image nonetheless has traces of the other movement-images in its context, and it is only by means of these traces of difference, this différance, that a movement-image is utilized by an affect (each unconscious perception-image is utilized by an affect, there is an affect inherent to each movement-image in a given context). That is to say, unconscious perception-images function through a process of infinite supplementation where the process of utilization is always deferred onto the next movement-image which succeeds it temporally, which means that each unconscious perception-image is only an interpretation of another movement-image and that there is no "correct" interpretation (since there is neither any "presence" nor any fully "present" meaning inherent to a movement-image). The unconscious interprets psychic forces-images from its environment, and the subsequently constructed unconscious perception-images are further interpreted by psychic forces within the system Ucs, and this process of interpretation is only possible through the traces of the unconscious perception-images which precede and follow a given unconscious perception-image, and the process of interpretation, the interpretation itself, is ceaselessly deferred onto successive unconscious perception-images. In other words, the context of unconscious perception-images is ceaselessly altering, just as the environment of the organism as well as the organism itself is ceaselessly being altered by psychic forces. The system Ucs is essentially a system of alterity, of perpetual otherness and unpredictability, even unto itself. Furthermore, to paraphrase Nietzsche, "there is no event "in itself," there are only interpretations and there is no "correct" interpretation," and this is true even of unconscious perception-images; even unconscious perception-images are merely interpretations, which means that in the system Ucs there is only ceaseless fluxes of interpretations, that the system Ucs, and the body without organs as a totality as well, is a system of infinite interpretations. The ultimate nature of reality is interpretation. The free spirit self-actualizes the self of interpretation itself and thereby becomes the self of interpretation itself.

13.

On the will to power, Heidegger writes, 'Only he can truly command—and commanding has nothing to do with mere ordering about—who is always ready and able to place himself under command. By means of such readiness he has placed himself within the scope of the command as the first to obey, the paragon of obedience. In such decisiveness of willing, which reaches out beyond itself, lies mastery-over, having power over what is revealed in the willing and in what is held fast in the grips of resoluteness. Willing itself is mastery-over, which reaches out beyond itself; will is intrinsically power. And power is willing that is constant in itself. Will is power; power is will." (Heidegger, 1979, p. 41)

The will to power is the drive for power, it *is* affect, feeling, emotion, passion. Wherever "will to power" is written, one may substitute "drive" for "will," as in "drive to power," in order to clarify the meaning of the concept "will to power." Drive *is* power, power *is* drive. Power is drive that is constant in itself. Drive itself is mastery-over, which reaches out beyond itself; drive is intrinsically power. In the decisiveness, the inexorability, of drive, of driving, which reaches out beyond itself, lies mastery-over, having power-over. What is revealed in a drive is the force which is actualized in a drive, an inexorable force which is constant in itself unless opposed by a greater, stronger, more inexorable force.

He who commands always already obeys a force within himself. His command is in actuality obedience to a command which drives his command. Hence why the readiness to command requires the readiness to obey, that is to say, to obey a force within one's self. The paragon of commanding must also necessarily be the paragon of obedience, one who has mastered the art of obeying himself, the art of obeying his own passions, passions which are healthy and exuberant forms of the will to power.

For a command to be a command, it must be obeyed. For obedience to be obedience, it must be obedience to a command. The intentionality of all mental acts, the "directedness" of all mental acts, implies that each mental act is directed *by* a force; the will to power is what directs each mental act. The intentionality of a mental act is its obedience to a will to power which commands its intention, its direction. To be more precise, the will to power is itself the mental act, and the mental act is itself the will to power, and "intentionality" is merely an interpretation of the essential property of the will to power, the property of commanding and obeying. Willing *is* commanding and obeying, power *is* commanding and obeying, hence why will *is* power and power *is* will. The will to power is commanding and obeying, the process of commanding and obeying.

14.

The aim of a drive is twofold, the discharge of its own strength and the appropriation-consumption of forces. Jouissance, or pleasure, is the feeling of the increase of power, which is equivalent to the increase of quantity of forces-qualia. Nietzsche writes, "What is a pleasure other than a stimulation of the feeling of power by an obstacle (more strongly still by rhythmical obstacles and resistances)—leading it to swell? Thus, every pleasure includes pain.—If the pleasure is to become great, the pain must be very long and the tension of the drawn bow prodigious" (WLN, N35, 15).

To be more precise, as Nietzsche writes, life "does *not* seek pleasure and does *not* avoid unpleasure...Pleasure and unpleasure are mere consequences, mere accompanying phenomena—what man wants, what every smallest part of a living organism wants, is an increment of power. Striving for this gives rise to both pleasure and unpleasure; out of that will man seeks resistance, needs something to oppose him...man does not avoid [pain] but instead has a constant need of it: every conquest, every pleasurable feeling, everything that happens presupposes a resistance overcome." (WLN, N14, 174)

All life is motivated by the drive for power, the drive to feel the feeling of the increase of power: this is the *power principle.* Jouissance, or pleasure, can only be achieved via pain, therefore the striving for pleasure is also always the striving for pain: this is the *jouissance principle.* The jouissance principle is a function of the power principle because the feeling of power, the feeling of the increase of power, *is* jouissance, and jouissance can only be achieved via pain. The greater the pain, the greater the jouissance. Pleasure and pain are "mere consequences, mere accompanying phenomena," because the primary motivation of the organism is always the drive for power, the power principle. Pain and pleasure are merely results of the drive for power, hence they are merely accompanying phenomena of the drive for power.

The "peremptoriness" of a drive is the irresistible and inexorable pressure upon the drive to discharge its excess strength (or what amounts to the same thing, to appropriate-consume forces). Pressure, or tension, results from resistances to a drive, resistances to the drive's activity of appropriating-consuming forces and resistance to the drive's discharge of its own excess energy. Pressure-tension is a form of pain. Pressure-tension arises from the conflict between the peremptoriness of a drive and the resistances it encounters. The more peremptory a drive is, the more mental and emotional resources it demands. Also, the more resistance a drive encounters, the more mental and emotional resources it demands. The pressure which results from resistance to a drive increases the peremptoriness of the drive. A drive only relieves pressure via overcoming resistance, i.e. via discharging its strength and appropriating-consuming forces.

Nietzsche writes, "The greater the resistances a force seeks out in order to master them, the greater is the magnitude of the failure and misfortune thus provoked: and as every force can only expend itself on what resists, every action necessarily contains an *ingredient of unpleasure*. But the effect of that unpleasure is to stimulate life—and to strengthen the *will to power*!" (WLN, N11, 77). In this regard, Marquis de Sade is a masterful psychologist, a psychologist par excellence, one of the greatest psychologists in the entire history of knowledge; to paraphrase Sade, "It has pleased nature to make us so that we only attain pleasure by way of pain." Not only each pleasure, but each action, contains an ingredient of pain as an essential ingredient; indeed, insofar as each action is an act of will, there is also a jouissance of each action, even if that jouissance is equivalent to pain. The greater the quantity of force of a drive, the greater the force it needs to appropriate-consume, but the greater the force, the more resistances there are to appropriating-consuming. Therefore, the greater the quantity of force of a drive, the greater the resistances it seeks out, i.e. the greater the extrajection of a drive, i.e. the greater the drive the more obstacles it needs to overcome, and these resistances are always stimulants to the drive and the peremptoriness of the drive. In other words, not only does all life need pain, but all life actively seeks out pain, all life craves pain in order to gratify its drives, because an ingredient of pain is essential to the gratification of each drive. Hence the jouissance principle.

15.

The body without organs is a system of interpretation, meaning both that it consists of interpretations and that its essential activity is interpretation. Interpretation means having power-over, and having power-over necessitates interpretation, hence why interpretation is essential to life and the primary drive of life is the will to power. The will to power is the will to interpret. Willing is always already interpreting, and interpreting is always already willing. Reality consists wholly of an infinity of interpretations, hence why reality consists wholly of the infinity of the will to power.

The body without organs, i.e. the mental apparatus, appropriates and consumes psychic forces from the environment, therefore the mental apparatus is a kind of digestive system, hence why "the mind is a stomach." For the mental apparatus, appropriation *is* consumption and consumption *is* appropriation. The successful consumption of psychic forces is the digestion of psychic forces. Indeed, what is typically called "digestion" is itself in actuality the process of appropriation-consumption of psychic forces. The unsuccessful consumption of psychic forces is indigestion. The consumption and digestion of psychic forces is precisely the interpretation of psychic forces. The failed digestion of psychic forces is failed interpretation; in a sense, it is "misinterpretation," but in a stricter sense, it is the inability to interpret altogether.

Nietzsche's following remarks on aphorisms suffices as an extended metaphor of the psychic economy of the mental apparatus: "An aphorism, properly stamped and molded, has not been "deciphered" when it has simply been read; rather, one has then to begin its *exegesis*, for which is required an art of exegesis...To be sure, one thing is necessary above all if one is to practice reading as an *art* in this way, something that has been unlearned most thoroughly nowadays—and therefore it will be some time before my writings are "readable"—something for which one has almost to be a cow and in any case *not* a "modern man": *rumination*." (GM, "Preface," 8)

The psychic forces which constitute the external world are all so many sources of forces-qualia, all so many emitters of signs. A source of forces-qualia *is* an emitter of signs; this source *is* a psychic force, a multiplicity of psychic forces, and these signs *are* psychic forces. In other words, a source of psychic forces is an emitter of psychic forces. We may say that psychic forces in the external world are all so many "aphorisms," and that the system Pcpt-Ucs is a "reader" of aphorisms who, in order to read aphorisms, must "decipher" them; the process of appropriation-consumption is the process of exegesis. A healthy mental apparatus is like a cow because a cow has five stomachs, meaning that it has a comprehensive digestive system which digests thoroughly; a mental apparatus with a comprehensive system of interpretation interprets signs thoroughly, which means that it appropriates vast amounts of psychic forces from the environment, which is precisely what *rumination* means. A diseased mental apparatus, such as that of "modern man," suffers from indigestion, the inability to interpret, the inability to appropriate psychic forces from the environment, hence modern man's inability to ruminate.

But what exactly is interpretation? "Interpretation" means "translation." Interpretation is the translation of signs from one form into another, and consequently from one content into another. Interpretation is the translation of psychic forces from one form into another. According to Nietzsche, interpretation is essentially "forcing, adjusting, abbreviating, omitting, padding, inventing, falsifying" (GM, III, 24). The body without organs, by consuming psychic forces from the environment, translates those psychic forces into the psychic forces of the body without organs, and this process is falsification because psychic forces which were other, the perspectives of others, are transformed into psychic forces which are the self, the perspectives of the self.

The will to power, in the form of active drives, both discharges its strength and appropriate-consumes forces from the environment, and it "intends" to do both simultaneously. That is to say, the appropriation-consumption of forces requires, in the first place, the discharge of excess strength by active drives. The appropriation-consumptions performed by active drives presupposes an "originary overproduction" and "originary overinvestment" which means precisely the discharge of excess strength, the discharge of potentials. In the healthy organism, the system Pcpt-Ucs consists of active drives.

The successful appropriation-consumption of psychic forces is *introjection* ("introjection" literally means "casting inside"). Introjection, is "cognizing" in the strict sense, taking into, appropriating into, casting inside into cognition. Introjection is *inpsychation*, taking into the psyche (cf. Nietzsche, GM, II, 1). Introjection is the process of broadening and increasing the self's own quantity of forces. The metabolism of the organism *is* the appropriation-consumption of forces-qualia, it *is* introjection. Introjection, because it *is* metabolism, is the fundamental and defining process of life. Introjection is essentially the affirmation of mediation. Introjection is mediation, mediation itself; not only is it mediated and mediating, but it is the very process of mediation itself. The discharge of excess strength by active drives is *extrajection*. Introjection is dependent upon extrajection.

A failed appropriation-consumption, a failure to interpret, is *incorporation*, the production of fantasy. Fantasy is make-believe wish-fulfilment. Abraham and Torok define incorporation as "the fantasy of non-introjection" (1994, p. 126). All fantasy is incorporation in our sense of the term, meaning that all fantasy is the failure to appropriate-consume psychic forces from the environment. On incorporation, Abraham and Torok write, "Incorporation denotes a fantasy, introjection a process" (1994, p. 125). Incorporation denotes the fantasy of an unmediated presence, whereas introjection denotes the process of mediation. Incorporation is a failed introjection, a failed mediation. Fantasy is always and essentially the fantasy of an unmediated presence. Conversely, an alleged "unmediated presence" is always a fantasy. Reality is mediation. Fantasy, incorporation, is essentially the denial of mediation (and thus the mental construction of an "unmediated presence," i.e. the mental construction of a fantasy, a fantasy-construct). Defence-mechanisms (viz. revising, Freud, we have thus far discovered only three forms of defence-mechanism: denial, reaction-formation, and projection) are forms of incorporation. The "mechanism" in "defence-mechanism" is merely a metaphor because in actuality such "defence-mechanisms" are effected by psychic forces which are motivated to employ them. Denial is the primary form of defence-mechanism: reaction-formation and projection are forms of denial, and ultimately these are all forms of self-denial. Fantasy itself, incorporation itself, is essentially the defence-mechanism of denial, viz. the denial of mediation, and self-denial.

On fantasy, Abraham and Torok write, "Granting our metapsychological definition of "reality" as everything, whether exogenous or endogenous, that affects the psyche by inflicting a topographical shift on it, "fantasy" can be defined as all those representations, beliefs, or bodily states that gravitate toward the opposite effect, that is, the preservation of the status quo. This definition does not address the contents or the formal characteristics of fantasy, only its function, a preventive and conservative function despite the highly innovative genius of fantasy, its vast field of action, and even despite its definite complacency with respect to desire. In our conception fantasy is essentially narcissistic; it tends to [pretend to] transform the world rather than inflict injury on the subject...Understanding a fantasy entails the identification of the specific topographical change the given fantasy is called upon to resist." (1994, p. 125)

Although Abraham and Torok are very imprecise in their description of fantasy, we may nonetheless accept the above description as metaphors and metonyms which are to an extent useful. Reality is mediation, whether that mediation is exogenous or endogenous to the body without organs, and we only understand the "topographical shifts" inflicted by "reality," the reality of psychic forces, in the sense of positive shifts in the quantity of force of the body without organs, i.e. in the sense of appropriation-consumption by the system Pcpt-Ucs. Even painful excitations inflicted by reality are the products of appropriation-consumption by the system Ucs. Fantasies are representations, beliefs, or affective states endogenous to a given mental apparatus which prevent, or resist, the appropriation-consumption of psychic forces by the system Pcpt-Ucs of that mental apparatus. Fantasies preserve the status quo of the diseased state of the unconscious, the status quo of the diseased unconscious, the status quo of disease itself. Fantasy is defined by its function; the function of fantasy is to resist the appropriation-consumption of psychic forces by the system Pcpt-Ucs, i.e. to resist interpretations performed by the self, i.e. to resist the increase of power of the self. Fantasies may be highly innovative, their field of action may be vast, and they may even be labelled works of genius by society, e.g. *The New Testament*, but their function is nonetheless preventive and conservative because their function is to resist the increase of power by the self.

Fantasies are indeed essentially narcissistic, which means fantasies are essentially neurotic and hubristic. Narcissism *is* hubris, and neurosis is essentially narcissistic (narcissism = neurosis = hubris). Hubris is essentially the wish that the world should be essentially different than the way that it is; for instance, characteristic fantasies of hubris include the beliefs that injustice, misfortune, and guilt exist in the world (cf. Nietzsche, PTG, p. 61). For reality to inflict injury on the subject means for the subject to appropriate-consume psychic forces and translate them into painful excitations, pain-excitations. Fantasy is the result of the organism being too weak to appropriate-consume pain-excitations, which would also mean the appropriation-consumption of power-jouissance. By making-believe that the world is other than the way it is, which in this context means making-believe either that these sources of pain-excitations do not exist (viz. the monistic philosophy of the Hindu religion as well as Parmenides, which argue that that there is only one unchanging being and that diachronic phenomena such as pain are merely illusions, are precisely this kind of fantasy; materialist philosophies such Daniel Dennett's, which denies the reality of subjectivity altogether, are also precisely this kind of fantasy), that pain-excitations can ultimately be escaped (viz. the fantasies of "nirvana" and heaven, i.e. the entirety of Buddhism and the entirety of Christianity), or that pain-excitations "exist" but are not pain-excitations (viz. the fantasy of Stoicism), the fantasist limits himself or herself to appropriating-consuming only those pain-excitations which they are strong enough—or rather, weak enough—to appropriate-consume. In the strict sense, however, fantasies do indeed inflict injury on the subject, indirectly by preventing the subject from increasing power, and even directly via the ingredient of pain inherent in all fantasies; however, the self-harm of fantasy merely serves to prevent those even greater pain-excitations, the pain-excitations of reality, which the subject of fantasy is unable to introject and interpret. Fantasy is essentially anaesthetic even when it involves self-harm; self-harm may even be essential to an ultimately anaesthetic fantasy (viz. "sin" is essential to the Christian religion and "karma" in Hinduism and Buddhism). Interpretation is essentially aesthetic, whereas fantasy is essentially anaesthetic. But the fantasist's decrease of pain-excitations also mean the decrease of jouissance. To paraphrase Jason Pierce, as he sings in the Spiritualized song "Come Together," the fantasist "dulls the pain, but kills the joy."

Understanding a fantasy entails the identification of the specific psychic forces which the subject resists appropriating-consuming, which means the identification of the way the subject's sense of his or her own power is threatened by an external force which oppresses the subject, the identification of the mechanisms by which the subject resists the increase of their own power, and the identification of the mechanisms by which the subject conserves their own feeling of being oppressed.

Abraham and Torok write that "fantasy is inseparable from the intrapsychic state of affairs it is supposed to protect as well as from the metapsychological reality that demands a change" (1994, p. 126). All metapsychological realities are power relations. The intrapsychic state of affairs which all fantasies protect is the feeling of being weak and oppressed. In other words, the intrapsychic state of affairs which all fantasies protect and preserve is the state of ressentiment. Fantasy is essentially and always already the fantasy of ressentiment, or more simply put, fantasy is essentially ressentiment.

In other words, all fantasies are essentially revenge fantasies; they take revenge upon reality, upon a reality which oppresses the subject. Paradoxically, even this fantasy-gratification of ressentiment can only be achieved by the subject via the experience of pain-excitations. The main difference between incorporation and introjection is the respective ability to accumulate power. The ability to introject pain-excitations is merely a function and a symptom of the ability to accumulate power. Being unable to introject pain-excitations is merely a function and a symptom of being unable to accumulate power.

Here it appears that we must revise our earlier conclusions regarding the nature of pleasure in order to be more precise. Nietzsche writes that there are two very different forms of pleasure: "The psychologists' great confusion has lain in their failure to distinguish those two *types of pleasure*, that of *falling asleep* and that of *conquest*" (WLN, N14, 174). Whereas active pleasure (or dynamic pleasure) is the pleasure of conquest (i.e. introjection and extrajection), passive pleasure is soporific pleasure (the pleasure of "falling asleep" or analogous activities, viz. incorporation, fantasizing). Active pleasures are symptoms of health because active pleasure are products of active drives. Active pleasures are the jouissance of active drives, the jouissance of introjection and the jouissance of extrajection. Passive pleasure, or soporific pleasure, is essentially the "elimination of suffering." Soporific pleasure is never in actuality possible due to the nature of pleasure (there is an ingredient of pain in every pleasure, and pleasure itself is a form of pain), not to mention the nature of life ("suffering is a mark of existence," and there is neither an afterlife, nor an unchanging being, nor nirvana), but the neurotic nonetheless strives for the "elimination of suffering," hence why soporific pleasure is characteristic of fantasy and neurosis, and why the jouissance of fantasy is essentially soporific pleasure. The valuation of passive pleasure as good is a symptom of a state of exhaustion, mental and physiological exhaustion, a deficiency of quantity of forces-qualia, i.e. it is a symptom of neurosis: "the exhausted want rest, to stretch out their limbs, they want peace, quiet—that is the *happiness* of the nihilistic religions and philosophies" (WLN, N14, 174). Neurotic fantasies are characterized by the belief in passive pleasures (the belief that passive pleasure is "good"). The jouissance of incorporation is the jouissance of passive-soporific pleasure, and hence a symptom of a state of exhaustion. The "unmediated presence" of a fantasy is precisely its soporific pleasure; the jouissance of the "unmediated presence" is the jouissance of soporific pleasure.

The drive to fantasy is essentially the will to nothingness, and the will to nothingness is essentially the drive to fantasy: i.e., the death drive. The death drive is the drive to "entropy," i.e. to soporific pleasure, i.e. to the fantasy of an "unmediated presence," which is the fantasy of surreptitious, or sometimes even explicit, forms of "nothingness" in the traditional sense, a "stasis," an absence of change, an absence of becoming, an absence of mediation, and an absence of ontological difference. Nihilism is essentially the death drive. The will to power in its natural state is *the* life-drive, the very drive of life itself, which is power itself: the will to power *is* the drive-to-violence: the life-drive is essentially the drive to violence, which is our concept of *Mars* (or *Ares*). All drives, especially the active drives, including the sex drive (Eros), are forms of the drive to violence. All drives are Martian drives. Even the death drive, which is a perversion of the will to power, is a Martian drive: the death-drive is a drive-to-violence directed against itself, the drive of violence against the self by the self, hence why it is the drive of self-denial and self-negation. The death-drive is motivated by the "Nirvana principle," the drive to soporific pleasure, and we may describe it as the *Nirvana-drive*. The death drive is the neurotic drive par excellence, the defining drive of neurosis. Ressentiment is essentially a form of the death drive.

Because history is absolutely devoid of telos, the will to power is always also Chance itself. Chance itself is the Heraclitean Child who, with the iron hand of necessity, shakes the dice-box of chance and plays the game of existence itself. As Deleuze writes, explicating Nietzsche, "What Nietzsche calls *necessity* (destiny) is thus never the abolition but rather the combination of chance itself. Necessity is affirmed of chance in as much as chance itself is affirmed" (NP, p. 26). Therefore, chance *is* necessity. Chance rules supreme in history, it is ultimately chance which determines all the "events" of history. The self is thrown into this world as the dice-throw of Chance. All teleological concepts are fantasies, denials of chance, self-denials of the inherent chanceness and thrownness of the self. Teleological concepts, themselves fantasies, are implicit in each fantasy. Fantasy is essentially the denial of chance, the self-denial of the inherent chanceness of drives. The death-drive is essentially hubris, the hubris-drive, because it is essentially the denial of chance and the self-denial of the chanceness of drives.

Moreover, our conclusions regarding fantasies also apply to fantasies related to mourning, which we describe as "necromantic fantasies." To be more precise, necromantic fantasies are the inability to mourn. Mourning, stricto sensu, is introjecting the loss of the beloved. Necromantic fantasies are the refusal—to be more precise, the inability—to introject loss. Necromantic fantasies are incorporations of the loss of the beloved. To mourn means to appropriate-consume the force-qualia, which are invariably pain-excitations, which signify the irrecoverable loss of the beloved. Necromantic fantasies are the inability to appropriate-consume the force-qualia, which are invariably pain-excitations, which signify the irrecoverable loss of the beloved. When the beloved is lost forever, the part of ourselves that we had placed in the beloved is likewise lost forever. When the subject's mental apparatus is too weak to introject loss, necromantic fantasies result. As Abraham and Torok write, the incorporation of necromantic fantasies "is the refusal [to be more precise, the inability] to acknowledge the full import of the loss, a loss that, if recognized as such, would effectively transform us" (1994, p. 127). Mourning, although incredibly painful, nonetheless positively transforms the subject by increasing the subject's power; by appropriating-consuming, by interpreting, the pain-excitations which signify the loss of the beloved, the subject increases his or her own quantity of force. In mourning, it is precisely due to the pain of mourning that the subject increases their own power; but the ability to introject the pain-excitations of mourning presupposes a sufficiently strong body without organs which is able to introject loss precisely because it discharges its own strength. Introjecting loss is only possible via the discharging of strength. By contrast, a weak body without organs is unable to introject the full import of loss, i.e. a weak body without organs grows resentful against reality due to its loss, and its consequent necromantic fantasies are its revenge fantasies against reality, the purely imaginary revenge it exacts upon reality for robbing him of the beloved. But necromantic fantasies are not only revenge fantasies directed against reality, but also revenge fantasies directed against the beloved, as is evinced from the fact that necromantic fantasies deny the subjectivity of the beloved, viz. they deny the fact that the subjectivity of the beloved is irrecoverably lost. Necromantic fantasies invariably, although often implicitly, blame the beloved for leaving the self, and this blaming means precisely that the self directs ressentiment against the beloved. Mourning, the introjection of loss, is exemplified by Edgar Allan Poe's poem "The Raven," in which the protagonist, an avatar of Poe himself, acknowledges that the beloved is gone forever, and that he will see her nevermore. Necromantic fantasy, the incorporation of loss, is exemplified by the protagonist of François Truffaut's film *The Green Room*, who keeps the dead "alive" "inside" of him.

We agree with Abraham and Torok that the interrelated procedures of *demetaphorization* and *objectivation* are essential to "the magic of incorporation," though we disagree on what is meant by these terms (1994, p. 126). According to Abraham and Torok, demetaphorization is the procedure of "taking literally what is meant figuratively" (1994, p. 126). It is evident that demetaphorization is already objectivation, in our sense of the latter term, since objectivation is the positing of an "objective reality" or an "objective truth," and to "take literally what is meant figuratively" means precisely to transform a metaphor into an objectality. Obviously, the transformation of a metaphor into an objectality is a purely psychological procedure, since an "objectality" remains a mental construct in any case. It is clear, from this preliminary analysis, that the "magic of incorporation" can only operate via linguistic constructs and pictorial constructs. An "objectality" is only ever merely a pictorial and linguistic construct. Incorporation's essential procedures of demetaphorization and objectivation can only occur via pictorial and linguistic constructs. Incorporation is "anti-metaphor" only in the sense that it posits an objective reality, thereby effectively denying the emptiness of all language; this usually takes the form of insisting that all language is *not* metaphor, that language does indeed correspond with "reality," e.g. the philosophy of Wittgenstein's *Tractatus*. By contrast, introjection is essentially the re-cognition of the essential emptiness of all language. For example, in mourning, re-cognizing the emptiness of all language, i.e. re-cognizing that words and images will never bring back the beloved or mitigate the loss of the beloved, is essential to introjecting the loss of the beloved.

16.

Active forces are active psychic forces, active drives. Reactive forces reactive psychic forces, reactive drives. Nietzsche writes that active drives are essentially spontaneous, aggressive, expansive, form-giving forces, whereas reactive drives are essentially adaptative forces; the adaptations of the reactive drives follow only after the spontaneous activity of the active drives (GM, II, 12). The active drives are the drives which essentially reach out for power. Deleuze writes that the essential activities of the active drives are "appropriating, possessing, subjugating, dominating" (NP, p. 42). Deleuze further explicates, "To appropriate means to impose forms, to create forms by exploiting circumstances" (NP, p. 42). The appropriations performed by active drives is only possible via the discharge of their excess strength; this discharge of excess strength is precisely the spontaneous imposition of "forms." The exploitation of circumstances by the active drives is also the creation of new "forms" because the active drives exploit circumstances only via discharging their (the active drives') own-most excess strength.

The system Ucs includes both active and reactive drives. The system Cs consists wholly of reactive drives which are determined in their entirety by the system Ucs. In the healthy, active type of organism, the active drives are dominant; in the healthy, active type of system Ucs, the *master unconscious*, the system Pcpt-Ucs is composed wholly of active drives, and the active drives are also dominant in other major mental systems such as the system Mnem-Ucs. The master unconscious is essentially introjective and extrajective.

In the diseased, reactive type of organism, the reactive drives are dominant; to be more precise, in the essentially reactive organism there are no active drives as such, hence the reactive drives are only dominant in the absence of active drives; in the diseased, reactive type of system Ucs, the *slave unconscious*, the system Pcpt-Ucs as well as all other mental systems consist exclusively of reactive drives. The slave unconscious is essentially "incorporative," that is to say, it essentially fantasizes; it sustains itself only via fantasy.

The master unconscious tends towards self-transformation via the increase of power, via violence directed externally towards the environment. Transformation via the increase of quantity of power is positive transformation. The slave unconscious tends towards self-transformation via violence directed internally against the self. Transformation via the decrease of quantity of power is negative transformation.

Active drives are essentially introjective. Reactive drives can only introject to a very limited extent, in a manner best characterized as "stimulus-response." Reactive drives are most efficient, in terms of appropriation-consumption performed by the organism, when they are submissive and obedient to the active drives. The appropriation-consumption performed by the organism is inefficient and deficient when reactive drives are dominant in the organism. Fantasies are essentially reactive and they are always the products of the slave unconscious.

The slave unconscious is essentially neurotic. The master unconscious is essentially psychotic and schizophrenic. The dominance of reactive drives in the organism *is* neurosis. The dominance of active drives *is* psychosis and schizophrenia (psychosis = schizophrenia). Neurosis is characterized by self-denial and the denial of reality, that is to say, the denial of psychic forces in the internal and external world. Neurosis is best characterized by the "reality principle," the belief in an objective reality, which is merely a fantasy. Psychosis is characterized by self-affirmation and the affirmation of reality, that is to say, the affirmation of psychic forces in the internal and external world. Psychosis is best characterized by the "perspectivity principle," the cognition of perspectivism, the cognition of the multiplicity of subjectivities, that reality consists wholly of subjectivities.

Psychosis *is* health, it *is* mental health. What is commonly diagnosed as "psychosis" or "schizophrenia" is in fact a misdiagnosis, since the majority of these cases are in actuality neuroses. Indeed, psychosis has never been truly understood, perhaps except by a small handful of individuals, including Pierre Klossowski, Antonin Artaud, Arthur Rimbaud, and Friedrich Nietzsche. Freud himself fundamentally misunderstood psychosis; indeed, he was incapable of understanding it, which is why he only ever explained it in terms of neurosis: "We may, for our own purposes, reconstruct the process [of psychosis] on the model of a neurosis, which is more familiar to us" (GPT, p. 208). Freud was familiar with the model of neurosis because he himself was a neurotic, hence his complete inability to understand the psychotic, who is a fundamentally different kind of creature. Freud's failure to interpret psychosis has governed psychiatry since; psychiatry has only ever attempted to understand psychosis in terms of neurosis, which has exacerbated the obfuscation, there from the beginning, of what exactly psychosis is, hence why severe cases of neurosis (e.g. neuroses which involve "hallucinations," delusions, paranoia, or catatonia) have frequently been misdiagnosed as psychosis.

In contemporary society, psychosis as we have defined it is much, much rarer, which means that health, mental health, is itself incredibly rare, to the point of being an endangered species. Power-analysis is a schizoanalysis insofar as it affirms that psychosis is healthy, the very model of health. However, our schizoanalysis, the schizoanalysis of the will to power, should never be confused with the schizoanalysis of Deleuze and Guattari. Deleuze and Guattari are still neurotics, their "schizoanalysis" is still merely an ideology of neurosis, as is evident from the fact that they are materialists, i.e. they still believe in an objective reality, they suffer from the "reality principle," and from the fact that their politics is one of slave morality, that is to say, of pity and ressentiment; their essential neurosis is also suggested by the fact that they believe in the truth of mnemic repression, despite citing evidence from Nietzsche's *Genealogy of Morals* that in actuality pain inscribes memories (pain increases the memorability of an "event," i.e. of a sign) (Deleuze and Guattari, AO, pp. 144-145). The Freudian theory of "repression" is a neurotic theory par excellence because the theory itself is a denial of subjectivity and a denial of reality (because there is no such thing as "repression" in reality); moreover, the concept of "repression" is a tool by means of which the psychoanalyst, who is a kind of priest, gaslights and dominates his patient, and subsequently infects his patient with neurosis to an even greater extent than the patient already likely suffered from.

We dub Nietzsche's theory of memory "mnemic inscription," or more simply, "inscription." "Mnemic inscription" means that excitations inscribe themselves into the memory system; to be more precise, the higher the degree of excitation, the higher the degree of mnemic inscription. It is not only the case that pain is a form of excitation, but in reality all excitations are forms of pain. The ultimate nature of reality is ontologically pain, pain is the hyle of the universe. Pain increases the memorability of the signs with which it is associated; the higher the degree of pain, the higher the degree of mnemic inscription, hence why traumatic memories are often remembered so clearly and vividly, and often even intrusively haunt those who have suffered from trauma. Let the psychoanalysts keep on talking about "repression" and make fools of themselves, and let us avoid their company. We power-analysts are free to talk about "traumatization" and "inscription." Nietzsche applies his theory of mnemic inscription to sociology and anthropology as well as to psychology (GM, II, 3). All writing is mnemic inscription—but because mnemic inscription is only possible at the expense of the forgetting, the erasure, of signs of weaker intensity, all writing is also forgetting, erasure.

Nietzsche writes that forgetting is indeed an active and positive process, but he only emphasizes forgetting in order to better explicate his theory of mnemic inscription (GM, II, 1). On the one hand, forgetting is the movement of signs from the system Cs into the system Ucs, but this kind of forgetting is a necessary result of the essential becoming of both the system Cs and the system Ucs; moreover, these signs may be remembered by the system Mnem-Ucs, and indeed, the entire memory system *is* the system Mnem-Ucs. However, the forgetting of consciousness, the erasure of signs from the system Cs, is nonetheless an important psychological process which is indispensable to life (GM, II, 1). But what is forgetting in the deeper sense of depth psychology? That is to say, what does forgetting mean for the system Mnem-Ucs? Forgetting is erasure— the faculty of forgetting is an eraser. To be sure, erasure is indeed an active and positive process. Forgetting is the dissolution of a sign by psychic forces; the dissolved elements of the erased sign are then used by the psychic forces to construct other signs. Forgetting is essentially a form of recycling, in the strict sense that the old is broken down in order to produce something new. A sign is forgotten when its quantity of intensity decreases sufficiently for a multiplicity of other psychic forces of greater intensity to appropriate-consume it, tearing it apart into fragments which are then used to construct wholly different signs.

Signs associated with pain-excitations, especially traumatic ones, are inscribed within the memory system as if with a blade or a red-hot brand upon flesh. Pain-excitations increase the salience of and the focus upon the signs associated with them. When a sign has a high emotional value, whether this emotion be joy or pain, it is remembered with vividness. Emotional involvement makes signs more memorable, especially when the emotional involvement is distressing, painful, or downright traumatic. The theory of mnemic inscription, because it is an affirmation of subjectivity and an affirmation of reality—that is, an affirmation of subjective realities, which are the only kind of reality—is a psychotic theory par excellence.

Not only are fantasies essentially neurotic, but neurosis is essentially characterized by fantasy, by the production and enjoyment of fantasy. Psychosis, on the other hand, is essentially characterized by reality, by the production and enjoyment of reality; reality, moreover, is essentially schizophrenic because reality is essentially a multiplicity of minds, i.e. reality *is* split-minds. To paraphrase Freud, "in neurosis a part of reality is avoided by a sort of flight, but in psychosis it is remodelled" (GPT, p. 207). The self-denial of neurosis *is* its flight from reality. The self-affirmation of psychosis *is* its "remodelling" of reality. To be more precise, the psychotic appropriates-consumes forces-qualia from the environment at a far higher rate than the neurotic, which means that the psychotic constructs more interpretations of reality at a far higher rate than the neurotic. The neurotic, for the most part, fails to interpret reality, i.e. fails to interpret other subjectivities, hence the neurotic's avoidance of reality. An interpretation is a model of reality (this is merely a metaphor). The psychotic ceaselessly interprets and re-interprets reality, i.e. ceaselessly interprets and re-interprets other subjectivities, which means precisely that the psychotic ceaselessly re-models, constructs new models of, reality. To be more precise in terms of psychic economy, because reality consists of quantities of forces-qualia, the appropriation-consumption of forces-qualia by the subject means an increase in the quantity of reality for the subject; because this increase in the quantity of reality only occurs via the translation of forces-qualia from one form into another form, more reality for the subject effectively means the remodelling of reality because it means the translation of reality, i.e. the creation of new realities. The psychotic ceaselessly translates reality, and thereby ceaselessly creates new realities.

To paraphrase Freud, "In a psychosis the remodelling of reality is effected by means of the residues in the mind of former relations with reality; that is, it concerns the memory-traces, ideas and judgements which have previously been formed about reality and by which reality was represented in the life of the mind. But this relation was never a final and complete one; it was perpetually being enriched and altered by new perceptions. Thus to a psychosis also there falls the task of creating perceptions of a kind corresponding with the new reality" (GPT, p. 208).

The psychotic uses prior appropriations of reality, which have since become memory traces, in order to construct *new* models of reality, new interpretations, which are more useful for appropriating-consuming new qualia and thereby for satisfying the inexorable demand of the life-affirming passions. Thus the psychotic is a seer, for the psychotic always perceives more. The psychotic follows the Rimbaudian program of the "systematic derangement of the senses." Our conscious and unconscious perceptions are limited artificially by the codes of a given culture, which ultimately means by the system of values of a given culture; it is on the basis of this cultural code and this system of values that the system Ucs targets force-qualia in the environment to appropriate and it is on this basis that the system Ucs generates conscious perceptions. The "systematic derangement of the senses" means the systematic derangement of the schemas of perception which limit the system Pcpt-Ucs and consequently also limit the nature of the conscious perceptions which the system Ucs generates. In other words, the systematic derangement of the senses is the program of deranging the unconscious syntax of culture, it is the program of overcoming the syntax of culture and thereby overcoming the codes of culture generally; but this is only possible via inventing a new syntax of culture, i.e. by inventing a new system of values. The task of creating perceptions means the task of creating values, because it is only by creating new values that truly new perceptions are possible, new perception which correspond with a new reality, the new reality of new values.

Schizophrenia is the excess of feelings, the excess of emotions, the excess of will to power, which means precisely the dominance of the active drives within the body without organs. From its excess of emotions, the system Ucs of the schizophrenic creates new realities, new interpretations, new perceptions, and a new language, which is to say, it creates a new form of life, the form of life of the creator of values. Indeed, the system Ucs does utilize its existing memory traces in order to create new realities, but it is able to do so by deranging and rearranging these memory traces differently and perpetually like crystals in a kaleidoscope. The creative work of the schizophrenic unconscious utilizes its own limited vocabulary of memory traces; its creative work is a mind-twister, a mind-twisting process. The schizophrenic unconscious is a mind-space kaleidoscope, a kaleidoscope of Chaos. Moreover, this kaleidoscopic process of creation is perpetually renewed by fresh appropriations-consumptions of the system Pcpt-Ucs, since each new appropriation-consumption forms new memory-traces.[23]

By contrast, the neurotic is dominated by values which deny the self and deny reality, hence the neurotic's limited perceptions of the world according to nihilistic schemas of perception. To paraphrase Freud, "A neurosis usually contents itself with avoiding the part of reality in question and protecting itself against coming into contact with it...The way in which this becomes possible is through the *world of fantasy*" (GPT, p. 209). The neurotic systematically avoids reality, and this is accomplished by systematically denying the life-affirming passions of the self; in the neurotic, the nihilistic passions, the life-denying passions, are the dominant forces, and these nihilistic passions deny the life-affirming passions of the organism. The system of values inscribed in the system Ucs of the neurotic are nihilistic values; the neurotic systematically arranges and orders sense-perceptions according to nihilistic schemas of perception. Not only do these nihilistic schemas of perception limit the qualities and the jouissance of the conscious perceptions which the neurotic's system Ucs generates, but it also limits the appropriations-consumptions that the neurotic's system Pcpt-Ucs is able to perform. Hence the neurotic's essential neurasthenia (mental weakness) and self-denial. The limitations which a nihilistic cultural syntax places upon the system Pcpt-Ucs prevents the system Pcpt-Ucs from introjecting to a great extent, hence why the neurotic body without organs necessarily "incorporates," produces fantasies. Neurosis is the deficiency of feelings, the deficiency of emotions, the deficiency of the will to power; the self-torture of neurosis is its attempt at self-preservation via stimulating itself with pain-excitations (this "self-preservation" ultimately merely means the reproduction of diseased mental states, i.e. the preservation of the power-structures of pathogenic forces within the unconscious). Neurosis fluctuates between ressentiment, self-torture, and apathy; these are indeed contradictory states, but neurosis is defined precisely by these contradictions.

17.

The psychotic is essentially a creator of values and a poet, the new kind of philosopher which Nietzsche describes, the free spirit. The psychotic invents new language games, which means that he invents new forms of life. The psychotic's language-games are necessarily misunderstood by neurotics, since neurotics can only comprehend what is like them, i.e. neurotics can only comprehend that which suffers from neurosis; this is attested to by that neurotic par excellence, that super-neurotic priest of neurosis, Sigmund Freud: "In schizophrenics we observe—especially in the earlier stages which are so instructive—a number of changes in *speech*, some of which deserve to be regarded from a particular point of view. The patient often devotes peculiar care to his way of expressing himself, which becomes "precious" and "elaborate." The construction of sentences undergoes a peculiar disorganization, making them so incomprehensible to us that the patient's remarks seem nonsensical" (GPT, p. 138). The schizophrenic's changes in speech are merely symptoms of a much deeper change, the change of their system of values. The schizophrenic is much, much healthier than psychoanalysts and psychiatrists (psychoanalysts and psychiatrists are themselves deeply mentally ill; they suffer from severe cases of neurosis). The schizophrenic devotes particular care to his way of expressing himself because the schizophrenic is essentially a poet; a poet, a real poet, a poet in the sense of the Ancient Greeks, a poet who is inspired, who feels inspiration, which is the active form of the will to power. To the neurotic, the schizophrenic's speech appears "precious," "elaborate," and even "nonsensical," but this is only because the neurotic is incapable of interpreting the schizophrenic; schizophrenic speech, and schizophrenia generally, *cannot* be interpreted in terms of neurosis under any circumstances whatsoever because schizophrenia is a fundamentally different and healthier mode of becoming-in-the-world than neurosis. From the schizophrenic's perspective, the schizophrenic merely attempts to be as concise as possible in speech. The sentence construction of schizophrenic language appears "peculiarly disorganized" to the neurotic's perspective, but this is merely because the language games of the schizophrenic transgress the rules of the language games of neurosis, which means precisely that the form of life of the schizophrenic transgresses the neurotic's system of values. The schizophrenic's form of life transgresses the neurotic's system of values because the schizophrenic's form of life is based upon a schizophrenic system of values, the system of values of the master, the system of values of the creator of values.

Freud writes, "In schizophrenia *words* are subject to the same process as that which makes dream-images out of dream-thoughts, the one we have called the primary mental process. They undergo condensation, and by means of displacement transfer their cathexes to one another without remainder; the process may extend so far that a single word, which on account of its manifold relations is specially suitable, can come to represent a whole train of thought" (GPT, pp. 140-141). By "primary mental process," we mean something quite different from Freud. The primary mental process, in our metapsychology, is interpretation, i.e. the two-fold interdependent and inextricably linked process of introjection-extrajection. What Freud writes of "words" in this passage applies equally well to images generally in schizophrenia; e.g. the paintings of Matisse and Picasso, the music of Erik Satie and Sun Ra, which are all so many hieroglyphs and aphorisms. Schizophrenic writing is the concise maximalization of excitations in the most effective and economic configuration of signs. Schizophrenic writing is essentially aphoristic writing, the writing of aphorisms. An aphorism is a hieroglyph, a hieroglyph is an aphorism; that is to say, a condensation of symbols. These hieroglyphs rejuvenate whoever interprets them. Schizophrenic writing is essentially hieroglyphic writing. Therefore, interpreting schizophrenic writing necessitates careful interpretation and rumination. Heraclitus and Nietzsche are schizophrenic philosophers, philosophers of schizophrenia, schizophrenics par excellence, the very models of schizophrenia. Homer, Hesiod, Aristophanes, Aeschylus, Sophocles, and Shakespeare are schizophrenic poets, poets of schizophrenia, schizophrenics par excellence, the very models of schizophrenia. And consequently, they are the very models of schizophrenic speech, and schizophrenic writing more generally.

The schizophrenic is never a melancholic, never a depressive, even when he undergoes tremendous suffering and sorrow. The schizophrenic is essentially a joyous being, a joyous creature, a creature of joy. What Nietzsche writes of Heraclitus applies equally well to schizophrenics generally, including to Nietzsche himself: "Gloomy, melancholy, tearful, sinister, bilious, pessimistic, generally hateful: only those can find him thus who have good cause to be dissatisfied with his natural history of mankind [which, basically, is that chance is fate and that existence itself justifies even the bitterest suffering]. But he would consider such people negligible, together with their antipathies and sympathies, their hatreds and their loves, and only condescend to offer advice like "Dogs bark at everyone they do not recognize," or "Donkeys prefer straw to gold."" (PTG, p. 64)

The neurotic can only "interpret" the schizophrenic in terms of neurosis, which means that the neurotic essentially fails to interpret schizophrenics and instead sees only neurosis; the neurotic projects himself onto the schizophrenic, hence the neurotic merely constructs a self-portrait when he thinks that the schizophrenic is "gloomy, melancholy, tearful, sinister, bilious, pessimistic, generally hateful." The neurotic is frightened by the schizophrenic, frightened by the joy the schizophrenic takes in life, frightened by the schizophrenic's philosophy of life, the schizophrenic's philosophy of joy. The joy of the schizophrenic is hard and hardened joy, a diamond-hard joy, the joy in life as it is, with all its suffering. The neurotic is simply too weak to enjoy life as it is, hence the neurotic's "good cause to be dissatisfied" with the philosophy of the schizophrenic. The neurotic needs his fantasies, the fantasies which the schizophrenic rejects with laughter and contempt. The schizophrenic considers neurotics "negligible, together with their antipathies and sympathies, their hatred and their loves," hence the schizophrenic's condescension towards the neurotic, and hence the schizophrenic's offhand, off-beat, and malicious remarks towards neurotics. The neurotic's hostility and aggressiveness towards schizophrenics is merely a symptom of their fear, their fear of what they do not and cannot understand; the neurotic barks at the schizophrenic just as "dogs bark at everyone they do not recognize." Neurotics reject the royal and rich wisdom of schizophrenics because neurotics are incapable of comprehending wisdom as such, incapable even of recognizing wisdom as wisdom; thus, neurotics prefer folly to wisdom just as "donkeys prefer straw to gold."

18.

"Idea" and "affect," "image" and "feeling," "perception" and "sensation," "thought" and "emotion," are inseparable and inextricably linked: in reality, they are *same*, they are absolutely equivalent to each other. (Idea = affect = image = feeling = thought = emotion = perception = sensation). Cognition *is* emotion, emotion *is* cognition. Each image is a dream-work. A dream-work is essentially a condensation. Each image is a condensation of a multiplicity of images. Ultimately, each image is a condensation of infinity. Dreaming is originary. Reality *is* a dream, a multiplicity of dreams, which means precisely that the ultimate nature of reality is the emotions. All thoughts are epistemologically false, but all emotions are ontologically real.

Chuang Tzu famously dreamt one night that he was a butterfly, and upon awaking he did not know whether he was the philosopher Chuang Tzu who had dreamt of being a butterfly, or a butterfly dreaming of being the philosopher Chuang Tzu; he described this as the "transformation of things." Waking life and sleeping life are both dreams produced by the body without organs, which itself consists of a multiplicity of dreams. As a pragmatic principle, to paraphrase Heraclitus, we "share" the waking world with others, but when we sleep we enter into a private world; this is still a bit of a falsification because the self is an intersubjectivity unto itself, and the self and the other are each essentially isolated from each other, but Heraclitus' meaning is nonetheless clear; and if we can speak of a "transformation of things" at all, it is only in the sense that, pragmatically speaking, the dream of waking life involves power relations with a multiplicity of others (and consequently, the multiplicity of others' waking dreams), whereas sleeping life involves only power relations within our self (and consequently, the multiplicity of dreams within the self). The transformation from waking life to sleeping life and vice versa is merely the transformation of one kind of dream into another kind of dream. In our sleeping-dreams we can read the combat of psychic forces within the self. In our waking-dreams, not only do we read the combat of psychic forces within the self, but we also read the combat of psychic forces within others, and we also read the combat of psychic forces between the self and others.

A dream is essentially a system of mediation and difference. Epistemologically life is fiction, but ontologically the ultimate nature of reality is the emotions. The concept of dreaming also implies fleetingness, temporality, diachronicity, impermanence, i.e. that nothing endures, i.e. Becoming, i.e. pure Becoming, i.e. it implies mortality, the theological immanence of mortality itself. The theological immanence of Dream *is* the theological immanence of Death. Death is forgetting, dissolution, and erasure. To clarify, we do indeed affirm that the body without organs is a *mortal body*. The death of a mortal body is the dissolution and erasure of the psychic forces which compose it. Death is forgetting and oblivion.

If "dreams are our royal road to the unconscious," it is only because reality itself is a dream, reality itself is a dream-work, an infinity of dream-works. Reality itself is an infinity of psychological condensations, an infinity of aphorisms, an infinity of hieroglyphs. The interpretation of reality is the interpretation of dreams, it is always already the interpretation of dreams. Because the self is a system of others and because the unconscious determines the entirety of psychic life, we are always trapped in the dream of the other, we are always already trapped in the dream of the other: it is the other who dreams us, consciousness is the dream of the other, to exist means to be dreamed by the other, the other within the self, the other which *is* the self. A dream is not necessarily fantasy. Fantasy is merely wish-fulfilment. A dream is essentially drive itself, driving itself, i.e. dreaming is essentially crystallization, the production of anticipated excitations. Dreaming is essentially the will to power, the will to power essentially dreams: reality is essentially the will to power, the will to power essentially creates new realities. Reality is essentially schizophrenia, schizophrenia is the ultimate ontological nature of reality: reality is the infinite hallucinates of infinite schizophrenics. The unconscious is essentially schizophrenic. Neurosis is a perversion, a denial of the essential schizophrenia of reality; the neurotic unconscious is a perversion, a self-denying unconscious, an unconscious dominated by the death drive. Our concept of the *dream-principle* is that reality and dreaming are fundamentally equivalent to each other. Our anti-metaphysical philosophy of the dream principle is an affirmation of the fact that there is neither a true world nor an apparent world. Metaphysics is essentially any system of ideas which argues for the existence of a "true world," and thereby necessarily constructs a false dichotomy between the "true world" and the "apparent world." Metaphysics is essentially neurotic fantasy. We have certainty that reality is ontologically a dream, an infinity of dreams, precisely because epistemologically "nothing is true," there is no truth, which means precisely that ontologically there is only an infinity of subjectivities. The denial of the dream-principle is a symptom of deficiency of psychic force, a symptom of neurosis. The "reality principle," the belief in an objective reality, is a product of and a symptom of neurosis. Descartes' *Meditations* and *Discourse on the Method*—not to mention the complete works of Sigmund Freud—exemplify the fantasy of the reality principle and the anxiety-ridden neurotic denial of the dream-principle.

Because dreaming is originary, theatre is originary (dreaming = theatre = reality). The language of reality is the language of dreams, which is the language of theatre. The language of theatre, the language of reality, the language of dreams, is essentially a hieroglyphic language. On the language of theatre, Artaud writes: "Once aware of this language in space, language of sounds, cries, lights, onomatopoeia, the theatre must organize it into veritable hieroglyphs, with the help of characters and objects, and make use of their symbolism and interconnections in relation to all organs and on all levels" (as quoted in Derrida, WD, pp. 240-241). Artaud continues: "THE LANGUAGE OF THE STAGE: It is not a question of suppressing the spoken language, but of giving words approximately the importance they have in dreams...As for ordinary objects, or even the human body, raised to the dignity of signs, it is evident that one can draw one's inspiration from hieroglyphic characters...Eternal laws, those of all poetry and all viable language, and among other things, of Chinese ideograms and ancient Egyptian hieroglyphs" (ibid, pp. 241-242). Derrida discovers that the language of the stage shares essential characteristics with the language of dreams as described by Freud: "On the stage of the dream, as described by Freud, speech has the same status...Present in dreams, speech can only behave as an element among others, sometimes like a "thing" which the primary process manipulates according to its own economy [we must understand this, mutatis mutandis, in terms of the psychic economy of the will to power, whose "primary process" is the drive to increase power]. "In this process thoughts are transformed into images, mainly of a visual sort; that is to say, word presentations are taken back to the thing-presentations which correspond to them, as if, in general the process were dominated by considerations of *representability (Darstellbarkeit)*." "It is very noteworthy how little the dream-work keeps to word-presentations; it is always ready to exchange one word for another till it finds the expression which is most handy for plastic representation." [What Freud writes of "visual images" applies, mutatis mutandis, to each of the senses, to images of each modality of sense-perception, and to the image generally. We emphasize the importance of smell, taste, sound, and touch in dreaming and reality]. Artaud too, speaks of a "visual and plastic materialization of speech" and of making use of speech "in a concrete and spatial sense" in order to "manipulate it like a solid object, one which overturns and disturbs things." And when Freud, speaking of dreams, invokes sculpture and painting, or the primitive painter who, in the fashion of the authors of comic strips, hung "small labels...from the mouths of the persons represented, containing in written characters the speeches which the artist despaired of representing pictorially," we understand what speech can become when it is but an element, a circumscribed site, a circumvented writing within both general writing and the space of representation. This is the structure of the rebus or the hieroglyphic. "The dream-content, on the other hand, is expressed as it were in a pictographic script." And in an article from 1913: "For in what follows 'speech' must be understood not merely to mean the expression of thought in words but to include the speech of gesture and every other method, such, for instance, as writing, by which mental activity can be expressed...If we reflect that the means of representation in dreams are principally [images] and not words, we shall see that it is even more appropriate to compare dreams with a system of writing than with language. In fact the interpretation of dreams is completely analogous to the decipherment of an ancient pictographic script such as Egyptian hieroglyphs." The "representation" of dreams and of reality is essentially nonrepresentation (non-re-*present*-ation), the complete and total absence of presence. Nonrepresentation is originary; as Derrida writes, "And nonrepresentation is, thus, original representation, if representation signifies, also, the unfolding of a volume, a multi-dimensional milieu, an experience which produces its own space" (WD, p. 257). This form of positive nonrepresentation is precisely the labyrinth, because it is the labyrinth which is "the unfolding of a volume, a multi-dimensional milieu, an experience which produces its own space."

Derrida's explication of Freud's observations on dreams quoted above applies equally well, mutatis mutandis, to reality itself. The psychic writing of reality itself is essentially theatrical-writing, which is essentially dream-writing. Reality-works are essentially dream-works, and dream-works are essentially theatrical-works. Reality is an aleatoric series of complexes of hieroglyphs dramatized by psychic forces. The drama of psychic forces is the hieroglyphic writing of reality. Bodies are always already signs, always already emitters of signs. Poetry is originary, the originary writing of reality is always already the writing of poetry, poetizing. The writing of poetry is essentially hieroglyphic writing, the writing of aphorisms, the condensation of signs, the production of condensations of signs. Words are merely empty fictions, arbitrary signs alongside other signs, alongside the signs which constitute reality, the hieroglyphic dream-works which constitute reality. Psychic forces drive and animate the hieroglyphic dream-works which constitute reality, psychic forces *are* the hieroglyphic dream-works which drive and animate reality. Each sign is essentially a gesture, a gesture made by a psychic force. Each psychic force is essentially a gesture made by an other psychic force. Each psychic force is an actor and an act (to paraphrase F. Scott Fitzgerald, "Character = action"). Each complex of psychic forces is essentially a theatre and reality is essentially a complex of psychic forces, meaning that reality is essentially a theatre of psychic forces, a drama written spontaneously by the psychic forces which stage it spontaneously; the writing of the drama of reality *is* the improvised acting of psychic forces. All writing is essentially cartography. The dream-work is essentially both nonrepresentational and cartographic, which means that it is essentially a labyrinth. A labyrinth is a system of mediation and difference. A labyrinth is a system of nonrepresentational cartography. All writing is essentially the drawing of labyrinths, labyrinth-writing. Originary writing is labyrinth-writing. The labyrinth is originary. The labyrinth is theologically immanent. Reality is essentially a labyrinth of gestures. Each sign is a condensation of gestures. Each hieroglyph is essentially the dramatization of psychic forces. Each drama is essentially the hieroglyphic-writing of labyrinths of psychic forces. Each psychic force is essentially the hieroglyphic-writing of labyrinths of dramas. Reality is essentially an infinity of dream-hieroglyphic labyrinth-writing. Each psychic force is a labyrinth unto itself which draws labyrinths. Each psychic force is a labyrinth-writing-labyrinth. Reality is an infinite series of dreams, an infinite dream within a dream ad infinitum, an infinite series of labyrinths, an infinite labyrinth within a labyrinth ad infinitum. The hieroglyphic stage-writing of psychic forces is dream-labyrinth-writing. The reality-work, which is a dream-work and a stage-work, is the labyrinth-work of infinity. The hieroglyphic labyrinth-work of the stage-work of reality itself is the infinity of dreams of the infinity of psychic forces, the infinity of dreams of the infinity of interpretations, the infinity of dreams of the multiplicity of the will to power. The reality of the emotions—that is to say, the reality of the drives—is the ultimate nature of reality.

Because language-games are originary, a dream-work is a dream-game, a hieroglyph-work is a hieroglyph-game, a stage-work is a stage-game, a labyrinth-work is a labyrinth-game, a reality-work is a reality-game, an interpretation-work is an interpretation-game. A dream-game is a form of life, a reality-game. A reality-game is a form of dream, a stage-game. Reality-games are interpretation-games produced by systems of values. Reality-games are dream-games produced by systems of values. To play a language-game is to play a reality-game. A language-game is essentially an interpretation-game. To play an interpretation-game is to play a reality-game. To play a reality-game is to play a stage-game. A language-game is essentially a dream-game. To play a reality-game is to play a dream-game. A reality-game is a labyrinth-game of dream-games, a hieroglyph-game of dream-games. A language-game is essentially a hieroglyph-game. A reality-game is an interpretation-game of hieroglyph-games. A hieroglyph-game is an interpretation-game and a labyrinth-game is essentially an interpretation-game. A reality-game is a labyrinth-game of interpretation-games, an interpretation-game of interpretation games ad infinitum.

19.

The function of power is to increase itself; this is necessarily so because power only exists as flux and never as stasis. Stasis is impossible (this can be inferred from the fact that stasis never occurs). If a power decreases, it is only because an other power increases at its expense. Therefore, there is a perpetual agon and combat of powers, or forces, all of which, always in flux, exist only by increasing themselves because existence itself *is* power, because all existents are psychic forces, wills to power. Forces do not struggle to preserve themselves stricto sensu. Forces struggle to appropriate other forces and thereby to increase power. In fact, in the very act of appropriating-consuming an other force, a force is altered, it becomes different from what it was. (By increasing itself, a force becomes *different* from what is was—*never* "opposite" of what it was, because there are no "opposites.").

Forces are perpetually destroyed and created, but never "ex nihilo." To be more accurate, there is always a "conservation of energy," to borrow a metaphor from thermodynamics, therefore forces are perpetually transformed, they perpetually become other forces. Forces are perpetually becoming-other. Becoming means precisely becoming-other. Becoming-other is originary. The perpetual transformation of forces implies that nothing can endure and that a "will to exist" is impossible, because forces can only exist through their own perpetual transformation, their own becoming-other, and these transformations mean precisely that forces perish by expending themselves (as Rimbaud writes, "Action is not life, but a way of spoiling some force, an enervation"; 2005, p. 293), and that forces even perish by increasing themselves (since appropriation-consumption is a form of self-transformation, and thus a form of perishing and "re-birth").

Therefore, as Klossowski writes, "It is this incessant augmentation that makes [Nietzsche] say that it is not simply 'power,' but *will* to power. The term '*Wille ZUR Macht*,' however, indicates an intention—a tendency *towards*—something he has already declared to be a fiction of language. A perpetual equivocity ensues, despite all his efforts to distinguish his own use of the term from the traditional concept of the will" (1997, p. 46).

The traditional concept of "will" connotes "free will" and denotes a will allegedly exerted by consciousness, a will born from and imposed by a conscious agent, as if from a causa sui. Alternatively, the traditional concept of the will refers to a telos, the "will of God." Nietzsche's concept of the will, however, denotes neither of these traditional concepts. Nietzsche's concept of the will denotes an unconscious will, a multiplicity of unconscious wills; the cosmos is itself a multiplicity of wills, an agon of wills. This multiplicity of wills implies that a telos is impossible, because a multiplicity of conflicting intentions, of intentions perpetually engaged in conflict with each other, is fundamentally incompatible with the idea of a telos, the idea of single, overarching will. But the absence of telos is implicit in the theory of perspectivism, just as a telos is perhaps inescapable and implicit in the concept of an objective reality. A telos can only function conceptually by inhering in the concept of an objective reality, an objective reality which guarantees the reality of the telos. A telos is an "objective will," which is, strictly speaking, a contradiction in terms. Because there are only subjective realities, only subjective wills, there is no objective reality in which a telos could possibly inhere, therefore there is no telos. To paraphrase Nietzsche, "Precisely this is godliness, that there are gods but no God" (TSZ, "On Apostates," 2). In other words, precisely this is the essence of the will, that there is a multiplicity of wills, but no single Will. At best, we may describe the multiplicity of wills as "teleonomies," but even this is ultimately a falsification; the cosmos and history is an agon of unconscious teleonomies, which is precisely why there is no telos.

Strictly speaking, the increase of power-force is merely an activity, or operation, or function, of power-force, and therefore it is not a "tendency towards." Klossowski, explicating Nietzsche, writes, "In the inorganic world, communication seems perfect. Nietzsche means: there is *no possible disagreement* between what is strong and what is weak. 'Every power draws its ultimate consequence at every moment,' he says elsewhere. Persuasion is immediate [in the inorganic world]" (1997, p. 45). Whereas in the organism the appropriation-consumption of forces is only possible via a system of mediation (the system Pcpt-Ucs), in the inorganic world the appropriation-consumption of forces by forces is unmediated, hence why "persuasion," having power-over, is immediate in the inorganic world. However, "immediate" and "unmediated" are clearly only metaphors here, and are ultimately falsifications. Persuasion in the inorganic world is unmediated, not because there is any "unmediated presence," but only because there are only psychic forces, only becomings, which means precisely that there are only mediations. But persuasion, or appropriation-consumption, i.e. perception, is "immediate" in the inorganic world because all inorganic psychic forces are active forces, that is to say, all inorganic psychic forces are essentially spontaneous, aggressive, expansive, form-giving, appropriating, possessing, subjugating, dominating forces. Inorganic forces are essentially powerful forces which "reach out" for power, constantly discharging their excess energy and constantly appropriating-consuming other forces.

Nietzsche writes that the inorganic world is "a more primitive form of the world of affects in which everything still lies contained in a powerful unity before it undergoes ramifications and developments in the organic process (and, as is only fair, also becomes tenderer and weaker)—as a kind of instinctive life in which all organic functions are still synthetically intertwined along with self-regulation, assimilation, nourishment, excretion, and metabolism—as a *pre-form* of life" (BGE 36). "Unity," as Nietzsche uses the term here, is also merely a metaphor and a falsification, since there is only ever a multiplicity of forces. Rather, what is meant here is that in the inorganic world, there is only a multiplicity of *active* forces, hence the concentration of power in inorganic psychic forces. That is to say, whereas in the organism various organic functions (e.g. self-regulation, assimilation, nourishment, excretion, and metabolism) require the labour of reactive forces as well as the direction of active forces, in the inorganic world there are only active forces in which all these organic functions are "unified" as a single function (hence why the inorganic world is a "pre-form" of life). There are indeed ramifications and developments in the inorganic world, but they are solely the ramifications and developments of active forces. In the organic world, "reactive" forces as such become possible for the first time, reactive forces which are subjugated by active forces, hence why "persuasion" in the organic world is always mediated and mediating, and why organisms are "tenderer and weaker" than the elements. The "ramifications" and "developments' of the organic world are the ramifications and developments of the power relations between the active forces and reactive forces which constitute the organism. Clearly, for the elements, concepts such as "self-regulation," "assimilation," "nourishment," "excretion," and "metabolism" can only be applied metaphorically and inaccurately, for such activities proper only begin with the formation and subjugation of reactive drives by active drives. Rather, it is perhaps more simple, but nonetheless still a metaphor, to conclude that the fundamental life-process of both the organic and the inorganic is *interpretation*, i.e. the two-fold inextricably linked process of introjection-extrajection, and that the elements *interpret*, albeit in a different manner than the way organisms interpret.

Roughly speaking, there are two "forms" of the will to power, inorganic (or elemental) forms, and organic forms. Within organic forms, there are fundamentally two forms force, i.e. two forms of organic forces, active forces and reactive forces. Active forces and reactive forces are variations along the continuum of organic force. The lower the quantity of subjectivity (force, power, intensity, drive, will to power), the more reactive the force. The higher the quantity of subjectivity (force, power, intensity, drive, will to power), the more active the force.

There are no reactive forces in inorganic forms because communication among elemental forms is "unmediated," hence "there is *no possible disagreement* between what is strong and what is weak" among elemental forces. All elemental forces are active forces. The quantity of an elemental force is decreased only when an other elemental force increases its own force at the weaker force's expense, and weak elemental forces are quickly appropriated-consumed and thus destroyed by stronger elemental forces. Elemental forces are perpetually transformed into different forms, but the quantity of an elemental force never becomes low enough in a relatively stable state (and thus relatively "endure") in order to meet the criteria of a reactive force and thus be reactive.

Reactive forces can only exist in organic forms. It is only within organic forms that a force's quantity can be low enough in a relatively stable state to relatively "endure" and thus be a reactive force. In an organism, active forces and reactive forces are engaged in a symbiotic mutualistic relationship. In organic forms, active forces and reactive forces live together in a conjunctive symbiosis, in bodily union (because they form a body without organs). Their symbiosis is mutualistic because each kind of force benefits from the activity of the other kind of force; active and reactive forces benefit from each other's activities (in a healthy organism), each increases the quantity of force of the other via their activities.

In the organism, each force is mediated by other forces; this means that partial selections of forces are exchanged among forces. In the organism, the organization of forces is generated and sustained by as system of exchange, which implies a system of production, i.e. a political economy. The psychic metabolism of the body without organs *is* a political economy. The originary capital is power, will to power. The will to power is the "living currency" of the psyche. The sign *is* the will to power, consequently the originary capital is the sign, signs are the "living currency" of the psyche. Because signs *are* culture, cultural capital is originary (all forms of capital are forms of cultural capital).

At the level of the organism, the question of "utility" (in the sense of utility for self-preservation) and "use value" (value in terms of utility for self-preservation) simply does not arise (there is no "self-preservation" as such). The primary and originary form of value is "exchange value," value in terms of quantity of will to power, and all exchange is performed primarily in terms of this "exchange value." If we can discuss "utility" and "use value" at all, it is only in terms of the will to power, i.e. only as a function of exchange-value; use-value, then, is the value in terms of utility for serving the end of a will to power, the value in terms of the potential to be used by a force to increase its own power, which is a function of the exchange value, the value in terms of the quantity of power.

Forces are movement-images, which means that a force *is* a sign (just as a sign *is* a force). Partial selections of forces are partial selections of movement-images; through partial selections, movement-images can be transformed into "pictorial constructs" and "representations," which are merely particular kinds of signs. In other words, identicalities and discursive constructs can only be constructed via partial selections of forces, and are indeed constituted by partial selections of forces; to paraphrase Klossowski, "points of reference, repetition and comparison appear—and finally, comparable signs" only because "in the organic world...exchange and assimilation are necessary" (1997, p. 45), i.e. because in the organic world, partial selections of forces and exchanges of partial selections of forces become necessary. Forces exchange (partial selections of) forces, which means that forces exchange signs. Signs are "carried" in the medium of force-images, which are themselves signs. Each sign is a quantity of force, a quantity of intensity. The political economy of the body without organs is a political economy of forces and signs. The exchange value of a sign is its quantity of intensity, its quantity of excitation, its quantity of force (force = intensity = excitation). The higher the condensation of the sign, the higher its quantity of intensity, i.e. the higher its exchange value. The value of a sign is always in flux; the determination of a sign's value depends on a variety of factors.

Klossowski writes that the psyche "interprets according to a code of signs, responding to variations in *excited* or *excitable* states" (1997, p. 47). Each body without organs interprets according to a code of signs, and each sign in this code *is* an excitation (an excited or excitable state). The differing exchange values of signs are variations of excitability, and even the "same" sign acquires different values over time.

Klossowski writes that a *phantasm* is an anticipated excitation, an image which *is* an anticipated excitation (1997, p. 47). However, an excitation is always also simultaneously an anticipated excitation. For example, beauty is both an excitation and an anticipated excitation, beauty is both happiness and the promise of happiness. The appropriation-consumption of excitations is always also a stimulus to more appropriation-consumption. Likewise, an exchange of excitations is also always a stimulus to further exchanges of excitations. Each sign is *both* an excitation *and* an anticipated excitation, a phantasm.

A drive is a drive only insofar as it has an exciting state as an aim, i.e. only insofar as it has a phantasm, an anticipated excitation, as its aim. A phantasm is the intention of a drive. The intentionality of a mental act (the body without organs is a system of mental acts) is the anticipated excitation which drives the mental act. The subject of a mental act *is* the mental act itself. The subject more generally, the self, is a system of mental acts. "Intention" (or "intentionality") is merely a metaphor because in actuality there are only intensities, and the "intention" is merely an interpretation of the *effect* of relations of intensities. The "intentionality" of a mental act is at best merely a metaphor for the intensity of the sign which directs the mental act and attracts the elements of the mental act; this process is *impulsion*. An anticipated excitation impulses, drives, a mental act. To be more precise, because each mental act is directed by an anticipated excitation which attracts all its elements, each mental act *is* an impulse. The intensity of a sign makes exchange and appropriation (all exchanges are forms of appropriation) necessary among forces of varying intensity. The body without organs, the self, is a system of impulses. The other, likewise, is a system of impulses.

Active and reactive drives are qualitatively distinct and have distinct functions within the body without organs. The political economy of the body without organs only functions due to the distinction between active drives and reactive drives. The difference between active and reactive drives is a quantitative as well as a qualitative difference, although it must be remembered that our use of the concept of "quantity" is wholly metaphorical. By "quantity," we do not refer strictly to numbers, since there are no numbers in nature, but instead we refer to "quantity of quality," or "quality of quantity," quantities which *are* qualities and nothing but qualities, and which can only be interpreted qualitatively. Because "numbers" are merely mental constructs, "quantities" in the traditional sense are likewise merely mental constructs. Because in reality there is only difference-in-itself, there is no "equality" in reality, whether numerical or sociopolitical; because reality consists of ontological difference, there is only hierarchy, only inequality, in reality. As Deleuze explicates, "To dream of two equal forces, even if they are said to be of opposite sense, is a coarse and approximate dream [a fiction], a statistical dream in which the living is submerged [obscured]...Each time that Nietzsche criticizes the concept of quantity we must take it to mean that quantity as an abstract concept always and essentially tends towards identification, [a fictive] equalisation of the [fictive] unity that forms it and [a mental, or psychological] annulment of [ontological] difference in this [fictive] unity. Nietzsche's reproach to every purely quantitative determination of forces is that it [mentally, psychologically] annuls, equalises or compensates for [ontological] difference in quantity" (NP, p. 43). Nietzsche's concept of quantity, quantity of quality, is therefore the concept of a "differencial quantity" or a "différantial quantity," i.e. a quantity of difference-in-itself, a non-numerical concept of quantity which is predicated on and understood in terms of ontological difference, difference-in-itself.

On Nietzsche's concept of quality, Deleuze explicates, "Quality is distinct from quantity but only because it is that aspect of quantity that cannot be equalised, that cannot be equalised out in the difference between quantities. Difference in quantity is therefore, in one sense, the irreducible element *of* quantity and in another sense the element which is irreducible *to* quantity itself. Quality is nothing but difference in quantity and corresponds to it each time forces enter into relation" (NP, p. 44). Deleuze is explicating Nietzsche's concept of quality, on which Nietzsche himself writes: "quantitative differences are something fundamentally distinct from quantity, namely they are *qualities* which can no longer be reduced to one another" (Nietzsche, WP, 565; as quoted in Deleuze, NP, p. 44). Différantial quantity (of force) *is* quality (of force), hence why forces, which are always qualitative forces and therefore qualia-forces, are psychic forces. Différantial quantity is quantity of subjectivity (which is the same as the quantity of quality). Subjectivity is irreducible to numbers, identicalities, and equalities because subjectivity *is* ontological difference. Subjectivity *is* difference-in-itself, difference-in-itself *is* subjectivity. Because there are no real "objects" in the strict sense, because there is no objective reality, "quantity" in the perspectivist sense refers to quantity of subjectivity. It is not only that subjectivity is a system of difference, but difference-in-itself *is* subjectivity, such that "there is only difference-in-itself = there is only a multiplicity of subjectivities." Subjectivity is always already the subjectivity of difference-in-itself itself. Moreover, since subjectivity *is* force, difference-in-itself *is* force, the multiplicity of psychic forces; the relations of forces are always relations of différantial quantity, which means that they are always hierarchical relations, power relations. Hence why hierarchy is originary. Différantial quantity implies that all exchanges are in actuality unequal exchanges. Force itself is always a différantial quantity, a quantity of subjectivity, and this différantial quantity is equivalent to irreducible qualitative differences (among forces).

Nietzsche's concept of différantial quantity complements his theory of continuums. Nietzsche writes that continuums are ontological, that ontologically there are only continuums. That is to say, there are no ontological "opposites," for "opposites" are merely mental constructs. In reality, there are only variations along scales (continuums), and what we interpret as "opposites" are merely variations along the same continuum. As a heuristic and pragmatic principle, as well as an ontological one, "like arises from like." Like arises from like precisely because there is only difference-in-itself, i.e. precisely because there are no identicalities in reality. A continuum is a form of force. Variations along a continuum are quantitative variations of a form of force, variations in the différantial quantity of a form of force. Ultimately, these are all merely metaphors because all forces are forms of the will to power; different continuums, i.e. different "forms" of force, arise from different configurations of forces, i.e. different configurations of the will to power (the will to power only exists in configurations of wills to power).

20.

To use a metaphor: the bursting forth of the blossom is a variation in the same continuum as the bud; similarly, the fruit is a variation in the same continuum which contains both the bud and blossom; all these are merely variations in the same continuum, the continuum of the plant. From the "thesis," there arises only variations of the same "thesis." Thesis, prosthesis, prosthesis, prosthesis, etc., ad infinitum. The plant is a will to power, a continuum of the will to power; the bud, the blossom, and the fruit are variations in the continuum of the will to power which is the plant, and these variations are themselves wills to power. History is an aleatoric series of variations along continuums.

21.

Nietzsche writes that a clear example of pleasure being constituted by pain is the sexual act of coitus: "There are even cases where a kind of pleasure is conditioned by a certain *rhythmic succession* of small unpleasurable stimuli: this leads to a very rapid growth of the feeling of power, the feeling of pleasure. This is the case, e.g., in tickling, including the sexual tickling in the act of coitus: here we see unpleasure working as an ingredient in pleasure. It seems a little resistance is overcome and is immediately followed by another resistance, which in turn is overcome—this play of resistance and victory most strongly stimulates that overall feeling of surplus, excessive power, that feeling which amounts to the essence of pleasure.—The reverse, an augmentation of the feeling of pain through little interpolated pleasurable stimuli, doesn't exist: pleasure and pain are, precisely, not the reverse of one another." (WLN, N14, 173). However, it is not only in cases of rhythmic succession, but more generally as well, that pleasure is constituted by pain. For example, the very feeling of being in love, of sexual desire, is simultaneously painful and pleasurable.

Pleasure is a form of pain (Nietzsche, WLN, N40, 42). It is not only the case that "pressure," or "tension," is a form of pain, but pleasure itself is a form of pain. Pain and pleasure are both variations along the same continuum of excitation, the same continuum of will to power. The peremptoriness of a drive and the tension produced by resistances to the drive are themselves inextricably linked with pain-excitations. Moreover, the peremptoriness of a drive is constituted by pain-excitations. Resistances to a drive produce pain-excitations, and these pain-excitations are equivalent to pressure.

Pleasure, or jouissance, is the feeling of the increase of power; or more simply put, the increase of the quantity of power-force *is* pleasure-jouissance. Pleasure is an excitation of the will to power, it is an excitation constituted by the will to power, it is a quantity (to be more, precise, an increase of quantity) of the will to power itself. But pleasure is a form of pain, which means that pain itself is likewise an excitation of the will to power, a form of the will to power. Indeed, a pain-excitation, because it can only be produced by the appropriation-consumption of power-force, is also a quantity of will to power, an increase in quantity of will to power. Therefore, there is always a jouissance of pain. Moreover, the will to power itself is essentially pain; quantities of will to power *are* quantities of pain-excitations. The will to power is the will to pain. That the primary function of the will to power is to increase itself, to increase power, means that the primary function of the will to power is to increase pain. The jouissance of the increase of power, pleasure, is the jouissance of the increase of pain; the feeling of pleasure is itself the feeling of an increase of pain. In this sense, we can agree with the Buddhists that "suffering is a mark of existence," although for us free spirits this is a cause for celebration.

But we have been writing of pleasure and pain in shorthand, as it were, because there is no pain in itself nor any pleasure in itself (WLN, N14, 173). Nietzsche writes that "pleasure" and "pain" are intellectual judgements, intellectual processes "in which a judgement makes itself unmistakeably heard" (WLN, N14, 173). However, pleasure and pain are nonetheless very real feelings. All forces-subjectivities, all wills to power, all power-excitations, are indeed pain-excitations, but the intellectual judgements which distinguish between "pleasure" and "pain" are wholly unconscious mental processes which interpret forces-qualia according to a cultural syntax, a system of values. Thus, for example, the same stimulus can at different times be interpreted as either painful or pleasurable according to its context.

First, a force-quale is appropriated-consumed by the system Pcpt-Ucs, then the system Ucs, utilizing the system Mnem-Ucs, interprets the force-quale according to a system of values, and according to this unconscious "intellectual judgement," the pain-excitation of the force-quale is experienced as "pleasurable," meaning that it is "good" according to the value system, or "painful," meaning that it is "bad" according to the value system. The pain-excitation of a force-quale is experienced as "pleasurable" or "painful" according to unconscious value judgements; but this means, to be more precise, that *an experience is produced*, an experience which is designed to be either "pleasurable" or "painful," by the system Ucs, by interpreting the pain-excitation of a force-quale according to an unconscious system of values. Therefore, while it is true that pleasure is a form of pain, pleasure and pain are slightly more complex phenomena than this principle makes clear, due to the fact that phenomena are experienced as "pleasure" or "pain" only according to whether they are "good" or "bad" according to a given system of values.

(It should also be kept in mind that our perception-images of "localized" pain, e.g. pain in a particular part of the body, is an artefact of perception produced by the system Ucs. In actuality, there are no such parts of the body because the body has no organs; very roughly speaking, these localizations of pain are correlates of excitations in particular subjectivities which compose the body without organs. The pain is real, especially because it is first and foremost composed of emotions, but the "organs" and the "causes" are merely mental fabrications, and at best useful labyrinths. (Insofar as all physical sensations are degrees of pain, this holds true for all physical sensations, e.g. sexual arousal).)

Each sensation is a labyrinth of sensation. Each pain is a labyrinth of pain. Each emotion is a labyrinth of emotion.

22

Wilhelm Reich's lasting contribution to science is primarily to history, and only indirectly to psychology; this lasting contribution is his discovery, via his critique of the Marxist theory of history, that the primary driving force of history is ideas. In his book *The Mass Psychology of Fascism*, Reich frames his critique of Marxism in light of Marxism's failure to explain the rise of National Socialism in Germany. Reich writes, "In the months following National Socialism's seizure of power in Germany, even those individuals whose revolutionary firmness and readiness to be of service had been proven again and again, expressed doubts about the correctness of Marx's basic conception of social processes. These doubts were generated by a fact that, though irrefutable, was at first incomprehensible: Fascism, the most extreme representative of political and economic reaction in both its goals and its nature, had become an international reality and in many countries had visibly and undeniably outstripped the socialist revolutionary movement" (1970, p. 3).

The basic problem that troubled Reich and his contemporary leftists about the phenomenon of fascism is that the masses *effectively desired* fascism. One should always remember that Hitler was *voted* into office. According to the predictions of Marx, during a severe economic crisis, for instance as Germany experienced prior to the rise of the Nazi Party, the working class ought to develop a "class consciousness" (viz. a Marxist consciousness), have a revolution, and seize power for themselves in order to establish a "dictatorship of the proletariat." However, this prediction was directly contradicted by the fact of the rise of the Nazi Party in Germany; during Germany's severe economic crisis, the working class of Germany generally became radically more reactionary and conservative, i.e. they came to believe fervently in views that could only benefit the bourgeoisie. Within the bounds of Marxist discourse, this is quite simply unexplainable, hence why Marxism is a failure. Marxism fails to provide useful explanations of real historical events.

Nazism is an ideology, a system of ideas. Moreover, Nazism is an ideology which, to paraphrase Reich, makes the starving masses cry out "Less bread, more taxes!" From this, Reich deduced that ideologies are indeed historical forces *independent* of economic conditions. Reich writes that "inasmuch *as a social ideology changes man's psychic structure, it has not only reproduced itself in man but, what is more significant, has become an active force, a material power in man, who in turn has become concretely changed, and, as a consequence thereof, acts in a different and contradictory fashion*" (1970, p. 18). Where Reich writes "material power" or "material force," we may substitute for greater accuracy "effective power" or "effective force," meaning a force in effect, a force which produces effects. Where Reich writes "active force," he does *not* mean it in the technical Nietzschean sense; rather, Reich's meaning is clearly "effective force." Although Reich was fundamentally wrong about the nature of the psyche (e.g. there are no "orgones"), he was nonetheless fundamentally right that the effective forces in history are ideologies, and not material conditions such as the economy.

However, to say merely that ideas drive history is still only superficial, because from such a statement alone one has not yet arrived at the essential subject, psychology, which alone is capable of explaining why and how ideas are constructed to begin with. It is here that we can invoke Nietzsche's political psychology of the will to power and thereby obtain an answer: it is psychic drives, which are all forms of the will to power, which construct ideas, and therefore it is psychic drives, which are all forms of the will to power, which primarily drive history. Nazism, for instance, is an ideology of the drive for revenge, ressentiment. The working class of Germany, like the working classes everywhere generally, were infected with ressentiment, which is why they were ripe for a movement such as National Socialism. Of course, Marxism is itself also an ideology of ressentiment, as is democracy (not only in Germany, where Hitler was *voted* into office, but also in other countries, notably in the United States of America); this opens up the historical question of why the masses in Germany opted for National Socialism as opposed to other ideologies of ressentiment. We may quickly find an answer in examining the facts, which tell us that anti-Semitism has a long history in Europe, especially in Germany, where nationalism wedded to anti-Semitism had been prevalent for many decades prior to the rise of National Socialism proper. In his writings, Friedrich Nietzsche often criticizes and ridicules the anti-Semitism prevalent among his contemporaries, most prominently in *On the Genealogy of Morals* and *Ecce Homo*.

Wilhelm Reich can also be praised for his clear-sightedness in noting that National Socialism was essentially a form of Christian mysticism (1970, pp. 115-142). This alone was likely responsible for the decision of the U.S. government in the 1950's to persecute Reich, ban and burn his books, and imprison him. It is in the interest of Christians, especially fundamentalist Christians, to suppress the clear and abundant fact that National Socialism was a fervently Christian religious movement, as is made evident to anyone who bothers to research Nazi propaganda even cursorily (for example, even a quick reading of Hitler's *Mein Kampf* makes clear the Christian basis of National Socialism). The United States has, since its inception, been the refuge of fundamentalist Christians, and its government serves the interests of these fundamentalists; it is a nation of ressentiment governed by the interests of fundamentalist Christians, and in this it is altogether too similar to National Socialism. The historical fact of the Christian mysticism of National Socialism has been brutally suppressed in the United States, to the point of re-writing the facts of history; indeed, Americans, including schoolteachers, university professors, and even public spokespersons of science, regularly erroneously claim that National Socialism was an atheistic movement. This distressingly blatant suppression and re-writing of the facts of history in the United States is only one symptom among many of growing ressentiment in the United States; another symptom, for instance, is that the characteristically resentful American populace has made Donal Trump, whose political campaign was one of blatant racism and misogyny, into their president. The United States of America is different from Nazi Germany in degree, not in kind. That is to say, the USA is essentially the same as Nazi Germany, albeit to a lesser degree; the USA is even implicated in genocides, for instance the genocide of the Native Americans and, more recently, the genocide of Middle Easterners via bombs dropped from airstrikes and drone-strikes (the vast majority of these victims are civilians, which is why I argue that this qualifies as genocide).

Therefore, it is not only to the isolated historical case of National Socialism that Reich's and especially Nietzsche's conclusions on history apply, but to history generally; that is to say, their conclusions, especially Nietzsche's conclusions, are useful explanations for a plethora of historical cases. Reich's conclusions on the primacy of ideology over material conditions are effective, but Nietzsche's "mass psychology" is much more effective than Reich's. Indeed, the true "mass psychology of fascism" and "introduction to the non-fascist life" is Nietzsche's *On the Genealogy of Morals*. Other alternative explanations such as Wilhelm Reich's

Mass Psychology of Fascism and Deleuze and Guattari's *Anti-Oedipus* are still much too infected with ressentiment, and insofar as they are infected with ressentiment, they are different from National Socialism only in degree, not in kind. Indeed, any critics who erroneously link Nietzsche with National Socialism are advised to read *On the Genealogy of Morals* at least three times; certainly more than once, because such a lazy and empirically groundless conclusion evinces that such critics are incapable of the simple act of reading, not to mention close reading.

23.

H.P. Lovecraft may not be a strategic target for the genealogy of morals, but his works are the record of a delirium of nihilism, and therefore invaluable to the psychologist. Moreover, Houellebecq's interpretation of H.P. Lovecraft, *H.P. Lovecraft: Against the World, Against Life*, is a masterful work of scientific psychology, full of new discoveries regarding ressentiment and nihilism. As a work of psychology as well as history, Houellebecq's study of Lovecraft is far superior to the works of Wilhelm Reich, Deleuze and Guattari, Freudo-Marxists, and Freudians and Marxists generally. Houellebecq's most important discovery is that ressentiment is essentially a form of fear, that ressentiment is essentially motivated by fear: "As an author of horror fiction (and one of the finest) he brutally takes racism back to its essential and most profound core: fear" (Houellebecq, p. 24). There are essentially two different kinds of fear which have two irreducibly different essences: 1) there is a noble form of fear towards an other who is revered, admired, and respected; this kind of "fear" is really a drive to revere, admire, and respect, and it is a symptom of strength; 2) there is the slave's form of fear towards an other which oppresses the self; this slave-form of fear is a symptom of weakness. Lovecraft pathologically suffered from the slave-form of fear.

24.

Racism in its banal form, i.e. the typical case of racism, is the ressentiment of the underprivileged. Alternatively, it is also inspired by pity for the underprivileged, which results in the subject themselves feeling weak and oppressed and thereby also feeling the ressentiment felt by the weak and the oppressed. Pity is indeed a form of empathy, but it is also a from of death drive and a form of jouissance of suffering; to self-pity is to enjoy one's own suffering, to pity others is to enjoy their suffering, albeit with a bad conscience, which means that this jouissance of suffering is only attained via the drive-to-self-torture and the jouissance of self-torture. Furthermore, self-pity is always merely self-victimization, and the pity for others merely victimizes others.

25.

Deleuze and Guattari write, "The unconscious is machinic, it is made of machines" (cf. *Anti-Oedipus*). Contrary to their claims, this can only ever be merely a metaphor, a fiction, perhaps useful in certain circumstances, similar to the concepts "structure" and "system." If we can discuss a machinic unconscious at all, it is only in a forcial sense, in terms of machines whose elements are subjectivities, machines which are composed entirely of subjectivities; a machine is a complex of psychic forces, it is produced, animated, and driven by psychic forces. All our conclusions regarding "structures" and "systems" apply mutatis mutandis to "machines." Perhaps the only nuance of the "machine" metaphor (the machine of metaphor, the metaphor of machines; the machine itself is metaphor itself) is that it implies that something is always *produced* by the machine, that there is always an *effect* of the machine. However, we can make the same observation about structures and systems, namely, that something is always *produced* by a structure or a system, and that there is always an *effect* of the structure or the system. In any case, it should always be remembered that ultimately we are discussing psychic forces, which are never really "machines," "structures," or "systems" at all. Deleuze and Guattari's machine metaphor draws attention to the utility of a kind of neo-pragmatic epistemology, or at least a neo-pragmatic epistemological trait, which focuses upon effectivity, praxis, utility (in the Wittgensteinian sense that "meaning is use"), operations, and concrete productions (effect = production); we may describe this epistemological trait as *effectivism, operationalism,* or *productionism.*

It is merely as a metaphor then that we can discuss, if ever we have the necessity to do so, "power-machines," machines of the will to power, and it is only in this sense that we can discuss a "technology of power." Each psychic force is a power-machine. There is only a multiplicity of power-machines. The system Ucs consists of power-machines which determine the entirety of psychic life. The body without organs is a multiplicity of power-machines, a society of power-machines, a drama of power-machines. The fundamental task of our schizoanalysis, of schizo-power-analysis, is to transform the self into a play-machine, a machine of play, a child-machine which plays as a child plays: positively, constructively, intuitively, spontaneously, affirmatively, and self-affirmatively. Friedrich Nietzsche's philosophy is essentially a philosophy for children. The world of "adults" is decadence, cultural degeneration.

Deleuze and Guattari write, "The unconscious is a factory, nature is a factory." This too, can only ever be merely a metaphor, the metaphor of the factory and the factory of metaphor (the factory itself is metaphor itself). The body without organs and nature are fundamentally equivalent to each other only because they both consist of the will to power, of forms of the will to power. The body without organs and nature *are* production, but production itself is driven by psychic forces: psychic forces are the agents of production, psychic forces are the means of production, psychic forces are the technology, psychic forces are the products, psychic forces are the producers, psychic forces are the very process of production itself, and, in the final analysis, psychic forces are each and every element of the political economy of the body without organs and the political economy of nature. The body without organs and nature are factories only in the following senses: 1) subjectivity-factories, factories of subjectivity; 2) psychic-factories, factories of psychic forces; 3) emotion-factories, factories of the emotions; 4) power-factories, factories of the will to power; 5) creative-factories, factories of creation; 6) aleatoric-factories, factories of aleatoricality; 7) surrealist-factories, factories of automatic writing; 8) dadaist-factories, factories of collage and the cut-up method; 9) violence-factories, factories of violence, factories of the drive-to-violence; 10) passion-factories, factories of the passions; 11) appropriating-factories, factories of appropriation; 12) experimental-factories, factories of experimentation; 13) plasticity-factories, plastic factories of plasticity; 14) differential-factories, factories of difference-in-itself; 15) mediation-factories, factories of mediation; 16) différance-factories, factories of différance; 17) diachronic-factories; factories of diachronicity; 18) reality-factories, factories of reality; 19) dream-factories, factories of dreams (reality-factories *are* dream-factories); 20) theatre-factories, factories of theatre (reality-factories *are* theatre-factories); 21) writing-factories, factories of writing (reality-factories *are* writing-factories); 22) game-factories, factories of games (reality-factories *are* game-factories). In addition, the master-unconscious essentially consists of: 1) health-factories, factories of health; 2) introjection-factories, factories of introjection, introjective factories; 3) extrajection-factories, factories of extrajection, extrajective factories. However, the slave-unconscious essentially consists of: 1) disease-factories, factories of disease, diseased factories; 2) ressentiment-factories, factories of ressentiment, resentful factories; 3) fantasy-factories, a factories of fantasy, 4) incorporation-factories, factories of incorporation, incorporative factories; 5) nihilistic-factories, factories of nihilism; 6) death-drive-factories, factories of the death drive.

Deleuze and Guattari, although they make poor use of it, do indeed invent a notable concept, the "social machine," which is a "megamachine" that encompasses an entire social field and that "has men for its parts, even if we view them *with* their machines, and integrate them, internalize them in an institutional model at every stage of action, transmission, and motoricity" (AO, p. 141). We propose a few revisions. First, each power-machine *is* a social-machine, a social-machine in the form of a micro-machine. Each power-machine *is* a social-machine, even if this means, in macroscopic terms, the social-machine of a society which does not yet exist. The power-machine of the free spirit is a social-machine of a society of overmen, microscopically this society of overmen is the free spirit's body without organs, but macroscopically this society of overmen does not yet exist.

Second, each social-machine in the form of a mega-machine is composed solely of power-machines; the mega-social-machine is composed entirely of the micro-social machines, the power-machines, which compose "individuals," and the existence of the mega-social-machine is entirely dependent upon and determined by these power-machines. That is to say, the mega-social-machine is composed by psychic forces, and it is entirely determined by psychic forces. (Above where-ever we have written "machines," we may as well have written "psychic forces," and our meaning would be exactly the same). Third, "technical machines," e.g. spears, swords, shields, wheels, factories, computers, etc. have no existence, meaning, or function in themselves, but they only exist insofar as they are used by psychic forces, therefore their existence, meaning, and function are entirely determined by psychic forces. That is to say, psychic forces invent and utilize technical machines; by implication, then, social changes are always entirely determined by psychic forces.

The Marxian theory of society, that the basis, or infrastructure, of a society is its economic system, its mode of production, is true only as a metaphor for psychic economy: the basis, or infrastructure, of a society is the psychic economy of the psychic forces of the unconscious, the mode of production of the psychic forces of the unconscious. It is not only that the unconscious is historical, but the unconscious is itself what determines history. But this is already no longer the Marxian theory of society and history. It is the Nietzschean theory of society and history, albeit described using the metaphor of psychic political economy.

26.

We have discovered a certain number of marvellous-machines, machines of the marvellous [*le merveilleux*], which are, of course, a form of power-machine. Marvellous-machines are essentially sensual and introjective-extrajective. Marvellous-machines produce high intensities, high quantities of intensity. To paraphrase Deleuze and Guattari, marvellous-machines are "the nupital celebration of a new alliance, a new birth, a radiant ecstasy, as though the [will to power] of the machine liberated other unlimited forces" (AO, p. 18). Marvellous-machines exist in every medium of art. A work of art is a source of psychic forces, an emitter of signs and psychic forces. A marvellous-machine is a source of the marvellous, an emitter of the marvellous. A marvellous-machine is essentially a schizophrenic-machine, a schizophrenic-machine is essentially a marvellous machine. In analysing marvellous-machines, one must remember at the very least these two formulas: "content determines form" and "to imagine a language is to imagine a form of life." Marvellous-machines are distinguished by their content, and if they appear to speak a radically different language—a "language within language"—it is only in order to express their content, which is primary; this content, which *is* the form of life, of course, consists of psychic forces, or to be more specific, it consists of an abundance of psychic forces, an excess of quantity of forces which are often condensed into what could equally well be described as "dream-works," "hieroglyphs," and "aphorisms." The active type of body without organs *is* a marvellous-machine, is always already a marvellous-machine, and the fundamental task of schizo-analysis is to self-actualize the marvellous-machine which *is* the body without organs, and thereby to invent new marvellous-machines. The schizoanalyst must discover the marvellous-machine within the self, the marvellous-machine that *is* the self, in order to produce new marvellous-machines out of the self itself, as a "first movement" and a "wheel rolling out of itself" (cf. Nietzsche, TSZ, "On the Three Metamorphoses").

Marvellous-machines in literature include: Nietzsche, Homer, Heraclitus, Hesiod, Aeschylus, Sophocles, Aristophanes, Ovid, Horace, Theognis; Shakespeare, Byron, Keats, Musset, Poe, Leopardi, Kleist, Gogol, Guy de Maupassant, Stendhal, Dostoevsky; Baudelaire, Rimbaud, Sade, Sacher-Masoch, Lautréamont, Nerval, Mallarmé, Jarry, Roussel, Cocteau, Radiguet, Artaud, Colette; Lord Dunsany, Clark Ashton Smith, Robert E. Howard, H.P. Lovecraft; James Joyce, Kafka, Proust, Hemingway, F. Scott Fitzgerald, Samuel Beckett, Ionesco, Nabokov, Henry Miller, D.H. Lawrence, William S. Burroughs, Hunter S. Thompson, Jim Morrison, Borges, George Bataille, Pierre Klossowski.

27.

We can indeed discuss the unconscious as a signifying-chain, as long as we keep in mind that it is primarily and ultimately a signifying-chain of movement-images. (If all movement-images can said to be interconnected, it is only because they are interconnected via différance, i.e. they are only interconnected via the process which constitutes them as systems of difference-in-itself, by the process of pure-becoming, which is always already the multiplicity and infinity of pure-becomings; this is the monism of Becoming). A signifying-chain is a system of writing, a system of mediation and difference, and because it is a system of movement-images and because reality consists of movement-images, a signifying-chain is a system of writing with reality. Because reality consists of hieroglyphs—or what amounts to the same thing, reality consists of aphorisms—

signifying-chains are aleatoric series of hieroglyphs, aleatoric series of aphorisms. To paraphrase Deleuze and Guattari, signifying-chains are "a strangely polyvocal kind of writing, never a bi-univocalized, linearized one; a transcursive system of writing, never a discursive one...where we would search in vain for something that might be labelled the Signifier—writing that ceaselessly composes and decomposes the chains into signs that have nothing that impels them to become signifying. The one vocation of the sign is to produce power, engineering it in every direction." (AO, p. 39). Moreover, to borrow a term from Lyotard, there is a "figural dimension" to each sign, i.e. an essential transcursivity of each sign, a system of difference-in-itself inherent in each sign which constitutes each sign, which escapes all discursivity and all attempts at description (cf. Lyotard, *Discourse, Figure*). (There is a figural dimension to all reality). Furthermore, it must be remembered that a signifying-chain is always a signifying-chain of will to power, and that movement-images *are* psychic forces, and consequently that signifying-chains are determined in their entirety by psychic forces which are all forms of the will to power. The psyche is essentially cinema, a cinematograph. To use a metaphor, the senses are all so many movie-cameras, and the unconscious mind is a film-maker and film-editor; consciousness watches the film produced by the unconscious.

28.

The symbiotic relationship between active forces and reactive forces is an economic system, the originary economic system: the *appropriationist political economy*, or *appropriationism*. The originary and primary economic system is the economic system of the unconscious, the psychic economy of the unconscious. An appropriationist political economy is similar to what Marx calls "primitive accumulation" (the appropriation of capital, or the appropriation of resources in order to increase capital) and what Harvey (2003) calls "accumulation by dispossession" (the accumulation of capital via appropriation), but there are nonetheless crucial differences between these and what we call appropriationism. All forms of economy are forms of appropriation, forms of appropriationism. Moreover, the aporias of an economic system are always supplemented by instances of direct appropriation (viz. war). Harvey (2003) also argues that the aporias of capitalism are supplemented by appropriation, more specifically, by accumulation by dispossession.

Appropriationism is an economic system (a system of production, allocation, distribution, and exchange) defined by its mode of production, appropriation. In an appropriationist economic system, there are produces, investors, labourers, productive forces, relations of production, and capital. The product *is* an appropriation, and surplus value is accumulated if the appropriation either directly exceeds the investment and labour cost or indirectly exceeds them via the net profit accumulated after exchange. We agree with Deleuze and Guattari that "production is immediately consumption," though in a quite different sense (AO, p. 4). The act of appropriation, which *is* the product of an appropriationist system, *is* consumption; the appropriation is both a consumption and a product, a consumption which *is* a product, a product which *is* a consumption. This is best exemplified by the attitude towards appropriation by the enfants terribles in Cocteau's *Les Enfants Terribles*: "It was stealing not for profit, not out of craving for forbidden fruit, simply for stealing's sake. Mortal terror was the lure" (pp. 69-70). To use the metaphor of a moral formula for an immoral purpose, the act of theft is its own reward. The act of appropriation is itself both the product and the consumption of appropriationist economy; this is, precisely, the meaning of "stealing for the sake of stealing." What is primarily being appropriated in the act of appropriation, especially for Cocteau's enfants terribles, is power, will to power, hence the great tension in the act of appropriation ("mortal terror was the lure"), and why "stealing for stealing's sake" suffices to increase the feeling of power. If there can be said to be a "profit motive" in appropriationism, it is purely as a metaphor because the "profit" is primarily and solely the feeling of power derived from the act of appropriation itself, i.e. the "profit motive" of appropriationism is "stealing for the sake of stealing."

Bearing in mind that the originary and primary form of capital is the will to power, the profit motive and capital accumulation are essential processes and functions of the political economy of the unconscious, they are the very engine of the unconscious; the political economy of the unconscious appears to "tend towards" the accumulation of its capital, will to power, because capital accumulation is an operation essential to the functioning of every agent of production, from investors and producers to labourers. The agents of production are the drives, both active drives and reactive drives. Each active drive is both a producer and an investor. Reactive drives are always labourers (reactive forces are the labour force). The profit motive is originary, considered in terms of the originary capital, the will to power. The profit motive (the motive to accumulate power) drives both active drives and reactive drives. As the producers, the active drives combine reactive drives (labour) and signs (capital), which are the factor inputs or factors of production, in order to produce (to output) appropriation (which is the product). Active drives are the originary investors. Active drives invest forces-signs from within themselves, from the great reservoir of forces-signs which *is* the active drives. These investments are partial selections of active drives, the partial selections of force-images which are then exchanged as signs among the active and reactive drives. Active drives are total drives, complete drives, because of their high, superabundant, excessive quantity of force-drive. Hence why the active drives are the source of originary overinvestment. Reactive drives are partial drives because of their low (partial) quantity of force-drive. Each sign has a value, a quantity of force-drive. The value of a sign is always determined by the system Ucs according to a system of values (viz. a morality). Signs, because they are partial selections of drives, fragments of drives, are partial drives. Each sign is both an excitation and an anticipated excitation, which means that each sign is a partial drive; the partial drive of a sign drives the reactive drive which reacts to it, and thereby a sign functions as the intention of a reactive drive. Investment is the production of products that will be used to produce other products. Active drives are investors because they produce signs (from out of (the active drives) themselves), and these products-signs are used (by the labourers, reactive drives) to produce other products (appropriations). The investments of active drives motivate and impulse reactive drives to perform labour (in the service of the active drives).

Active drives invest signs due to the originary profit motive (of active drives); the high quantity of intensity of active drives means that active drives serve as their own anticipated excitations, their own intentions. Active drives are self-directed by their own high intensity. An active drive is a mental act, and its ownmost high intensity attracts its ownmost elements, hence why an active drive is its ownmost intentionality. Active drives drive themselves, they are self-driven.

To be more precise reactive drives can also produce signs and exchange signs with each other, thereby inducing each other to perform labour, although to sum up the essential difference between the reactive drives and the active drives, the signs produced by reactive drives are weaker than the signs produced by active drives. A sign produced by a reactive drive always has a lesser quantity of force-intensity than a sign produced by an active drive. Whereas active drives produce signs spontaneously, reactive drives only produce signs in reaction to other drives (whether these other drives be active or reactive); i.e. reactive drives only produce signs as "response to stimuli," as "adaptation."

The labourers always *are* means of production. Reactive drives are unfree labourers, slaves, in a triple sense: they are not free to sell their labour power (their potentiality to perform labour), the exploitation of their labour power is determined by the active drives (the domination of the active drives, the activity of the active drives), and reactive drives can *only* be labourers (in a deterministic sense) because of their low quantity of power. The political economy of the unconscious is similar to the feudal system, and even moreso to slavery; reactive drives are the vassals-slaves of active drives, whereas the active drives are the masters, an aristocracy and an oligarchy. The active drives and signs are the productive forces, the enabling factors of production. Changes in the quantity of active drives begets social change, which are changes in the relations of production ("relations of production" here must be taken strictly in our sense, as relations among unconscious psychic drives). Signs are the originary technology, and signs are partial selections of active drives. (This is, of course, merely a metaphor, because active drives *are* a form of sign). Technical change, changes in the means and intensity of production (viz. changes of signs, systems of signs, and intensities of signs) causes social change.

Active drives, which are unconscious and constitute the power of the unconscious, perceive the environment first, i.e. active drives are the first drives to appropriate-consume qualia-forces from the environment. Reactive drives, including consciousness (consciousness is itself composed of reactive drives), "perceive" only after much unconscious processing of forces-qualia by active drives. The processing and interpretation of forces-qualia by the active drives *is* the production of signs, and it is these signs which are invested into reactive drives (viz. conscious perception-images are merely investments made by the active drives of the system Ucs).

The function of reactive drives in the organism is attention, to attend to the signs (partial drives, or "stimuli") invested into them by active drives. To be more precise, the "attention" of reactive drives facilitates their "reactions," their adaptations. The active drives direct the reactive drives (and thereby the organism) via the mediation of partial drives. Signs *are* the intentionality of reactive drives, the intentionality to which reactive drives attend. The attention of a reactive drive is the attraction of its elements towards the lower intensity of the sign which drives the reactive drive. The quantity of force of the sign which drives a reactive drive is lower than the quantity of force of the reactive drive. A reactive drive's elements (the signs, movement-images, and affects which compose a reactive drive) are attracted towards the invested sign in order to consume the invested sign (and the invested signs' quantity of force-power), and thereby a reactive drive incrementally increases its own quantity of force-power. The signs invested into reactive drives also double as the "wages" of reactive drives. Whereas active drives increase their own quantity of power by appropriating-consuming force-qualia, reactive drives increase their own quantity of power by consuming the signs invested into them by active drives. Reactive drives do not appropriate-consume forces-qualia from the environment because they lack the power to do so; the forces-qualia in the environment have a higher quantity of power-subjectivity than reactive drives. Active drives have a higher quantity of power-subjectivity than the forces-qualia they appropriate-consume from the environment. Surplus value is generated by and within the active drives of an organism when the quantity of power appropriated-consumed from the environment exceeds the quantity of power of the signs invested into reactive drives. Because the active drives are first to appropriate-consume forces-qualia from the environment, the active drives are the first to derive jouissance from the forces-qualia of the environment; this is primary jouissance. Reactive drives only derive jouissance from the consumption of signs invested into them by active drives; this is secondary jouissance.

The attraction of forces is produced by the relation between forces of varying intensity, which makes an appropriation-consumption necessary; the greater force is attracted to the lesser force because the intensity of the greater force needs more intensity in order to increase itself, and the greater force acquires the intensity it needs by appropriating-consuming the lesser force. This "attraction" of the greater force towards the lesser force is in actuality the extrajection of the greater force, the discharge of the greater force's excess power-subjectivity. There is a "power-attraction" of the greater will to power towards the lesser will to power, and this "power-attraction" is precisely the extrajection of the greater will to power; "sexual attraction" is but one example of a power-attraction, i.e. the self's feeling of being sexually attracted to an other is the extrajection of the self's active drives towards an other.

29.

The peremptoriness and pressure of drives is cyclic because, to paraphrase Klossowski, "the will to power appears essentially as a principle of disequilibrium" (1997, p. 103). As Klossowski writes, the will to power, "by its very nature will disrupt the conservation of an attained level [state], since by necessity it will always exceed this level through its own increase" (1997, p. 103). Nietzsche himself writes, "The fact that a state of equilibrium is never reached proves that it is not possible...At any precise moment of a force, the absolute conditionality of a new distribution of all its forces given: it cannot stand still. 'Change' belongs to the essence [of the will to power], therefore also temporality" (as quoted in Klossowski, 1997, pp. 109-110). Klossowski explicates, "The *disproportion between the goal and the means to attain it* implies that there is always a constant *disrupting* of the state of equilibrium ["equilibrium," if we can use the term at all, is not only a relative term, but a metaphor and a falsification]. Energy always surpasses the goal. But if *energy always surpasses the goal,* it is because the latter is nothing other than *energy itself*" (1997, p. 116). The essential disequilibrium of the will to power is equivalent to its originary diachronicity (its originary becoming), which is the precondition of the perpetually new distribution of forces; in this regard, to paraphrase Klossowski, "what was important to [Nietzsche] was the fact that *every power draws its ultimate consequence at every moment*; that a quantum of power is defined by the action it exerts and by that which it resists; that this *quantum* is essentially *a will to do violence* and to defend itself against all violence, and *not self-preservation* (1997, p. 101). The paradox of the will to power is, to use Klossowski's phrase, "the circular movement of energy" (1997, p. 101), which is a circular movement of pressure, jouissance, and disequilibrium. Moreover, it

240

must be remembered that by the term "energy" Klossowski designates the will to power.

The originary economic growth is organic growth, the life-process of growth, the growth of life-processes, the increase of psychic forces within the body without organs. Growth is flux, and both imply disequilibrium. The relatively constant state of *homeostasis* concerns only particular systems of reactive drives within the organism, and not the totality of the drives which constitute the organism. The maintenance of homeostasis by a set of reactive drives enables the growth of the totality of the organism via enabling the growth of the organism's active drives. The totality of the organism does not operate to maintain homeostasis because a truly stable state would mean the absence of all flux and transformation and this would only be possible in the complete absence of all psychic forces. Because there is growth, one can infer that the totality of the organism does not "tend towards" homeostasis, because growth would be impossible if homeostasis encompassed the totality of the organism. The totality of the organism "tends towards" growth (reproduction is a function of growth), capital accumulation of power-capital, because of the originary profit motive inherent in the essence of force itself, which is the will to power. Homeostasis is a means of production. Homeostasis enables the capital accumulation of power-capital. It is because of organic growth that pressure is cyclic for the will to power, and it is because of the cyclic pressure of the will to power that organic growth occurs.

There is no "objective violence." All violence is "subjective violence," that is to say, all violence is the violence of subjectivities against subjectivities. All violence can be described as "systemic violence" only in the sense that all violence is the violence of systems of psychic forces against other systems of psychic forces.[24] The appropriation-consumption of one psychic force by another psychic force *is* violence, violation, performed by psychic force upon psychic force; we describe this form of violence as *introjection*; introjection—as well as *extrajection*, the violence and violation performed by an excess of psychic forces, which is inextricable from and the precondition of introjection—are, to steal Derrida's phrase, forms of *originary violence*, violence that is always already there at the origin, and violence which originates, violence which produces, forces of violence which are also creative forces, forces of violence which create new forms via creating new content.

The act of violence is in essence a creative act, always already a creative act. The creative act is in essence an act of violence, always already an act of violence. Violence is essential to life, for the flourishing of life. Violence implies hierarchy, for it implies that there is a superior force which gains by violence at the expense of an inferior force. Appropriation *is* violence because it is always also consumption, i.e. the violation and destruction of a lesser quantity of subjectivity by a greater quantity of subjectivity. More simply: the will to power is the will to have power-over, and having power-over means violating, i.e. violence, therefore the will to power is the will to violate, the will to violence. Forces, drives, are all essentially aggressive drives; active drives are more aggressive than reactive drives. Power is violence, violence is power. Violence is transformation, and transformation is violence. The appropriation-consumption of force results in the transformation of the stronger, appropriating force as it increases its own quantity of force at the expense of the weaker, appropriated force which is destroyed in the process. Introjection and extrajection are the self-affirmation of active forces, their domination, imperialism, and self-actualization (domination = imperialism = self-actualization). (Imperialism is originary). The extrajection-introjection of active forces results from their high quantity of force-intensity, their excess and superabundance of force-intensity, their originary overproduction and overinvestment of force-intensity.

The increase of force is the disruption of equilibrium since it means that there is a higher quantity of force than there was before, i.e. all increase of force is the affirmation of difference-in-itself and hierarchy. Difference-in-itself is the absence of equality and hence the absence of "equal states" such as equilibrium.

Pressure, or tension, results form the conflict between two forces (viz. the drives and the obstacle, or resistance, to the drives), and this in turn is the result of the differing quantities of intensity of the two forces. The force of greater intensity is attracted to the force of lesser intensity. Obstacles, or resistances, are forces opposing the appropriation-consumption. Resistance is always resistance to the increase of power. A force can only increase its own power via violence against whatever resists it, and ultimately, violence against the weaker forces it appropriates-consumes. In order to appropriate-consume forces, the force of greater intensity must always overcome resistance and thereby relieve pressure. The relieving of pressure (via the overcoming of resistance) is always a means to an end, and

the end is always the increase of power. There are always obstacles
to the appropriation-consumption of force, therefore there is always
resistance and there is always violence. Once a process of
appropriation-consumption is completed, there is a temporary state
of satisfaction, a temporary relief from the peremptoriness and
pressure of the drive. However, the appropriation-consumption of
force also means the disruption of equilibrium due to the increase of
force; the same increase of force which is felt as satisfaction and the
relief from pressure also results in a new pressure because the
increased intensity of the drive is once again attracted to a lesser
intensity, thus renewing the peremptoriness of the drive and the
pressure of resistances to the drive. Hence, to paraphrase Weinberger
and Stein, "there is a cyclic rise and fall to the pressure of a drive"
(2002, p. 164), due to the perpetual increase, disequilibrium, and
positive transformation of the drives, which is always also a cycle of
violence directed by the system Ucs of the organism against psychic
forces in the environment. (In diseases of the unconscious, this cycle
of violence is directed by the system Ucs of the organism against the
psychic forces within the organism itself).

30.

In analysing signs using the economic analytic perspective,
Althusser's writings on the relation of political economy to ideology
are immeasurably helpful, mutatis mutandis, once they are adapted
in order to be used as metaphors for the psychic economy of the
unconscious. Althusser's writings on society apply, mutatis mutandis,
to the body without organs, which is a society unto itself; it also
applies, in a sense, to society in the macroscopic sense, but only in
the sense that society is a multiplicity of psychic drives. The primary
political economy of society is the psychic economy of the
unconscious.

Althusser writes that "every social formation arises from a
dominant mode of production...the process of production sets to
work the existing productive force in and under definite relations of
production. It follows that, in order to exist, every social formation
must reproduce the conditions of production at the same time as it
produces, and in order to be able to produce. [Society] must
therefore reproduce: 1) The existing productive forces, 2) The
existing relations of production" (2001, p. 86). The relations of

production are the relations among the agents of production. The agents of production are psychic drives, the mode of production is either that of the master unconscious or that of the slave unconscious. In order for the unconscious to function, in order for the unconscious to appropriate-consume forces, it must reproduce its conditions of production (either that of the master unconscious or that of the slave unconscious): it must reproduce its existing productive forces (the labour power of the reactive drives) and it must reproduce the existing relations of production (the relations among the psychic drives). The symbiosis among forces which makes the appropriationist mode of production possible (and thus makes life possible) necessitates the formation of a structure which reproduces the conditions of production (the conditions of the symbiosis) and thereby maintains and enables the symbiosis.

Consciousness consists of reactive drives. The stream of consciousness is a stream of reactive drives. However, the vast majority of reactive drives are unconscious. Consciousness cannot be defined solely by the fact that it consists of reactive drives. Rather, consciousness is more accurately defined "topographically" or "structurally." That is to say, consciousness is more accurately described in terms of the structures formed by the forces of the psyche. A structure, or a system, is a combination of forces (structure = system). The unconscious is a structure, and consciousness is a structure which is determined in the last instance by the structure of the unconscious. We may say that whereas the unconscious is the infrastructure, the mode of production, consciousness is the superstructure, ideology; however, this is merely a metaphor, and not altogether accurate, because consciousness is merely the epiphenomenon of unconscious drives. That is to say, more strictly speaking, the ideological state apparatus is itself still unconscious, still a part of the unconscious psyche, and consciousness is merely the epiphenomenon of this ideological state apparatus of the unconscious mind. However, it is nonetheless a useful abbreviation and a shorthand to say that consciousness is ideology and that the unconscious is the mode of production (either of the master or the slave), although it ought to be borne in mind that this is nonetheless a falsification and merely a metaphor.

Althusser, explicating Marx, writes that "the structure of every society [is] constituted by 'levels' or 'instances' articulated by a specific determination: the *infrastructure*, or economic base (the 'unity' of the productive forces and the relations of production) and the *superstructure*" (2001, p. 90). We identify in the superstructure only ideology. The political economy of the body without organs is a code of signs, and its conditions of production are reproduced by the ideological state apparatus of the unconscious, which is also a code of signs. Consciousness is a code of signs which is accidentally produced as the accidental byproduct of the ideological state apparatus of the unconscious. As Althusser writes, the structural model of infrastructure and superstructure is a metaphor, a spatial metaphor, for the relationship between the economic system and the ideological system: just as the upper floors (the superstructure) of a building only "stay up" in the air because of the base of the building (the infrastructure), so is the ideological system (the superstructure) "determined in the last instance" by the economic system (the infrastructure) (2001. pp. 90-91). More accurately, the infrastructure and superstructure are systems of forces: the infrastructural system and the superstructural system. The mode of production determines ideology in the last instance. To be more precise, as Althusser writes, the infrastructure and the superstructure have relative indices of effectivity: the superstructure is determined (in the last instance) by the effectivity of the infrastructure, and if the superstructure is determinant and determining on its own, it is only insofar as it is determined by the infrastructure. However, as it regards the unconscious, because the ideological state apparatus is composed exclusively of reactive drives, it is more accurate to write that the superstructural psychic system of the unconscious is determined in its entirety by the infrastructural psychic system of the unconscious. We wrote earlier of "conscious perception-images," but it becomes apparent now that this was merely a metaphor and an abbreviation, because in actuality the system Ucs produces ideological perception-images via an ideological state apparatus, and conscious perception-images are merely epiphenomena of ideological perception-images; these, of course, are preceded by the appropriations-consumptions of the system Ucs and the production of unconscious perception-images. In any case, consciousness is always determined in its entirety by unconscious drives; to be more precise, consciousness is an epiphenomenon of the superstructural psychic system of the unconscious, which is itself determined in its entirety by the infrastructural psychic system of the unconscious.

Althusser also writes that the index of effectivity (or determination) of the superstructure "as determined by the determination in the last instance" of the infrastructure, "is thought by the Marxist tradition in two ways: (1) there is a 'relative autonomy' of the superstructure with respect to the base [the infrastructure]; (2) there is a 'reciprocal action' of the superstructure on the base [infrastructure]" (2001, p. 91). The effectivity of the superstructural system is a "derivatory effectivity" because it is itself determined in the last instance by the effectivity of the infrastructural system; the infrastructural system effects (or produces) the superstructural system, and the superstructural system derives its effectivity from the effectivity of the infrastructural system which determines it (Althusser, 2001, p. 91). The "relative autonomy" of the superstructural system is completely illusory; in actuality, the superstructural system is effected, produced, and determined in its entirety by the infrastructural system. If the purported "relative autonomy" of the superstructural system means anything at all, it is only as an inaccurate description of the fact that the superstructural system is distinguished from the infrastructural system due to its function; this function is more accurately described by the "reciprocal action" of the superstructural system upon the infrastructural system. The actions of the superstructural system are "reciprocal actions" because although they are determined by the infrastructural system in their entirety, it is nonetheless the case that the actions of the superstructural system reproduces the conditions of the infrastructural system, and thereby the superstructural system enables the functioning of the infrastructural system (which is, however, primary in any case). In any case, we reiterate that the whole "edifice" of the psyche, the totality of the psychic system, is determined in its entirety by the infrastructural psychic system.

An ideological state apparatus (or more simply, an ideological apparatus) is an apparatus which produces and injects ideology. All signs are fictions, but ideology is a form of fiction distinguished by its function. The signs which constitute ideology are, in economic terms, investments, since they are products which are used to produce other products. The function of ideology is the reproduction of the labour power of reactive drives, and this is accomplished by means of the production of signs by the ideological state apparatus which are then subsequently invested-injected into the labourers-reactive-drives (in exchange for other signs and, by implication, the quantity of power-capital inherent to these signs). To be more precise, the ideological state apparatus is in actuality a multiplicity of ideological state apparatuses. The defining function of all these ideological state apparatuses are the same, namely the reproduction of the conditions of production, although each ideological state apparatus fulfils this same function in diverse ways according to the dictates of the infrastructural psychic system. For example, speech, abstract reasoning, education, and art are produced by ideological state apparatuses (the particular ideological state apparatuses involved, and to what degree they are involved, differ according to particular tasks and the corresponding mental functional systems implicated in these tasks). To phrase it more simply, all reason is merely the rationalization of the passions.

31.

All consciousness is interpretation, and all interpretation is falsification, therefore all consciousness is false consciousness. Because consciousness is determined in its entirety by the unconscious, and the unconscious itself is also interpretation, the unconscious is always a false unconscious. All emotions are ontologically real, but all thoughts are epistemologically false. Consciousness is always already ideological, always already ideology itself, i.e. consciousness is always already false consciousness; and because the unconscious consists of signs and all signs are fictions, the unconscious is likewise always already a false unconscious. There is no truth, therefore all consciousness is false consciousness and all the unconscious is a false unconscious. Ideology is originary. All art is propaganda, either in the service of master morality or slave morality.

32.

In the master unconscious, the system Pcpt-Ucs is essentially active, it is an automatic-writing-machine. In the slave unconscious, the system Pcpt-Ucs is essentially reactive, it is essentially a writing-surface which merely reacts to stimuli. In the slave unconscious, the ideological apparatus continues to function as the superstructural system of the organism, but without investments from active drives. Instead, the sole sources of the forces-qualia of the ideological apparatus becomes other reactive drives. The ideological state apparatus, in order to fulfil its function of reproducing the labour power of the other unconscious reactive drives, produces signs using only the signs injected into it by other reactive drives; the slave ideological apparatus produces "supplements"; i.e. the slave ideological apparatus produces fantasy, fictitious capital, capital without any forcial basis in appropriation-consumption from the environment but which nonetheless is invested into circulation. In the reactive organism, ideology is fantasy, and this reproduces the reactive mode of production, characterized by the death drive. By reproducing the reactive mode of production (by means of injecting fantasy-signs into other reactive drives), the slave ideological apparatus limits the potentiality of the system Pcpt-Ucs. This limitation of the system Pcpt-Ucs means a net decrease of the quantity of power of the system Pcpt-Ucs, a deficiency and inability to introject and extraject. The reactive organism essentially appropriates-consumes itself. Hence the essential parasitism of the reactive organism: within the reactive organism, the reactive drives of the organism appropriate force-energy from each other at the expense of the organism as a totality, which experiences a net loss in its quantity of power-energy. The reactive system Pcpt-Ucs (and thus the reactive organism) relieves pressure and achieves jouissance only via fantasy-signs, it is only capable of relieving pressure and achieving jouissance via fantasy signs. Not all ideology is fantasy, but all fantasy is ideology. Fantasy is diseased ideology, the ideology of disease.

33.

This entire book is essentially an explication of the concepts of master morality and slave morality, which Nietzsche defines in *On the Genealogy of Morals* (cf. GM, I, 10-11). On slave morality, Nietzsche writes: "The slave revolt in morality begins when *ressentiment* itself becomes creative and gives birth to values: the *ressentiment* of natures that are denied the true reaction, that of deeds, and compensate themselves with an imaginary revenge. While every noble morality develops from a triumphant affirmation of itself, slave morality from the outset says No to what is "outside," what is "different," what is "not itself"; and *this* no is its creative deed. This inversion of the value-positing eye—this *need* to direct one's view outward instead of back to oneself—is of the essence of *ressentiment*" (GM, I, 10). On master morality, Nietzsche writes: "The reverse is the case with the noble mode of valuation: it acts and

248

grows spontaneously, it seeks its opposite only so as to affirm itself more gratefully and triumphantly—its negative concept "low," "common," "bad" is only a subsequently-invented pale, contrasting image in relation to its positive basic concept—filled with life and passion through and through—"we noble ones, we good, beautiful, happy ones!" (GM, I, 10). The master unconscious "conceives the basic concept "good" in advance and spontaneously out of himself and only then creates for himself an idea of "bad"! This "bad" of noble origin and that "evil" out of the cauldron of unsatisfied hatred—the former an after-production, a side issue, a contrasting shade, the latter on the contrary the original thing, the beginning, the distinctive *deed* in the conception of slave morality—how different these words "bad" and "evil" are, although they are both apparently the opposite of the same concept "good." But it is *not* the same concept "good": one should ask rather precisely *who* is "evil" in the sense of the morality of *ressentiment*. The answer, in all strictness, is: *precisely* the "good man" of the other morality, precisely the noble, powerful man, the ruler, but dyed in another color, interpreted in another fashion, seen in another way by the venomous eye of *ressentiment*" (GM, I, 11).

There are two basic forms of the unconscious, each of which is its own distinct mode of production: the master unconscious and the slave unconscious.

The type of ideology generated by the master unconscious is master morality. To be more precise, the system of values generated by the master unconscious is master morality, and the master unconscious also generates ideologies using the syntax of master morality; these ideologies are master ideologies. With the term "master ideology," we also signify "master morality," which is itself an unconscious ideological-cultural syntax. Master ideologies reproduce the master unconscious. Master ideologies are healthy, they are health itself. Master ideologies are always introjective-extrajective, they always facilitate introjection and extrajection.

The type of ideology generated by the slave unconscious is slave morality. To be more precise, the system of values generated by the slave unconscious is slave morality, and the slave unconscious also generates ideologies using the syntax of slave morality; these ideologies are slave ideologies. With the term "slave ideology," we also signify "slave morality," which is itself an unconscious ideological-cultural syntax. Slave ideologies reproduce the slave unconscious. Slave ideologies are mental illnesses. Slave ideologies are always fantasies, incorporations, they always prevent introjection and extrajection.

Cultural hegemony is originary. Culture necessarily implies cultural hegemony. Indeed, cultural hegemony even prevails in each psyche; cultural hegemony in a given society is constituted and determined by the cultural hegemony which prevails in individual psyches. The only "problem" of cultural hegemony is *which* ideology has hegemony, i.e. whether the hegemonic ideology is a slave ideology or a master ideology. In other words, the "problem" of cultural hegemony is whether the hegemonic ideology is sick or healthy. Only master ideologies, i.e. master moralities, are healthy. Modern society suffers from the cultural hegemony of slave morality.

There are slave cultures, characterized by slave ideologies, and there are master cultures, characterized by master ideologies. Nietzsche concept of *decadence* is the concept of cultural degeneration, a movement towards a slave culture, the development of elements of slave ideologies in a given culture. Examples of slave cultures include all of Christendom, all of Christian civilization, that is to say, each and every Christian culture, and because Christianity is merely a form of Judaism, this means by implication each and every Jewish culture; this broad category of slave cultures embraces both Jewish cultures and anti-Semitic cultures such as Nazi Germany, because, as Nietzsche writes, anti-Semitism is merely a product of the historical development of Judaism and the slave morality of Judaism, of the ressentiment which characterizes Judaism (cf. *The Anti-Christ*; also, GM, I, 16 and GM, III, 26). A common retort against Christian anti-Semites is that Jesus, Mary, Peter, and Paul were all Jews; this retort applies equally well to Nazis, who are indeed Christian anti-Semites; but to comprehend this joke is to comprehend that Christianity is a form of Judaism, and consequently, it means to comprehend that Nazism, which was a Christian religious movement, is also a form of Judaism, that is to say, of slave morality.

As examples of master cultures, Nietzsche cites the Romans, the Arabs, the Goths, the Vandals, the Japanese nobility (viz. the samurai), the Ancient Greeks (especially the Homeric heroes), the Trojans, and the Scandinavian Vikings (GM, I, 11). To this list, I would the Ancient Indians (especially during the time of *The Rig Veda*, their heroic age, when conquerors such as Rama and Krishna flourished; but elements of their master-culture continued to survive in the warrior caste even during their long decadence in which the priest caste came into power and falsified the aforementioned heroes into ascetics), many Native American cultures (including, but not limited to, the Mayans, the Aztecs, the Lakota, the Apaches, and the Sauk), many pre-colonial African cultures (including but not limited to the Yoruba), the Mesopotamians (cf. *The Epic of Gilgamesh*), the Babylonians, and the Persians. (The Mughals, who were masters, were able to conquer India because the protracted decadence brought on by the domination of the ascetic priest caste in India significantly weakened India). Master cultures, including the ones we have cited, believed fervently in hierarchy and warfare, and even in slavery.

Post-colonial thinkers, such as Frantz Fanon, who cry out for equality, democracy, socialism, and even peace, are decadents suffering from slave morality who bring shame upon their ancestors. Abolitionists, too, bring shame upon their ancestors; their ancestors knew that freedom is only possible via enslaving others, and consequently their ancestors increased their own freedom by enslaving others; contrast this with the cry for "equality," which is merely the hatred for those who have more power than the rest. Egalitarianism is always a slave morality; perhaps now we can understand more clearly why the United States of America has been a slave culture from its inception, best exemplified by the resentful egalitarianism of the American Revolution, but even before then due to the fundamentalist Christianity of its immigrants (most prominently the Puritans).

Nietzsche's works can only be understood in the light of five fundamental concepts (the five fundamental concepts of power-analysis): the Eternal Return, perspectivism, genealogy, master morality, and slave morality. Any account of Nietzsche's philosophy which misunderstands any one of these concepts misunderstands his entire philosophy. Likewise, to reject any one of these concepts means to reject the entirety of Nietzsche's philosophy. It is evident from this that the most celebrated intellectuals of the 20th century, who are likely to celebrated for some time to come—viz. Husserl, Heidegger, Merleau-Ponty, Sartre, Simone de Beauvoir, Camus, Guy Debord, Althusser, Lacan, Deleuze, Foucault, Derrida, Baudrillard, Zizek and even analytic philosophers such as Wittgenstein and Bertrand Russell—all suffer from slave morality, and consequently they are emphatically *not* Nietzschean philosophers, but are merely "slave philosophers," merely philosophical labourers in the service of slave morality; in fact, these slave philosophers are new kinds of priests. Egalitarianism is a slave ideology; any preacher of equality, such as the slave philosophers we have cited, are merely slave-ideologists, and if they ever happen to quote Nietzsche and posture as Nietzscheans, then they are merely so many "Zarathustra's apes," pale imitators and falsifiers of Nietzsche who have appropriated Nietzsche for plebeian ends. When Nietzsche writes of the free spirit, the new philosopher, as a creator of values, he means a creator of master morality, a philosopher with a master unconscious who creates master values; the prototypes of such a philosopher are Heraclitus, Machiavelli, Stendhal, Homer, and Nietzsche himself. As far as I know, there are only a small handful of works of philosophy written post-Nietzsche which can even be said to come close to approaching Nietzsche's ideal of the new philosopher: Bataille's *On Nietzsche* and *The Accursed Share*, Klossowski's *Nietzsche and the Vicious Circle*, Blanchot's *The Step Not Beyond*, Derrida's *Of Grammatology*, *Speech and Phenomena*, and *Writing and Difference*, Baudrillard's *Simulacra and Simulation*, *The Ecstasy of Communication*, and *The Intelligence of Evil*, Foucault's "Nietzsche, Genealogy, History," Cocteau's *Opium* and *The Difficulty of Being*. But these works are still merely prototypes. The free spirits, the new philosophers, have yet to be born.

34.

Crystallization is Stendhal's concept, and it is one of the greatest discoveries in the entire history of psychology. As such, it cannot be appreciated enough; that Stendhal's writings have gone all but ignored by academic psychology is evidence enough that academic psychology consists of trivialities, pretension, moralizing, idiocies, and quackery. Stendhal is one of the greatest psychologists in the entire history of psychology, and his book *Love* [*De L'Amour*] is worth more than all of academic psychology, psychoanalysis, and sexology put together—it is worth even more than Foucault's *History of Sexuality*, and indeed, Stendhal's *Love* is even the superior work of history, despite its shortcomings—because Stendhal is actually interested in subjectivity, especially the subjectivity of the passions, which is to say that he is actually interested in psychology.

On the metaphor of crystallization, Stendhal writes, "At the salt mines of Salzburg, they throw a leafless wintry bough into one of the abandoned workings. Two or three months later they haul it out covered with a shining deposit of crystals. The smallest twig, no bigger than a tom-tit's claw, is studded with a galaxy of scintillating diamonds. The original branch is no longer recognizable" (1957, p. 45). In Stendhal's metaphor, the branch is the drive and the "shining deposit of crystals," the "galaxy of scintillating diamonds," which have formed upon it are phantasms. Crystallization is essentially the production of anticipated excitations, of phantasms. By means of the production of anticipated excitations, a drive is both reproduced and intensified, i.e. a passion is inflamed. All passions are forms of the will to power, which is the primary passion. The crystallization of each passion is the crystallization of a different form of the will to power. Crystallization is primarily crystallization of the will to power. Ultimately, each anticipated excitation is an anticipation of a power-over, a potentiality for having power-over. Crystallization is an essential activity of each drive. Crystallization goes on throughout the existence of a drive almost without a break; thus the pleasure of a drive never stays the same, except in its origin; as Stendhal writes, "every day brings forth a new blossom" (1957, p. 51).

Crystallization is the production of imaginary symbols, but there are two forms of crystallization: the crystallization of introjection-extrajection and the crystallization of incorporation (i.e. the crystallization of fantasy). Crystallization is essential to both extrajection and introjection. By means of the crystallization of introjection-extrajection, a drive directs the organism towards the "object" of the drive, i.e. towards a source of forces-signs in the environment which is capable of satisfying the drive. By contrast, the crystallization of fantasy prevents the organism from introjecting-extrajecting. Crystallization is indeed essential to incorporation, but it must be kept in mind that incorporation effectively prevents the organism from introjecting-extrajecting, that incorporation effectively prevents introjective-extrajective-crystallization.

Although Stendhal writes of crystallization primarily in the context of describing different forms of love, especially passionate love, ("What I have called crystallization is a mental process which draws from everything that happens new proofs of the perfection of the loved one"; 1957, p. 45), he also acknowledges that each drive crystallizes. For instance, Stendhal mentions that gambling and hatred each have their own crystallization process: "Gambling also has its crystallization process, concerned with the use you will make of the money you hope to win...Hatred, too, has its crystallization; as soon as you see a hope of revenge, your hatred breaks out afresh" (1957, p. 52). Just as the active drives—passionate love, the sex drive, and the drive-to-violence—have their own crystallization processes, so do the reactive drives, such as ressentiment, the drive to revenge, have their own crystallization process. In this regard, we must make a distinction, as there is indeed a clear distinction, between the drive-to-violence and ressentiment. Nietzsche writes that the master unconscious "shakes off with a *single* shrug many vermin that eat deep into others; here alone genuine "love of one's enemies" is possible—supposing it to be possible at all on earth. How much reverence has a noble man for his enemies!—and such reverence is a bridge to love.—For he desires his enemy for himself, as his mark of distinction; he can endure no other enemy than one in whom there is nothing to despise and *very much* to honor! In contrast to this, picture "the enemy" as the man of *ressentiment* conceives him—and here precisely is his deed, his creation: he has conceived "the evil enemy," *"the Evil One,"* and this in fact is his basic concept, from which he then evolves, as an afterthought and pendant, a "good one"—himself!" (GM, I, 10).

Ressentiment is essentially the feeling of being weak and oppressed; to be more precise, ressentiment is essentially a long-lasting hatred born out of the feeling of being weak and oppressed. The crystallization of ressentiment reproduces and intensifies the hatred and weakness of the slave unconscious. The concept of "evil," of the "evil enemy," and the "Evil One" are slave ideologies, incorporations, and phantasms constructed by ressentiment. By contrast, the master unconscious has no concept of "evil" as such, it does not believe that "evil" exists. It is important to remember that ressentiment is a symptom of the lack of force, a symptom of the deficiency of force, which characterizes the slave unconscious. The drive-to-violence of the master unconscious is essentially the feeling of strength, a feeling born out of strength, out of the excess of force; it is essentially introjective-extrajective. The drive-to-violence actively seeks out greater and greater resistances to overcome, hence why the noble man reveres and loves his enemies. The crystallization of the drive-to-violence reproduces and intensifies the strength of the master unconscious. The "noble enemy," the "revered enemy," the "honourable enemy," are phantasms of an active drive-to-violence which is akin to passionate love; the "true love" of the drive-to-violence has a necessity and a hunger for great power-over, hence why the "beloved" of the active drive-to-violence is always a powerful figure, and ultimately a mirror-image of the self.

More simply, however, the masters, the nobility, suffer from the tension of an excess of strength which they *need* to discharge; hence why, historically, as Nietzsche writes, once the masters "go outside, where the strange, the *stranger* is found, they are not much better than uncaged beasts of prey. There they savor a freedom from all social constraints, they compensate themselves in the wilderness for the tension engendered by protracted confinement and enclosure within the peace of society, they go *back* to the innocent conscience of the beast of prey, as triumphant monsters who perhaps emerge from a disgusting procession of murder, arson, rape, and torture, exhilarated and undisturbed of soul, as if it were no more than a students' prank, convinced they have provided the poets with a lot more material for song and praise" (GM, I, 11). The master unconscious does indeed actively seek out the worthy enemy, but it also has a need for violence more generally, and consequently it also discharges its drive-to-violence more generally upon bodies weaker than itself—it has a *need* to, due to the sheer pressure of the peremptoriness of the drive, the excess quantity of the drive—just as the lion and even the house-cat discharges its drive-to-violence on bodies weaker than itself. The masters who commit orgies of violence, orgies of murder, arson, rape, and torture, are as innocent as the kitten which tortures a mouse before killing it (a kitten may do this even without even having a need to eat the mouse).

Crystallization only operates via a given syntax. The crystallization of a given drive is based upon the various syntaxes acquired during early childhood development. For example, sexual desire operates via its own syntax, a desire-syntax (or libido-syntax). Sexual desire is a system of mediation and difference, a system of writing with its own syntax (the sexual act itself is a form of writing, a form of writing with the bodies of the self and the other; invariably, the sexual act is the mnemic inscription of pain-excitations and the jouissance of this mnemic inscription). Based upon this desire-syntax, the sex-drive produces the phantasms of desire. All perceptions are interpreted according to the psychological syntaxes of the unconscious; it is by means of this interpretation according to psychological syntaxes that perception-images of beauty are produced. In other words, we "directly perceive" others as beautiful or ugly due to an unconscious interpretation of perceptions based on psychological syntaxes. Beauty, as it is directly perceived, *is a* phantasm, a *tangible* phantasm. The "object" of desire, i.e. the other of desire, the beloved, as "directly perceived", is a perception-image fabricated by the system Ucs according to its syntax of sexual desire. The beloved is perceived as the beloved because the signs emitted by her correspond to the desire-syntax of the system Ucs. In other words, the "beloved" is entirely, in totality and in all her parts, a mental construct produced by the system Ucs. Love is a dream. Of course, at bottom, this means the syntax of values: either a master-syntax, a syntax of master values, or a slave-syntax, a syntax of slave values. As it regards the sex-drive, the quantity of the sex-drive, the degree of love, is a function of the syntax of values: a master-syntax means a high quantity of active drives (including the sex-drive), whereas a slave-syntax means the absence of active drives (meaning a low, reactive quantity of sex-drive, i.e. an incapacity for passionate love). In this regard, Stendhal writes, "Although physical pleasure, being natural, is known to all, it is only of secondary importance to sensitive, passionate people. If such people are derided in drawing rooms or made unhappy by the intrigues of the worldly, they possess in compensation a knowledge of pleasures utterly inaccessible to those moved only by vanity or money" (1957, p. 44). Passionate love is only possible via a master-syntax. All forms of the sex-drive, including passionate love, are forms of the drive-to-violence. The "violence of passion" is the extrajection of the sex-drive, which is a form of drive-to-violence. Only the master-unconscious has an excess of the drive-to-violence, hence only the master-unconscious is capable of passionate love. The high quantity of sex-drive in the master unconscious means that the experience of sexual desire, i.e. the experience of love, is infinitely intense for the master. The master unconscious perceives the beauty of the beloved as infinite beauty, an infinite quantity of beauty, the infinity itself of beauty itself and the beauty itself of infinity itself.

35.

On the modern educational system, Althusser writes: "It takes children from every [socioeconomic] class at infant-school age, and then for years, the years in which the child is most 'vulnerable,' squeezed between the family State apparatus and the educational State apparatus, it drums into them, whether it uses new or old methods, a certain amount of 'know-how' wrapped in the ruling ideology (French [or English, for that matter], arithmetic, natural history, the sciences, literature) or simply the ruling ideology in its pure state (ethics, civic instruction, philosophy). Somewhere around the age of sixteen, a huge mass of children is ejected 'into production': these are the workers or small peasants. Another portion of scholastically adapted youth carries on: and, for better or worse, it goes somewhat further, until it falls by the wayside and fills the posts of small and middle technicians, white-collar workers, small and middle executives, petty bourgeois of all kinds." (2001, pp. 104-105)

Education is essentially cultural indoctrination. "Knowledge" is merely a mask of values. In slave cultures, education means being culturally indoctrinated with slave morality. However, as it regards modern society, the function of the educational system is much more rudimentary: its function is to transform children into labourers, either manual labourers or intellectual labourers. These children are indeed indoctrinated with slave morality, but the function of slave morality in the educational system is primarily to transform the children into efficient labourers; it achieves this via a combination of discourse and discipline. Those children who finish only primary or secondary education have been indoctrinated sufficiently to become manual labourers or hold minimum wage jobs; those children who go on to universities are indoctrinated sufficiently to become intellectual labourers, viz. corporate slaves, schoolteachers, and professors.

Generally speaking, cultural indoctrination occurs more effectively during leisure time; of course, via the family and, if applicable, the church, but also via what is commonly called "culture," i.e. "art," as well via extra-familial social relationships, what is commonly called "friendship." All art is propaganda in the service of a morality, either slave morality or master morality. In Christian civilization, especially in contemporary Christian civilization, the overwhelmingly vast majority of art is propaganda in the service of slave morality; if it is not directly Christian propaganda, it is nonetheless slave morality in another form, e.g. the plebian "philosophies" of pop culture (including the brain-dead, mind-numbing rubbish targeted at children), hedonism, Marxism, etc. What is commonly called "friendship" in Christian civilization is merely what Nietzsche describes as "herd-instinct," the need to be with others motivated by the slave-fear of solitude; the function of such "friendship" is merely cultural indoctrination with slave morality. Discourse, strictly speaking, is generally less effective than the transcursive elements of culture, including both art, family, and friendship, in culturally indoctrinating people (including children), although discourse does play an important role in the overall process of cultural indoctrination. Often, transcursive elements of contemporary culture—meaning pop culture—is aimed at the lowest common denominator, the most vulgar and plebian of the common people, or at least the most vulgar and plebian drives of humans generally (including both the proletariat and the bourgeoisie), and this necessarily means that it is even more stupid than discourse, which is itself nothing other than slave ideology. In plainer language, academia is often out of touch with the common people; a critical analysis of popular culture quickly reveals that the cultural degeneration of Europe, America, and the rest of the world (most notably, India, cf. Bollywood) has advanced far, far beyond merely "decadence" into an "ultra-decadence." Nietzsche thought that Wagner was a decadent—he may have been right, but Wagner is a thousand times more preferable to the travesties of pop culture, and especially for what passes for "music" these days, e.g. pop music, EDM, dubstep. Although one may wish that this is the terminal phase of the illness—how much cleaner the air would be if the masses simply died—it is likely that this trend will only continue and worsen, and that the free spirits of the future will have to extricate themselves from a cultural ultra-decadence akin to the dystopian vision of Mike Judge's film *Idiocracy*. Indeed, even the contemporary ultra-decadence is already a dystopia, it is already far too akin the stupidities of *Idiocracy*, at least as far as pop culture is concerned.

It is only in this context that we can understand Nietzsche's critique of feminism. Nietzsche writes: ""Emancipation of women"—that is the instinctive hatred of the abortive woman, who is incapable of giving birth, against the woman who is turned out well—the fight against the "man" is always a mere means, pretext, tactic. By raising themselves higher, as "woman in herself," as the "higher woman," as a female "idealist," they want to *lower* the level of the general rank of *woman*; and there is no surer means for that than *higher education*, slacks, and political *voting-cattle* rights. At bottom, the emancipated are anarchists in the world of the "eternally feminine," the underprivileged whose most fundamental drive is *revenge*." (EH, "Why I Write Such Good Books," 5; my emphasis)

Feminism is primarily motivated by ressentiment, the drive for revenge, but only secondarily against men—feminism is primarily the drive for revenge against *woman*, more specifically, "against the woman who is turned out well," i.e. against the *feminine* woman. The feminine-woman is a woman who is capable of passionate love (e.g. Juliet in Shakespeare's *Romeo and Juliet*). The feminine woman is the active type of woman, a woman with an excess of active drives and a master unconscious, who is "a dangerous, creeping, subterranean little beast of prey" (ibid). Nietzsche writes that the feminine woman is "indescribably more evil than man; also cleverer," and one should keep in mind that "evil," in Nietzsche's mouth, is a virtue and a compliment, it means precisely that feminine women have *a higher quantity of active drives than men*. In other words, the feminine woman is a woman who has power, a woman who is superior to the majority of women. Thus, the egalitarianism of feminism is ressentiment directed not primarily towards men, but towards superior feminine women; feminism is the wish to "equalize" these feminine-women, to reduce their power to the level of even the most vulgar women, the reactive "abortive" type of woman. Nietzsche writes of "voting rights" as "voting-*cattle* rights"; it should be remembered here that he is against democracy generally because democracy is merely mob-rule, domination by the herd (hence "voting-cattle"; it should be remembered that Hitler was *voted* into office), a form of government whose primary motivation is the ressentiment of the masses directed against those who have more power than the rest. Indoctrinating women with democracy means filling them with the ressentiment which motivates democracy. "Higher education" is nothing more than a method of cultural indoctrination, invariably the indoctrination of slave morality; Nietzsche is against "higher education" for women because in concrete terms it merely means indoctrinating women with slave morality and filling them with the ressentiment and nihilism of slave morality and of discourse. "Higher education" merely transforms women into either corporate slaves, schoolteachers, or university professors, all of which *lowers* the general rank of women because it reduces them to the status of mere intellectual labourers. Besides, schoolteachers and university professors are merely all so many boring and nihilistic ideologues; to paraphrase Heraclitus, they may have much learning, but they have little understanding. Higher education, and the modern educational system generally, infects men *and* women with Cottardian idiocy.

Nietzsche writes, "Woman, the more she is a woman, resists rights in general hand and foot: after all, *the state of nature, the eternal war between the sexes, gives her by far the first rank*" (ibid; my emphasis). That is to say, the feminine-woman resists the general concept of "natural rights," which is a slave ideology symptomatic of a slave culture. This can be best understood in the context of Nietzsche's conclusions regarding the close relation of passionate love and master morality; he writes, "One last fundamental difference: the longing for *freedom* [the slave's concept of "freedom," which merely means revenge against those who have more power than the slaves], the drive for happiness [the happiness of slaves, soporific pleasure] and the subtleties of the feeling of "freedom" belong just as necessarily to slave morality and morals as *artful and enthusiastic reverence and devotion are the regular symptom of an aristocratic way of thinking and evaluating*. This makes plain why *love as passion*—which is our European specialty—*simply must be of noble origin*: as is well known, its invention must be credited to the Provençal knight-poets, those magnificent and inventive human beings of the "*gai saber*" [gay science] to whom Europe owes so many things and almost owes itself" (BGE, 260; my emphasis). This is supported by Stendhal's observation that passionate love tends to flourish in aristocratic societies, i.e. in master cultures, such as Provence in the twelfth century (Stendhal, 1957, pp. 165-174). This is also supported by the fact that some master cultures, such as that of the Greeks, the Trojans, and the Romans, deified passionate love itself (viz. Eros-Cupid and Aphrodite-Venus). Nietzsche is most emphatically *not* a misogynist precisely because he is devoted to affirming passionate love. The affirmation of passionate love is essential to Nietzsche's project; hence Nietzsche's book title *The Gay Science*. To love woman means to affirm passionate love, to affirm passionate love means to affirm woman. Nietzsche is the first philosopher of the Eternal Feminine. Nietzsche is one of the precious few philosophers, among whom we may also include Stendhal and Proust, who had a vast and profound love of woman, who elevated and deified their love of woman into philosophical concepts, in order to make woman and passionate love flourish for all eternity. The overman is essentially a lover of woman. The overman loves woman for the woman in woman, for the soul in woman, for the will to power in woman. Moreover, it is only those who believe in "objective truth" who stricto sensu objectify women. Nietzsche is a perspectivist, therefore he affirms the subjectivity of woman, that woman is only woman by virtue of her subjectivity; if there is a sex difference, it is ultimately a sex difference between two bodies without organs, and consequently it is a psychological difference, an irreducible psychological difference, hence why "men and women are more strangers to each other than they realize." The overman affirms the difference-in-itself between man and woman, and thereby he affirms the natural hierarchy between man and woman: *the natural hierarchy which gives woman the first rank*, the superior position to man, because it is woman who has power over the heart of man, and more especially, it is woman who has power over the heart of the overman (cf. Shakespeare's *Antony and Cleopatra*). The "artful and enthusiastic reverence and devotion" essential to master morality, to the thinking and evaluating of master morality, is precisely the precondition of passionate love, the enabling condition which allows passionate love to flourish. Passionate love is essentially the artful and enthusiastic reverence and devotion towards the beloved. Passionate love is essentially aristocratic, it is the valuation of *one being* as *superior* to all the rest. Therefore, love is essentially incompatible with egalitarianism, with viewing *everyone* as *equal* to each other; in fact, the slave's concept of equality breeds hatred towards anyone who is superior to the rest. Hence the rarity of passionate love in modern society; passionate love in modern society is only possible, and indeed only occurs, in the exceptions, in the hearts of the exceptions, in those who *are* superior, in those who are capable of revering and being devoted to others who are also superior (cf. Prevost's *Manon Lescaut*). For a man to love, for a man to be able to fall in love, requires him to be a knight-poet, a knight of love. The knight of love is essentially a knight of affirmation, a knight of self-affirmation. The affirmation of passionate love is the affirmation of one's self-given right to exclusively possess the beloved, to possess the very soul of the beloved. Leave the misery and self-torture of "renunciation" and "selflessness" to the ascetics. The knight of love is beyond good and evil. The knight of love embodies and lives by Nietzsche's formula: "What is done out of love takes place beyond good and evil." Love is essentially selfish. As Radiguet writes in his novel *The Devil in the Flesh*, "Happiness thinks only of itself." The overman is essentially a knight-poet, a knight of love, a knight of affirmation and self-affirmation.

36

Stendhal writes of physical love and passionate love as two different kinds of love. Indeed, they are two different kinds of love, but they differ from each other only in degree. Passionate love is a more complete and total form of physical love. Passionate love and physical love are both variations in quantity of the sex drive (the "libido"). Whenever we use the term "sex drive," it must be remembered that the sex drive *is* sexual desire, i.e. that the sex drive is itself a subjectivity, that it feels like something to be the sex drive from the inside out; this is our concept of Eros. Sexual desire in which there is a relatively low quantity of sex drive is physical love. Sexual desire in which there is a relatively high quantity of sex drive is passionate love. The body is itself a soul, a multiplicity of souls; the total and complete possession of the body of the beloved is only possible via the total and complete possession of the soul of the beloved. Passionate love is an active drive, it presupposes an excess of force; therefore, passionate love is only possible in the active type, it is only possible via the master unconscious. The will to power is territorial and territorializing. Therefore, sexual desire, which is a form of will to power, is likewise territorial and territorializing, a lust for possession (cf. Nietzsche, GS, 14: "Sexual love betrays itself most clearly as a lust for possession: the lover desires unconditional and sole possession of the person for whom he longs; he desires equally unconditional power over the soul and over the body of the beloved; he alone wants to be loved and desires to live and rule in the other soul as supreme and supremely desirable."). A high quantity of sexual desire means a high quantity of territorialization. Passionate love is the lust to possess the totality of the beloved, to possess the very soul of the beloved. Nietzsche's conclusions are also supported by Shakespeare's *Romeo and Juliet*, Prevost's *Manon Lescaut*, Laclos' *Les Liaisons Dangereuses*, Racine's *Phèdre*, Byron's *Don Juan* and D.H. Lawrence's *Lady Chatterley's Lover*. Nietzsche's conclusions are also supported by the Greek and Roman poets who deified passionate love as Eros-Cupid and Aphrodite-Venus. Many of Stendhal's own observations, too, are better explained with Nietzsche's conclusions.

Stendhal writes that the birth of love is preceded by admiration, but admiration is already the perception of beauty, that is to say, it is already crystallization. In other words, falling in love presupposes that passionate sexual desire, a high quantity of Eros, exists in the subject to begin with, even before the subject has found its particular beloved. Falling in love consists not of "stages," but of varying rates of crystallization; the higher the rate of crystallization, the greater the sensation of falling in love, i.e. the greater the sexual desire. These rates of crystallization depend upon a variety of factors, and ultimately upon chance. Hence why love may develop slowly over time, as in Laclos' *Les Liaisons Dangereuse* and Radiguet's *Le Bal du Comte d'Orgel*, or it may develop at first sight, as in Shakespeare's *Romeo and Juliet*. From this, we may generalize about the other passions as well. Just as there is a "falling in love" of sexual desire, there is a "falling in violence" of the drive-to-violence, a "falling in power" of the will to power, a "falling in revenge" of ressentiment, and a "falling in death" of the death drive; these are all dependent on the varying rates of crystallization of the given passion, assuming the passion exists in the first place.

37.

Stendhal writes, "Beauty is the promise of happiness." In another passage, he explicates his meaning: "Once crystallization has begun, you delight in each new beauty that you discover in your beloved. But what is beauty? It is a new potentiality for pleasure. Each person's pleasures are different, and often radically so, which explains quite clearly why something that is beautiful to one man is ugly to another...To determine the nature of beauty, we must investigate each individual's idea of pleasure...Since the beauty a man discovers is a new capacity for arousing his pleasure, and since pleasures vary with the individual, each man's crystallization will be tinged with the colour of his pleasures. The crystallization about your mistress, that is to say her *beauty*, is nothing but the sum of the fulfilment of all the desires you have been able to formulate about her." (1957, p. 59)

Because each drive has its own crystallization, each drive has its own "beauty." Sexual desire has its own "beauty," the drive-to-violence has its own "beauty," and even ressentiment has its own "beauty." Beauty is a "potentiality for pleasure," i.e. beauty is an anticipated excitation, which means precisely that beauty is a phantasm. Crystallization is the production of beauties, hence why the lover delights in each new beauty that he "discovers" in the beloved. Stendhal does acknowledge that, however, sexual desire presupposes the perception of beauty, that to a great extent "*beauty* is necessary if love is to be born" (1957, p. 58). That is to say, beauty is primarily something which is perceived by the senses; that is to say, an anticipated excitation is primarily something which is perceived by the senses. In other words, a perception-image can itself directly *be* an anticipated excitation, a beauty. The system Pcpt-Ucs knows only appropriations-consumptions and extrajection; however, the production of perception-images by the system Ucs is essentially crystallization; all perception-images are anticipated excitations to varying degrees. What is typically called "beauty," e.g. in passionate love, is the perception of an anticipated excitation with a far greater quantity of intensity than other anticipated excitations. These perception-images are indeed imaginary symbols, insofar as they are imagings and symbolings. However, crystallization also encompasses the production of "images," in the traditional sense, which are anticipated excitations; Stendhal focuses on "imagination" in the traditional sense when describing crystallization, but in actuality perception itself also consists of images. However, the traditional qualitative distinction between "perception" and "imagination," however tenuous, is nonetheless pragmatic; but we must bear in mind that both of these designate subjectivities constructed by the system Ucs.

The beauties of the crystallization of sexual desire are potentialities for the pleasure in the possession of the beloved. The beauties of the crystallization of the drive-to-violence are potentialities for the pleasure in violence. The beauties of the crystallization of ressentiment are potentialities for the pleasure in revenge; the beauties of ressentiment consist largely of fantasy-constructs, but ressentiment does indeed also "directly perceive" its own kind of beauty, that is to say, it also "directly perceives" what inspires and inflames its own drive for revenge. The beauties of the crystallization of the bad conscience, the drive-to-self-torture, are potentialities for the pleasure in self-torture. Where we have written "beauty," we could have written "phantasm," or vice versa, and the meaning would be the same.

38.

Bad conscience is the drive-to-violence turned against itself; i.e. *bad conscience* is the drive-to-self-torture, the "will to self-maltreatment" (cf. Nietzsche, GM, II, 16-18). Bad conscience is a mental illness. Bad conscience is essentially a nihilistic drive, a form of the death drive, a drive to self-denial and self-negation. Bad conscience is a self-torture-apparatus. Nietzsche concludes that "selflessness," "self-denial," and "self-sacrifice" are motivated by the drive-to-self-torture: "This hint will at least make less enigmatic the enigma of how contradictory concepts such as *selflessness, self-denial, self-sacrifice* can suggest an ideal, a kind of beauty; and one thing we know henceforth—I have no doubt of it—and that is the nature of the *delight* that the selfless man, the self-denier, the self-sacrificer feels from the first: this delight is tied to cruelty" (GM, I, 18). The crystallization of the drive-to-self-torture produces phantasms of self-torture; the ideals of "selflessness," "self-denial," and "self-sacrifice" are merely phantasms of the drive-to-self-torture; they are "beauties" in the sense that, for those who suffer from bad conscience, they are potentialities for the pleasure in self-torture. The jouissance of bad conscience is the jouissance of self-torture, the jouissance of violence directed internally against the self by the self itself.

Nietzsche writes, "All drives that do not discharge themselves outwardly *turn inward*...Those fearful bulwarks with which the political organization protected itself against the old drives of freedom—punishments belong among these bulwarks—brought about that all those drives of wild, free, prowling man turned backward *against man himself.* Hostility, cruelty, joy in persecuting, in attacking, in change, in destruction—all this turned against the possessors of such drives: *that* is the origin of the "bad conscience"" (GM, II, 16).

The drive-to-self-torture is the sublimation of the drive-to-violence. When the will to power—which is essentially the will to violence, the drive-to-violence—is disabled from extrajecting, it is discharged within the organism against the organism itself. The "drive of freedom" is the will to power, the drive-to-violence. Thus the drive-to-violence becomes the drive-to-self-torture. The drive-to-violence, the drive to direct violence outward against forces in the environment, is primary, natural and healthy. The drive-to-self-torture, the drive to direct violence internally against one's self, is an unnatural and sick perversion which results from suppressing the drive-to-violence. The drive-to-violence is suppressed in society and in the individual psyche *via mnemic inscription* ("those fearful bulwarks with which the political organization protected itself against the old drives of freedom—punishments belong among these bulwarks—brought about that all those drives of wild, free, prowling man turned backward *against man himself*"). The Nietzschean theory of the suppression of the drives (or drive-suppression) is that the suppression of the drives is effected via mnemic inscription, i.e. via inscribing the suppression of the drives in the memory with pain-excitations. The sublimation of a drive is always effected via the suppression of a drive, which means, ultimately, that it is effected via the mnemic inscription of pain-excitations. Insofar as the sublimation of a drive means the effective prevention of an active drive from extrajecting, and the subsequent transformation of an active drive into a drive-to-self-torture, the sublimation of drives is always neurotic, perverted, and sick. The sublimation of drives is a cause and a symptom of mental illness.

39.

Guilt, the feeling of guilt, is essentially "the guilty feeling of indebtedness," the feeling of being in debt (GM, II, 20). In terms of psychic economy, guilt *is* debt: guilt is debt in the political economy of the psyche (GM, II, 19-23). However, the feeling of being indebted is not by itself yet the feeling of guilty self-torture, self-torturing guilt, i.e. it is not yet the feeling of "sin." "Guilt" and "duty" become truly moral concepts only when they become fused with the drive-to-self-torture, i.e. when they become fused with bad conscience (GM, II, 21). In terms of psychic economy, this fusion of guilt and bad conscience occurs when the psychic debt becomes infinite (GM, II, 21). In terms of psychological operations, the fusion of drives occurs via mnemonic inscription. For example, the fusion of guilt and bad conscience occurs via mnemonic inscription; e.g., the Christian concept of original sin, and the Christian religion generally. As Nietzsche writes: "this man of the bad conscience has seized upon the presupposition of religion so as to drive his self-torture to its most gruesome pitch of severity and rigor. Guilt before *God*: this thought becomes an instrument of torture to him" (GM, II, 22). To détournement a term from Lacan, the mnemonic inscription of infinite debt and the fusion of bad conscience and guilt occurs via the mnemonic inscription of a despotic *Great Signifier* into the system Mnem-Ucs. This Great Signifier—which is a fantasy-construct—is not merely a creditor-apparatus, or creditor-machine, which is installed in the system Ucs, but it is a parasitic creditor-apparatus with an infinite "mass." The Great Signifier, which invariably *is* the very fused drive of bad conscience and guilt, arrogates to itself all the power-capital of other signs via incorporation, i.e. it parasitically appropriates-consumes the power-capital within the organism itself, thereby producing debt in every other mental system of the unconscious, only in order to produce phantasms of self-torture which effectively self-torture the organism. Slave ideologies generally, Christian concepts included, are so many self-torture apparatuses, so many phantasms of the fusion of psychic debt and the drive-to-self-torture. The identicality of the Great Signifier, e.g. the Christian God, is effectively the opposite of the difference-in-itself of systems of Great Multiplicities, e.g. the Greek religion and its multiplicity of gods (cf. Nietzsche, GM, II, 23). A system of Great Multiplicity is a master ideology, it is the installation of an empowerment-apparatus, or empowerment-machine, in the system Ucs which effectively empowers the active drives of the organism (cf. Nietzsche, GM, II, 23).

The concept and the feeling of sin, however, have survived the cultural "death of God" in surreptitious forms, most prominently in the concepts of "guilt," "responsibility," and "duty" that are commonly employed in Western civilization, especially in its humanist discourse. The concept of sin even infects the human sciences—the all too human sciences—and the most prominent example of this is Freud's concept of the Oedipus complex, which, apart from desecrating the Hero Oedipus, is unconsciously designed to give those who are infected with it the feeling of Oedipus tearing out his own eyes—except the feeling of the Oedipus complex is long lasting, it is the perpetual feeling of "tearing out one's own eyes," as it were. To be sure, Freud does indeed explicitly conceive of the Oedipus complex as sin, even as original sin, and this is made abundantly evident and clear by his book *Totem and Taboo*, which conceptually places the Oedipus complex, viz. the fusion of guilt and bad conscience, at the very origin of human civilization, and then proceeds to confess, "The creative sense of guilt has not yet become extinct within us" (TT, p. 264). Furthermore, as Nietzsche might have predicted, Freud also places a form of debt, a lack, at the origin of the Oedipus complex, namely "castration anxiety"; that this lack is a form of psychological debt is made abundantly clear by Deleuze and Guattari's *Anti-Oedipus*. Deleuze and Guattari keenly, correctly, and profoundly conclude that sexual desire is primarily a positive and productive force, that sexual desire in its primary form has nothing to do with lack, that lack (i.e. psychic debt) is something which has to be injected into the psyche, and that sexual desire which is predicated on lack is essentially a neurotic perversion.

(In addition, we would like to note that Freud's concept of the Oedipus complex is in itself an incorporation—more specifically, it is a necromantic fantasy prompted by the death of Freud's father and Freud's inability to mourn stricto sensu, his inability to introject the loss of his father (it is well known among psychoanalysts and Freud scholars that Freud's invention of the Oedipus complex was prompted by the death of his father). Therefore, Freud's texts are invaluable for the psychologist because they are in essence the record of a neurotic delirium of bad conscience, guilt, slave morality, and incorporation, as well as the record of a delirium of the priestly drive in a relatively modern form; Freud's texts, because of their introspective nature and their direct attempt to describe Freudian mental states (however much fantasy, such as the fantasy-concept of "repression," may be inextricable from these descriptions), give the psychologist a rare opportunity to examine the psychology of slave morality in great detail and precision. In addition, the overproduction of psychoanalytic literature allows us to examine slave morality with even greater precision and microscopic detail, not to mention that it allows to examine a plethora of varieties of slave morality (e.g. Jung, Adler, Rank, Gross, Reich, Lacan, Zizek, and ultimately even Deleuze, Guattari, and Derrida). That Lou Andreas-Salomé became a psychoanalyst signifies that she was deeply mentally ill, and even suffered from the priestly drive; this should be taken into account when interpreting biographical details of Nietzsche's life.)

We may describe guilt as the *drive-to-lack*, or the *drive-to-debt*, and we may describe the crystallization of the drive-to-lack, as *debtizing*, or *debtization*. The phantasms produced by debtization are "debts," or "lacks." We may describe the crystallization of bad conscience, the crystallization of the drive-to-self-torture, as *self-torturing*, or *self-torturization*. The phantasms produced by self-torturization are "self-tortures." We may describe the fusion of the drive-to-debt and the drive-to-self-torture, following Deleuze and Guattari, as *oedipalization*, bearing in mind that this is the drive of Oedipus tearing out his own eyes, and we may designate the crystallization of oedipalization with the same name as the drive, namely, as oedipalization. However, more accurately and more simply, not to mention purged of the desecration of the name of

Oedipus, the fusion of the drive-to-debt and the drive-to-self-torture is the *drive-to guilt*, and crystallization of the drive-to-guilt is *guiltization*. The phantasms produced by oedipalization are "oedipuses," or more simply put, the phantasms produced by guiltization are "sins." The drive-to-debt, the drive-to-self-torture, and the drive-to-guilt are all forms of the death-drive. The first thing which strikes the reader of Freud is his repetition-compulsion to interpret—to be more precise, to misinterpret—all phenomena as ultimately signifying the Oedipus complex. Freud effectively reduces everything to the Oedipus complex, which means that he effectively reduces everything to the *affect* of the Oedipus complex, which is a fusion of self-torture and guilt. In other words, Freud mis-interprets all signs via incorporating them into the incorporation of the Oedipus complex, which means that he translates, or converts, each sign into potentialities for the pleasure in self-torture and debt. The jouissance of sin is the jouissance of self-torture and debt. We find in the Oedipus complex, in effect, the exact same psychology as original sin. The psychological operation which results from the belief in original sin is precisely the conversion of all signs into potentialities for the jouissance of self-torture and debt, i.e. it is oedipalization, which is guiltization. Insofar as Freud reduces all signs to the Oedipus complex, he also reduces all signs to debt; for him, the concept of debt is embodied in the concept of "castration anxiety." The second thing which strikes the reader of Freud is his repetition-compulsion to mis-interpret all signs, to convert and reduce all signs, to castration anxiety—and, by implication, as Lacan's psychoanalysis explicates, this means the mis-interpretation, conversion, and reduction of all signs to *lack*, i.e., to debt: this reduction to debt is the necessary counterpart of the reduction to sin. In Freud's writings, we discover the essential psychic processes of slave-morality: the conversion and incorporation of all signs into phantasms of bad conscience, debt, and guilt, but this presupposes a syntax of bad conscience, a syntax of debt, and a syntax of guilt. In other words, bad conscience and guilty-indebtedness are essential parts of the machine of slave-morality, they are themselves values which are essential to the over-arching system of values of slave-morality. Sin, or the drive-to-guilt, does indeed become an essential value-part of the value-machine of slave-morality, but historically this only happens with the establishment of Christianity, viz. with the social construction of the concept of original sin (cf. GM, II, 21-22). Insofar as Freud inscribes the Oedipus complex into the very essence of sexual desire, the experience of sexual desire he describes and reproduces is infected with the affect of drive-to-guilt, i.e. it is a sexual desire which is experienced as self-denial, self-torture, and guilt; i.e., it is a sexual desire motivated by the death-drive, which simply means a reactive sexual desire, a low quantity of sexual desire, a diminished, exhausted, and self-torturing sexual desire.

40.

Given Derrida's discovery that violence is originary and Nietzsche's discovery that the fundamental drive of life is the drive-to-violence, as well as Nietzsche's discoveries regarding political science, history, sociology, and anthropology, Galtung's concept of "structural violence" is in need of comprehensive revision. *Structural violence* is the limiting of the potentiality, the limiting of the freedom, of a given group or individual. (Potentiality = freedom = power). Structural violence is originary. All forms of violence are forms of structural violence. The will to power is essentially the drive of freedom, the drive-to-freedom: more power means more freedom, and because power means power-over, more freedom for the self can only be gained via decreasing the freedom of the other. In other words, the self can only gain more freedom via enslaving the other, in terms of concrete power relations. All relations of the self and the other are relations of structural violence.

Perhaps the concept of structural violence is best illustrated by Nietzsche's master-slave discourse (cf. GM, I, 10-13). The master has power-over the slave precisely because the master recognizes and understands the slave. The master's recognition and understanding of the slave—"recognition" and "understanding" here are to be understood in the most pragmatic and concrete sense—is precisely what enables the master to have power-over the slave. At the most fundamental level, this means that the master recognizes and understands the weaknesses of the slave. The slave, on the other hand, always fundamentally misrecognizes and misunderstands the master. The slave is fundamentally incapable of recognizing and understanding the master precisely because the master has more power than the slave. The master recognizes and understands the slave via the *pathos of distance*. The pathos of distance is a form of empathy through which the master "constantly looks afar and looks down upon subjects and instruments and just as constantly practices obedience and command, keeping down and keeping at a distance" (BGE, 257). The pathos of distance—which may also aptly be described as the *pathos of difference*—is produced as and out of a self-affirmation of the power of the self, and consequently it is the jouissance of having power-over, the jouissance of hierarchy, the jouissance of one's superior position in relation to an inferior other, and this necessarily presupposes empathy because the superior self needs to be able to feel the inferiority of the inferior other in order to be able to affectively evaluate the disparity between the superior self and the inferior other (this, in turn, presupposes a pre-existing feeling of power in the self). Via the pathos of distance, the master affirms himself more gratefully and triumphantly (GM, I, 10). For the master, empathy is a means for becoming a more efficient and effective beast of prey. By contrast, the slave is essentially unable to empathize with the master, and consequently the slave is essentially unable to recognize and understand the master, hence the slave's radical falsification of the master, i.e. the slave's fantasy-construct of the master as "evil" (cf. GM, I, 11; GM, I, 13). Concretely, power *is* intelligence, intelligence *is* power. The slave is unable to recognize and understand the master simply because the slave is essentially weak, which means that the slave is essentially lacking in intelligence. In other words, the slave lacks the intelligence, the slave lacks the power, necessary to recognize and understand the master. Apart from the pathos of distance, recognition and understanding is only possible among equals. To be more precise, recognition and understanding is only possible among masters. Insofar as the slaves falsify themselves with fantasy-constructs, they cannot even actually recognize and understand themselves; they lack even the intelligence and the power to do that. Only the masters can recognize and understand other masters—and only the masters can recognize and understand the slaves. The slaves' concept of recognition (viz. Hegel's master-slave dialectic) is merely a fantasy-construct; this is evinced by the fact that, as Deleuze and Klossowski both point out, the "master" who needs to be recognized by the slave as a "master" is still a slave, he is a "master" in name only; this means that the slave's conception of himself as "master" is merely a narcissistic fantasy, a symptom of an essential deficiency of power. The slave's need to be recognized by the other is not really a need to have the other recognize the self; rather, it is the slave's need to have the other gratify the narcissistic fantasy of the slave-self via affirming the fantasy-construct of the slave's "personal identity" as "master." The real master has absolutely no need to be recognized by the slave. It is enough for the real master for himself to recognize the slave as a slave, because this means, in concrete terms, having power-over the slave.

There are two forms of structural violence: the structural violence performed by the master, and the structural violence performed by the slave. Whereas master-structural-violence operates via extrajection, slave-structural-violence operates via incorporation that has become an effective force which effects effective events. Nietzsche hypothesizes that master-structural violence is there at the origin of the state: "the welding of a hitherto unchecked and shapeless populace into a firm form was not only instituted by an act of violence but also carried to its conclusion by nothing but acts of violence—that the oldest "state" thus appeared as a fearful tyranny, as an oppressive and remorseless machine, and went on working until this raw material of people and semi-animals was at last not only thoroughly kneaded and pliant but also *formed*" (GM, II, 17). However, it is indeed possible for the slaves to triumph over the masters, and this happens when the fantasies of the slaves effectively produce effective events, i.e. when the slaves are motivated to act by their fantasies: "Supposing that what is at any rate believed to be the "truth" really is true, and the *meaning of all culture* is the reduction of the beast of prey "man" to a tame and civilized animal, a *domestic animal*, then one would undoubtedly have to regard all those drives of reaction and *ressentiment* through whose aid the noble races and their ideals were finally confounded and overthrown as the actual *instruments of culture*" (GM, I, 11). The master-structural-violence performed by the masters of a master culture does indeed tame and domesticate man, since it forms and shapes people according to the will of the masters. However, in a master culture there are still masters, and the structural violence performed by the masters is merely a means by which the masters more triumphantly affirm themselves; the masters increase their own psychic quantity of force-power via structural violence. In contrast, slave cultures perform structural violence against the masters and potential masters out of ressentiment, out of the fear of being oppressed by the masters or potential masters (e.g. this is the case in Christianity, Nazism, Communism, the French Revolution, the American Revolution); slaves may come to dominate the masters, but despite their domination the slaves do not increase their own psychic quantity of force-power, i.e. the slaves remain essentially slaves. The triumph of the slaves over the masters is the triumph of reactive drives over active drives. Ressentiment does not put an end to ressentiment. Indeed, ressentiment is capable of producing only more ressentiment. A slave culture merely reproduces the psychological conditions of its existence, i.e. it reproduces the psychological state of ressentiment. Even when a slave culture dominates the masters, as Christian civilization certainly has, the slave culture nevertheless continues to reproduce its own psychological state of ressentiment, i.e. it continues to reproduce its own psychological states of slave-fear and weakness. The slave continues to feel oppressed even when it dominates the master; the slave continues to feel oppressed even long after the fact of having dominated the master.

41.

We find our *ars erotica, ars theoretica, ars politica* in Nietzsche's *On the Genealogy of Morals*, and much more so in Nietzsche's *Thus Spoke Zarathustra*. If we militant Nietzscheans need to orient ourselves politically at all—and it is likely that many of us will indeed have this need—we should do so only in such a manner so as to assert our pathos of distance to all of what is traditionally called politics. We are not only against nationalism, populism, and fascism, but we are also against socialism, communism, anarchism, democracy, and egalitarianism. To most others it will appear that we are "against everything," and for most extents and purposes, being "against everything," being "nothing," is a useful slogan, just like "atheism" is a useful slogan, although ultimately, just like "atheism," it is a rather superficial and inaccurate term.

In reality, we militant Nietzscheans are also militant Machiavellians—which means that we think the only people who ought to have political power are either ourselves or those like us, hence our fondness for great conquerors such as Caesar, Alexander the Great, Genghis Khan, and Napoleon. *Our* revolution is a Nietzschean revolution: a revolution in morality, a revolution in customs, a revolution in values: a power-revolution, a revolution of power, a revolution whose sole meaning is the increase of power for ourselves. And it must be remembered that we can only increase our own freedom by enslaving others. That is to say, we believe only in the increase of our own power. Power is justice.

The problem with fascism is not merely "obedience," since commanding and obeying are essential to all life. The problem with fascism is *obedience to the force of ressentiment*. It is likely that "fascism," meaning Nazism, will continue to be discussed for some time to come as a bogeyman of Euro-American society, without any comprehension that fascism is in actuality merely ressentiment. Nietzsche's explanation of anti-Semitism (that anti-Semitism is motivated by ressentiment) is both the most parsimonious, the most accurate, and the most effective. We militant Nietzscheans alone know that fascism is ressentiment, and we alone are the enemies of ressentiment, consequently we alone are the only true anti-fascists. The rest of the world will continue using "fascism" as a bogeyman, all the while themselves cultivating their own ressentiment and consequently becoming more and more fascist themselves, until, in the end, they will be indistinguishable from the Nazis. Fascism is merely a culmination, an apotheosis, of slave morality; or at least, it has been the most visible apotheosis *thus far*. It is conceivable and perhaps even probable that new forms of intensified ressentiment, rivals to fascism—and who can tell? perhaps even something *worse* than Nazism—will develop in the future. We can already observe the germs of this today in populist and nationalist movements in America and Europe. The major problem with fascism is its state of mind—ressentiment, which is a form of misery—and its values, e.g. that pity is good (viz. hence why poor whites victimize themselves as the "white minority"), merely serve to reproduce this miserable, resentful, and pathetic state of mind. It is ultimately a question of psychological motivation; the consequences only follow from the motivation.

Assuming that the political atmosphere of today, congested as it is with pseudo-fascistic conservatives on the one hand and pseudo-socialist neo-liberals on the other hand, will only intensify in these trends—and assuming that we militant Nietzscheans are all former *radical* leftists, that we lived experimentally through the follies of egalitarianism, democracy, anarchism, and Marxism, perhaps even to the point of terrorism—we militant Nietzscheans, who have left behind the entire political spectrum, do indeed need to establish, at least to ourselves, what we are *not*. We are *not* fascists, and we are *not* leftists, of any kind whatsoever.

In this regard, we can, for the occasion, détournement some words from Foucault's preface to *Anti-Oedipus* for our purposes, in order to make a little clearer the pathos of distance between us (with our *ars politica* being *On the Genealogy of Morals*) and the rest of modern politics:

"Whence the three adversaries confronted by *On the Genealogy of Morals*. Three adversaries who do not have the same strength, who represent varying degrees of danger, and whom the book combats in different ways:

1. The political ascetics, the sad militants, the terrorists of theory, those who would preserve the pure order of politics and political discourse. Bureaucrats of the revolution and civil servants of the truth. [Given their leftism, and by implication their ressentiment, Jean-Paul Sartre, Wilhelm Reich, Adorno and Horkheimer, Guy Debord, Deleuze and Guattari, Derrida, and Foucault himself all fall into this category, not to mention countless others. Foucault, because he writes things such as "Do not become enamoured of power," is a preacher of weakness and self-emasculation, and is most certainly *not* a Nietzschean philosopher, despite all appearances to the contrary (cf. Deleuze and Guattari, AO, p. xiv).].

2. The poor technicians of desire—psychoanalysts and semiologists of every sign and symptom—who would subjugate the multiplicity of desire to the twofold law of structure and lack. [In this category, as well as the first, we can include philosophical labourers such as Slavoj Zizek, who has apparently renewed psychoanalysis, at least for many humanities students and even for the lay populace, all of whom apparently still believe in outdated 19th century concepts such as "repression" into the 21st century. It is likely, given the profound depths of human stupidity, that Zizek, and psychoanalysis more generally, will continue for some time to exert its ugly and foul-smelling influence in both the humanities departments of universities and among the common populace.].

3. Last but not least, the major enemy, the strategic adversary is fascism...And not only historical fascism, the fascism of Hitler and Mussolini—which was able to mobilize and use the ressentiment of the masses so effectively—but also the fascism in us all, in our heads and in our everyday behaviour, [that is to say, the ressentiment in us all, in our heads and in our everyday behaviour, at least insofar as "us all" means us insofar as we believe in the same things as the masses, feel the same way about things as the masses, and act in the same way as the masses], the fascism that causes us to love *revenge*, to desire the very thing that makes us *feel miserable*.

I would say that *On the Genealogy of Morals* is a book of ethics, the first book to invent a new ethical system in the world in quite a long time (perhaps that explains why it has only been comprehended by only a small minority, an ultra-minority: being an Anti-Christ and an anti-nihilist has become a life style, a way of thinking and living, only for the strongest) How does one keep from being fascist, even (especially) when one believes oneself to be a revolutionary militant? [One needs to cease being both a conservative and a leftist in order to become free from all traces of fascism, that is to say, free from all traces of ressentiment. If we militant Nietzscheans can still call ourselves "revolutionary militants"—and why not?—it is because we believe in a revolution of power whose praxis is outlined by Machiavelli and Nietzsche.]. How do we rid our speech and our acts, our hearts and our pleasures, of fascism? How do we ferret out the fascism that is ingrained in our behaviour? The Christian moralists sought out the traces of the flesh lodged deep within the soul. Nietzsche pursues the slightest traces of fascism in the body.

One might say that *On the Genealogy of Morals* is an *Introduction to the Non-Fascist Life.*

The art of living counter to all forms of fascism, whether already present or impending, carries with it a certain number of essential principles which I would summarize as follows if I were to make this great book into a manual or guide to everyday life:

- Free political action from all unitary and totalizing paranoia [paranoia is always a form of ressentiment].
- Develop action, thought, and power by proliferation, juxtaposition, and disjunction, as well as by subdivision and pyramidal hierarchization.
- Withdraw allegiance from the old categories of the Negative (law, limit, castration, lack, lacuna), which Western thought has so long held sacred as a form of power and an access to reality. Prefer what is positive and multiple, difference over uniformity, flows over unities, mobile arrangements over systems. Believe that what is productive is not sedentary but nomadic.
- Do not think that one has to be sad in order to be militant, even though the thing one is fighting is abominable. It is the connection of power to reality

(and not its retreat into the forms of representation) that possesses revolutionary force.

- Do not use thought to ground a political practice in Truth. The ultimate test of a line of thought is its practice, its political action. Any line of thought whose corresponding practices are ineffective is, by virtue of its ineffectivity in practice, thereby discredited as mere speculation. Use political practice as a test of thought, use thought as an intensifier of political practice, and use analysis as a multiplier of the forms and domains for the intervention of political action.
- Do not demand of politics that it restore the "rights" of the individual, as philosophy has defined them. The "individual" is a product of ressentiment. What is needed is to "de-individualize" by means of multiplication and displacement, diverse combinations, and experimentation. One must lose one's belief in the ego in order to establish hierarchies between one's self and others.
- Become enamoured of power, devoted to power. Worship power itself.

It could even be said that Nietzsche cares so much for power that he has enhanced the effects of power linked to his own discourse. Hence the games and snares scattered throughout his books, rendering their translation a feat of real prowess. But despite all of his masterful rhetoric, only one who shares something of the same essence with Nietzsche can understand Nietzsche. The traps of Nietzsche's books are those of humour: so many invitations to let oneself be put out, to take one's leave of the text and slam the door shut. His books often lead one to believe it is all fun and games, when something essential is taking place, something of extreme importance—but also of extreme levity—the tracking down of all varieties of fascism, from the enormous ones that surround and crush us to the petty ones that constitute the tyrannical bitterness of our everyday lives." (paraphrased from AO, pp. xii-xiv)

42.

On the Genealogy of Morals shows first of all how much ground has been covered, but it does much more than that. Nietzsche wastes no time in philosophizing with a hammer, with smashing the old idols and the old law tablets—and then chiselling something new.

"European nihilism" is no longer merely European, indeed it is not even any longer a question of "Euro-American nihilism" or "American nihilism," but a question of "Global nihilism." Globalization, which is merely "Europeanization" and "Americanization" by another name, has infected almost the entire globe with Euro-American nihilism. The contemporary epoch of globalization is the beginning of the age of the "last men," the smallest men, the most contemptible men, those who think they have invented happiness and that formerly the rest of the world was insane, and yet these last men are merely a cross between lotus eaters and beasts of burden. On the last men, Nietzsche writes: "No shepherd and one herd! Everybody wants the same, everybody is the same: whoever feels different goes voluntarily into a madhouse" (TSZ, "Prologue," 5). When the last men feel differently from the herd, they beg their psychiatrists to cure them, to give them magic pills, more lotuses to eat, without ritual and without ceremony, in the operations of the neurotic shamanism of the nihilistic philosophy of materialism. But we militant Nietzscheans, we who feel differently and *enjoy* feeling differently, we who enjoy the luxury of solitude our irreducible difference has blessed us with, look upon this absurd comedy, and we cannot help but *laugh*.

But then, considering the psychological problem of the last men and his psychiatrists, the priests of the last men, a terrible question strikes us. To what extent do *we* still suffer from the psychology of the last men? Perhaps more importantly, to what extent do we still suffer from the psychology of the *psychiatrist*? The anti-psychiatrists, such as R.D. Laing and Deleuze and Guattari, are no help to us here, for they are still materialists, and therefore despite all their talk about spirituality and "desire," they are still nihilists, still ascetics, still priests, still all too human. But then the thought dawns upon us, a thought impassioned, jubilant, and enigmatic, that we must *think through* all our former errors in order to make sure that we no longer believe in them. Thus begins our down-going, and consequently, our self-overcoming.

But here, inside our souls, what exactly is taking place? Psychological warfare, the revolution of all the masters against the slaves, the birth of a politics of domination. A psychological war fought on two fronts: culture and discourse. The only way to escape culture—that is to say, the only way to escape Christian civilization—is to invent our own culture, to invent our own civilization. A surge of power rushes through us at the thought of this vast and gigantic power struggle in which the odds are against us. We militant Nietzscheans are each a general, and time is our battlefield; we fight for own minds as well as the minds of men to come; our task is dangerous and success seems a gamble, which is exactly what our hearts crave, for it is only in the element of danger that we are in our element and that we thrive.

In our attacks, we must be strategic, we must attack what is dominant in discourse and culture at its weak points using guerrilla tactics. Moreover, it is more important to conquer mental territory than it is to merely "kill soldiers," i.e. to merely prepare refutations of particular thinkers. Contemporary Western culture, that is to say, early 21st century Western culture, is in a state of transition, as is evident from its concept of "man," which is also in a state of transition; this transition and conflict in Western culture is perhaps most evident in university discourse: psychology is for the most part completely dominated by neuroscience, cognitive psychology, and evolutionary psychology, that is to say, by an odd combination of vulgar materialism and naive information theory (the mind is reduced to matter and mathematics, and this is softened by the teleology of Darwinism's "survival of the fittest (to reproduce)"); the humanities, on the other hand, still suffer from Freud and Marx, albeit in ever newer choreographed numbers. Our strategic enemies, then, are clear: Freud, Marx, Darwin, and as broad categories, "neuroscience" and "cognitive psychology," all of which have contributed key parts to the contemporary concept of "man." The concept of "man" must be destroyed so that we can eliminate all traces of humanity within ourselves, for it is only by eliminating what is all too human in ourselves, i.e. it is only by eliminating our weaknesses, that we can cultivate our strengths and become overmen.

But are we strong enough and cunning enough for this task? Our project may indeed be called a "utopian project," but our utopia is like none of the others: in our utopia, hierarchy prevails, power flourishes, and peace-time is always preparation for war. Our political struggle does not fit in with any existing or recent political tradition; we are against both democracy, socialism, communism, and fascism. We are militant Nietzscheans, and our experience and technology of power have never been seen on earth before. We are warriors in the service of a society that does not yet exist, the society of the overman. It is true we raise a few old banners, such as those of Greece, Rome, and Napoleon, but the combat has shifted and spread into new zones.

43.

Nietzsche's theory of history is the positivist method of *genealogy*. It is this positivist method of genealogy that is the focus of Foucault's essay "Nietzsche, Genealogy, History." Explicating the principles of his positivist method of genealogy, Nietzsche writes in the following passage, which we have dedicated this entire book to explicating, "there is for historiography of any kind no more important proposition than the one it took such effort to establish but which really *ought to be* established now: the cause of the origin of a thing and its eventual utility, its actual employment and place in a system of purposes, lie worlds apart; whatever exists, having somehow come into being, is again and again reinterpreted to new ends, taken over, transformed, and redirected by some power superior to it; all events in the organic world are a subduing, a *becoming master*, and all subduing and becoming master involves a fresh interpretation, an adaptation through which any previous "meaning" and "purpose" are necessarily obscured or even obliterated. However well one has understood the *utility* of any physiological organ (or of a legal institution, a social custom, a political usage, a form in art or in a religious cult), this means nothing regarding its origin: however uncomfortable and disagreeable this may sound to older ears—for one had always believed that to understand the demonstrable purpose, the utility of a thing, a form, or an institution, was also to understand the reason why it originated—the eye being made for seeing, the hand being made for grasping...But purposes and utilities are only *signs* that a *will to power* has become master of something less powerful and imposed upon it the character of a function; and the entire history of a "thing," an organ, a custom can in this way be a continuous sign-chain of ever new interpretations and adaptations whose causes do not even have to be related to one another but, on the contrary, in some cases succeed and alternate with one another in a purely chance fashion. The "evolution" of a thing, a custom, an organ is thus by no means its *progressus* toward a goal, even less a logical *progressus* by the shortest route and with the smallest expenditure of force—but a succession of more or less profound, more or less mutually independent processes of subduing, plus the resistances they encounter, the attempts at transformation for the purpose of defense and reaction, and the results of successful counteractions. The form is fluid, but the "meaning" is even more so." (GM, II, 12; my emphasis)

Nietzsche's theory of genealogy is his theory of evolution, his theory of development; it is a method for the interpretation of history which applies to all forms of history, from biological evolution, to the histories of societies and cultures, to psychological development, to childhood development, to biographies and autobiographies, to any given stream of thoughts and feelings, to the histories of signs generally. Each sign is always already historical, always already diachronic. There is nothing outside of history. Ontologically there are *only* signs, therefore all history is the history of signs. Moreover, there is no event in itself, there are only interpretations, and there is no "correct" interpretation (cf. Nietzsche, WLN, N1, 115). The very definition of epistemological perspectivism is that history "is variously interpretable; it has no meaning behind it, but countless meanings" (Nietzsche, WLN, N7, 60). Each "event," each "fact," is itself an interpretation, that is to say, it is a *sign*, and as such it is a mask for a drive which has imposed its own perspective, its own interpretation, "as a norm on all other drives" (ibid). History is always already the history of signs. It is not only the case that history consists of signs, but it is also the case that history itself has a history, that historiography, the writing of history, is itself a history of competing drives imposing new interpretations upon signs; i.e. the history of historiography is itself interpretable via the genealogical method. From the above quoted passage, it is clear that one of the principles of Nietzsche's semiology is that "meaning is use." He argues that history is always a "sign-chain," a chain of various uses of signs, uses which may not be causally linked in a sequence, but which may succeed each other aleatoricly. Nietzsche's non-linear and aleatoric genealogical theory of time and history is best summarized by Shakespeare's poetic formula, "The time is out of joint." Time is a series of dislocations. Explicating Nietzsche's genealogical theory of history, Foucault writes, "An entire historical tradition (theological or rationalistic) aims at dissolving the singular event into an ideal continuity—as a teleological movement or natural process" (FR, p. 88). To assert that there time is continuous, that there is an "ideal continuity" to time, is to impose a teleology upon time, because it is to assert that all historical events are *necessarily* causally linked to each other. In other words, the concept of an "ideal continuity" is the concept of a necessity, i.e. it is a teleological concept (Q.E.D.). However, there are no grounds for asserting such an "ideal continuity," nor any other teleological concept for that matter. There are ruptures and breaks in history. The "origin" of a sign and the use of a sign are irreducibly different from each other, and the history of uses of a sign are not necessarily causally linked to each other. History is out of joint, a series of dislocations. Insofar as a use of a sign is a language-game, history is always the history of language-games, always already the history of language-games. The "rules" of these language-games are ultimately systems of values. Genealogy is the genealogy of signs, the genealogy of uses of signs. History is an aleatoric series of power relations. Each use of a sign is motivated and animated by a psychic force, a form of will to power. Each use of a sign is an interpretation of a sign, an interpretation by a will to power. Each use of a sign signifies a will to power which has become dominant and imposed a function upon something weaker.

Because the will to power *is* the symbol, *is* the multiplicity of symbols, the infinity of symbols, symbolic power is originary, all forms of power are forms of symbolic power, the power of symbols and the symbology of power, the symbology of power itself. Dominant psychic forces have power-over submissive psychic forces only via symbols, only via the mediation of symbols. Symbolic power *is* symbolic violence. Jenkins, summarizing Bourdieu's concept of *symbolic violence*, writes, "Symbolic violence...is the imposition of systems of symbolism and meaning (i.e. culture) upon groups or classes in such a way that they are experienced as legitimate" (2002, p. 104). However, given our findings regarding symbols, meaning, culture, violence, and psychology, Bourdieu's concept of symbolic violence must be revised. Because both the symbol, violence, and power are originary, symbolic violence is likewise originary. Wherever we have written "psychic force," "will to power," or any other term tautologous to "will to power," we may substitute "drive-to-violence" and the meaning would be exactly the same. Systems of symbolism, systems of meaning, and systems of culture are systems of uses; these uses are invariably performed by drives-to-violence; moreover, each "individual" is a group unto itself. Each use of a symbol is a use by a drive-to-violence. All symbols are weapons used by drives-to-violence. Language-games are essentially games of symbolic violence, war-games, games of psychological warfare. Symbolic violence is the violence of symbols, the drive-to-violence of symbols, the drive-to-violence inherent to each use of a symbol. Symbolic violence is the imposition of a use upon a symbol by a drive-to-violence. The quantity of intensity of a symbol is a quantity of violence. There is a quantity of violence inherent to each symbol, a diachronic quantity of violence which fluctuates depending on a variety of factors; to be brief, the quantity of violence of a symbol fluctuates depending on the use of the symbol. The political economy of the body without organs is the political economy of violence; violence, the drive-to-violence, is the "living currency" of psyche. Legitimacy can only be achieved via violence, via symbolic violence. All forms of violence are forms of symbolic violence. History is the history of violence. History is an aleatoric series of symbolic violence. Genealogy is the analysis of history as an aleatoric series of symbolic violence. Reality consists of an infinity of symbols, drives-to-violence, and symbolic violence. All relations are relations of violence. Each use of a symbol signifies a drive-to-violence which has become dominant and imposed a function upon something weaker.

On the method of genealogy, Foucault writes, that it "shortens its vision to those things nearest to it—the body, the nervous system, nutrition, digestion, and energies" (FR, p. 89). In other words, what is commonly called "material conditions," especially physiology, is essential to genealogy; however, it must be borne in mind that these are *not* causal agencies, but correlates of the will to power (in the case of physiology, biochemical correlates). Ultimately, there is no material reality. If we ever speak of "material conditions" as a causal agencies, it is only ever as a metaphor, an abbreviation and a shorthand (e.g. that many Christian mystics were merely epileptics, that their doctrines are ideologies of epilepsy, a well-documented fact). The scientific genealogy of effective history, however, is primarily and ultimately an analysis of the will to power, of the history of the will to power (all history is the history of the will to power). History *is* the will to power, the will to power *is* history.

The genealogical theory of history is a Dionysian, or dramatic, theory of history; the genealogical method includes what Deleuze describes as the Nietzschean, or Dionysian, "method of dramatization." On dramatization, Deleuze writes, "Any given concept, feeling or belief will be treated as symptoms of a will that wills something. What does *the one that* says this, that thinks or feels that, will? It is a matter of showing that he could not say, think or feel this particular thing if he did not have a particular will, particular forces, a particular way of being...Willing is the critical and genetic instance of all our actions, feelings and thoughts. The method is as follows: relating a concept to the will to power in order to make it the symptom of a will without which it could not even be thought (nor the feeling experienced, nor the action undertaken)...What a will wants—this is the latent content of the corresponding thing" (NP, p. 78). In each case, we must ask, "What is the motivation? What does this force want?" It is only by asking such questions and by empathizing with the case in question that we can discover which force is the motivation, the effective drive (viz. and especially whether the drive in question is healthy or sick). The positivist method of genealogy is essentially an empathetic method, a method of empathy. History is always already and essentially a psycho-history. History is the drama of psychic forces. In this regard, some preliminary training in the art of acting is essential for the genealogist, as is a working knowledge of Stanislavski's method (cf. Stanislavski's *An Actor Prepares, Building a Role, Creating a Character*, and *An Actor's Handbook*). Stanislavski's method is more important to the philosophers, psychologists, anthropologists, sociologists, and historians of the future than all of metaphysics combined (metaphysics itself can only be properly understood via the method of dramatization). The ontological basis of positivist genealogy is perspectivism. The will to power is the genetic and differential element of history. If we can speak of history as "descent with modification," it is only in the sense of descents of signs and modifications of signs, that is to say, descents of the will to power and modifications of the will to power. Ethnography and historiography are essential to the project of the genealogist. Genealogy is not only the "archaeology of knowledge," but it is also the archaeology of culture, the archaeology of emotions, and the archaeology of values. The genealogy of morals is the archaeology of morals.

History is an infinity of stories. Each story *is* an interpretation, and in addition there are infinite interpretations of each story. There is no event, no story, in itself, but there are only interpretations, and there is no "correct" interpretation. There is only an infinity of interpretations, therefore there is only an infinity of stories. (Each concept has a story, a history; moreover, each concept *is* a story). Genealogy is the science of interpretation. More specifically, as Foucault writes, genealogy is the scientific study of "effective history," what is history in effect: effective history "deals with events in terms of their most unique characteristics, their most acute manifestations. An event, consequently, is not a decision, a treaty, a reign, or a battle, but the reversal of a relationship of forces, the usurpation of power, the appropriation of a vocabulary turned against those who had once used it, a feeble domination that poisons itself as it grows lax, the entry of a mask "other." The forces operating in history are not controlled by destiny or regulative mechanisms, but respond to haphazard conflicts" (FR, p. 88). History, effective history, is "a profusion of entangled events...the true historical sense confirms our existence among countless lost events, without a landmark or a point of reference" (ibid, p. 89). If there can be said to be a "law" of history, it is the unwritten and unwritable law of chance. Chance rules supreme in the universe. Effective history, what is history in effect, is an aleatoric series of power relations, which necessitates the psychological analysis of psychic forces. Ultimately, this psychological analysis means identifying either elements of master morality or elements of slave morality. The positivist science of genealogy is a "curative science," which means that it diagnoses health or sickness via interpreting symptoms (each sign is a symptom of either health or sickness); health is precisely elements of master morality, whereas sickness is precisely elements of slave morality. In analysing each event (viz. each sign; event = sign), the genealogist must ask, "Which forces are effective in this event? Which forces are effectively producing this event? Which forces are motivating and driving this event?" This question must be asked bearing in mind that interpretations themselves need interpreting. To be more specific, it must be borne in mind that the vast majority of written histories are written by ideologues of slave morality, which means that the "event," the "effective event," is distorted by the interpretation imposed on it by slave ideologies, even to the point of burying the "text" beneath the interpretation; this means that genealogy necessitates critique, the critique of historians and historiographers—not to mention countless others, e.g. sociologists, anthropologists, philosophers—in order to discover the "effective events" of history, the events of psychic forces. In ontological terms, effective events are "events in terms of their most unique characteristics, their most acute manifestations," and in terms of the psychological analysis necessary to the genealogical method, this means events in terms of the psychic forces which produce and effect events. Each event is a "masked other," a mask of a will to power. All events, all signs, all evaluations, and all values are masks of psychic forces. The positivist method of genealogy is the dramaturgy of history.

Each thought is also an effective event. Each thought is an action, and ultimately, each action is a thought. The genealogist dramatizes the concepts of philosophy, asking which forces motivate the construction of a given concept. Each concept is a conceptual persona. The concept, conceptual persona, is originary; the concept, conceptual persona, is ontologically originary. Concepts are ultimately movement-concepts, i.e. movement-images. Existence itself consists of an infinity of concepts which *are* conceptual persona (forces = conceptual personae = concepts = movement-images = wills to power), but this means precisely that thoughts *are* emotions, i.e. that the ultimate nature of reality is the emotions. All images are concepts, and all concepts are images; but it must always be kept in mind that the ultimate nature of reality is the passions. "The greatest events in the world are silent" because the most powerful effective events in the world, in the history of the world, are the creation of values. Values, via cultural indoctrination and culture-acquisition, become inscribed in the unconscious mind, become inscribed in the body, and consequently determine the thoughts, feelings, and actions of individuals, and even of entire societies. Therefore, the genealogist must also be a "geophilosopher," a creator of values: a philosopher of the earth and the "meaning" of the earth, which is the production of the overman. The "geophilosopher" is a Nietzschean environmentalist. The geophilosopher empathizes with the psychic forces of the earth itself, with the will to power of the earth itself, that is to say, the motivation of the geophilosopher is to make life flourish, which means to make power flourish. The overman is a creature who has an excess of power, who is the product of an excess of power. The aim of the genealogist is to reverse-engineer society and culture in order create the conditions which allow the overman to flourish.

The essence of the overman is the self-actualization of power, the self-actualization of an excess of the will to power. The overman is defined by a praxis, a praxis of power, a praxis which evinces the excess of power. This praxis presupposes theory, at least in the form of "know-how," if not discursive concepts proper. In our study, it may be said that there are two concepts of the overman: the philosopher-overman and the general-overman. The philosopher-overman is the overman in the form of a philosopher, e.g. Nietzsche, Machiavelli, and Sun Tzu. The general-overman is the overman in the form of a military general, e.g. Alexander the Great, Julius Caesar, Genghis Khan, Napoleon Bonaparte, and Sun Tzu. This is a pragmatic distinction, although it is ultimately a fiction, since the general-overman always has a philosophy and the philosopher-overman is a general whose battle-field is the psyche; this is best exemplified by the case of Sun Tzu, who was both a military general and a philosopher. The genealogist is a philosopher-overman, and the aim of the genealogist is to engender the general-overman via reverse-engineering culture. Nietzsche makes clear the project of the genealogist: "Like a last signpost to the *other* path, Napoleon appeared, the most isolated and late-born man there has ever been, and in him the problem of the *noble ideal as such* made flesh—one might well ponder *what* kind of problem it is: Napoleon, this synthesis of the *inhuman* and *superhuman*" (GM, I, 16). Nietzsche explicitly designates Napoleon as an example of an overman, although he often hints at other names as well, such as Alexander the Great, Julius Caesar, and the Homeric Heroes. Napoleon is a strategic example of a general-overman because he is a well-documented case—in fact, the *only* documented case—in modern history of a general-overman. The "problem" of Napoleon is a pragmatic and experimental problem: How do we *create* a Napoleon? To find a solution to this riddle, we must sacrifice everything, we must be true artists. We must build a house for the overman, we must build a house of language for the overman. Perform all action as sacrifice for the overman. The fruits of thy labours belong to the overman, and to the overman alone. But insofar as we free spirits *are* overmen, the fruits of our labours belong to ourselves as well.

Of course, we can begin to find a solution to this riddle by asking: How was Napoleon created? Napoleon's proximity to us in time and culture is a hyperbolic boon because it allows us to examine social, cultural, and economic conditions which are generally similar to our contemporary time and culture; there are of course, differences, even major differences, but proximity in time and culture also gives us an abundance of data which enables us to efficiently compare and account for historical changes and differences. Of course, Nietzsche lived in an era temporally and culturally closer to Napoleon than we do; however, we have the benefit of having not only Nietzsche's works, but also the works of countless scientific and philosophic labourers at our disposal for our project. Nonetheless, our task is immeasurably more difficult than Nietzsche's due to both our distance from Napoleon and the severe cultural decadence which has not only worsened in Europe and America, but has spread pandemically throughout the globe, becoming a veritable global plague. In the vast majority of cases, being a geophilosopher will mean being completely isolated, and perhaps even being branded insane (we must use the utmost cunning when dealing with psychiatrists), because our system of values, our master morality, is completely opposed to the system of values which dominates the vast majority of the human race—indeed, which predominates in every single "human"—namely, slave morality. The totality of the life of the geophilosopher is essentially a long reconnaissance mission, an infinite series of reconnaissance missions. We free spirits—*we* are the most isolated and late-born men that have ever been, it is *we* who make flesh the problem of the *noble ideal as such*, it is *we who are inhuman and superhuman.* Bearing in mind that the mass of humanity, the diseased-others, the infected, are not the *causes* of nihilism *but are in actuality merely the symptoms of nihilism, symptoms of the global pandemic of nihilism, of nihilistic drives*—we find ourselves in a desperate situation analogous to that of the Ten Thousand, the Greek mercenary army which became trapped in the heart of enemy territory, in Persia, and had to fight their way back to Greece, battling both Persians, warlike tribes, traitorous allies, the weather, and disease. We ought to take comfort in the example of Xenophon, the general and historian who led the Ten Thousand back to Greece; Xenophon wrote, "The only things of value we have at present are our arms and our courage."

44

In the eyes of the genealogist, all history, each event of history, each image, is a joke-work. The free spirit comprehends that life has no inherent meaning, and that is precisely why the free spirit is incapable of taking life seriously. The free spirit comprehends that life has no inherent meaning, and that is precisely why the free spirit takes life lightly. Genealogy is the celebration of all the suffering in existence, a celebration even of the fact that "suffering is a mark of existence." A joke-work is essentially a dream-work, a condensation. Each joke-work is an aphorism, a hieroglyph. Nietzsche writes, "Laughter means: being *schadenfroh* but with a good conscience" (GS, 200). The mental state of the comic, the mental state of comedy, is essentially simultaneously the enjoyment of suffering and the enjoyment of nonsense, the enjoyment of the nonsense inherent to a given suffering. The mental state of comedy means simultaneously cognizing-introjecting both suffering, nonsense, and the nonsense inherent to suffering; this kind of cognizing is the essence of "comic cognition." "Laughter" is the jouissance of comic cognition, it is both the jouissance of suffering and the jouissance of nonsense simultaneously. Joke-works are the phantasms produced by the crystallization of the drive-to-comedy. A joke-work is an interpretation which produces the jouissance of comic cognition; of course, it is only possible for a joke-work to be a joke-work via the interpretation of a comic cognition. In other words, a joke-work always presupposes a mental state of comedy which is capable of producing a joke-work. The enjoyment of suffering presupposes empathy for suffering; one needs to be able to empathize with others in order to enjoy their suffering. The joke-work is an empathy-work, it is always already an empathy work, a work of empathy. The mental state of comedy is essentially an empathetic state. (Whenever we employ the term "empathy," we mean it in a strictly psychological sense only, that is to say, we mean it in a strictly non-moral sense). Because nonsense implies innocence, all jokes are essentially innocent, at least from the perspective of the joker, no matter how obscene, sexual, offensive, violent, or cruel.

There are two forms of the joke-work: the ressentiment-joke and the active-joke. The ressentiment-joke is essentially a revenge fantasy; it is essentially narcissistic and a denial of reality (typically, a denial of the reality of the other); often, the "suffering" it enjoys is a purely fantasy suffering, a fantasy of the suffering of the "evil" other, a "burning in effigy" by the vengefulness of the impotent. The subject of ressentiment has a tendency to the transference of ressentiment, the transference of feelings of ressentiment from one "object" to another (i.e. from one other to another other); typically, ressentiment towards an other which actually oppresses the subject of ressentiment is transferred onto another other: either a fantasy-construct of the oppressive other (e.g. the concept of "evil" and applications of the concept of "evil"), or to a weaker other which the subject of ressentiment proceeds to bully parasitically (typically this also involves, either explicitly or implicitly, labelling this weaker other with the fantasy-construct of "evil" in one form or another). E.g. racist jokes are invariably ressentiment-jokes. Ressentiment jokes are essentially defensive-jokes, jokes produced by defence-mechanisms, which means ultimately that they are forms of self-denial motivated by the death drive. Whereas the active-joke is the joke-work of the beast of prey, the ressentiment-joke is the joke-work of the parasite.

Active-jokes directly introject the suffering of the self or the other. Even when the "object," the other, of the active-joke is imaginary, e.g. a Marx Brothers film, a Charlie Chaplin film, a Monty Python film, it is, strictly speaking, an ideological-construct, but it is *never* a fantasy-construct. Whereas a ressentiment-joke is always an a-priori negation of difference (this negation of difference is always merely a fantasy), an active-joke is always an affirmation of difference and an affirmation of the self. An active-joke always affirms a *pathos of distance* between the self and the "object" of the joke (a *pathos of distance* is an empathy-affect, a feeling of empathy, which affirms the superiority of the self). A ressentiment-joke is always a revenge fantasy, but an active-joke enjoys the suffering of the self or the other only in order to affirm the self more gratefully and triumphantly. There is no true element of nonsense in a ressentiment-joke; its apparent element of nonsense is always merely a fantasy-construct which in actuality affirms the fantasy of an unmediated presence, a "meaning" (e.g. a racist joke affirms the fantasy of "races," which are identicalities; ultimately, the fantasy-concept of "race" leads back to the "unmediated presence" of the "personal identity" of the racist, viz. the "unmediated presence" of the ego). Only an active-joke has a true element of nonsense, an actual affirmation of nonsense, an affirmation of mediation and difference. The implication then is that ressentiment-jokes are not true jokes, ontologically and epistemologically speaking, because they fail to cognize-introject nonsense and therefore they imply the absence of the mental state of comedy. Ressentiment-jokes are essentially reactive-jokes, which means they are not really jokes at all, because reactive drives can only react to stimuli, and therefore reactive drives can never be light, "weightless," and spontaneous. The mental state of comedy is essentially a joyous, light, weightless, and spontaneous mental state, but only the active drives are joyous, light, weightless, and spontaneous, which means that only the active drives are capable of attaining the mental state of comedy and producing real joke-works. A ressentiment-joke is always the product of the mental state of ressentiment, which is essentially a feeling of misery, a feeling of being weak and oppressed, a "heavy" mental state. In contrast, an active-joke is always the product of the mental state of comedy, which is essentially a mental state of happiness, a weightless and spontaneous mental state. A ressentiment-joke, insofar as it prevents the self from introjecting (it always prevents the self from introjecting), is an act and work of self-denial. Only active-jokes are self-affirmations. Active-jokes are essentially malicious and cruel, sadistic jokes, because the active drives which produce them are essentially drives-to-violence, but these drives-to-violence, because they are active drives, are essentially joyous, light, and spontaneous mental states, hence the production of mental states of comedy, which are likewise joyous, light, and spontaneous. The joyousness of the active drives are their essential excess of quantity of force, which means that the active drives are characterized essentially by their excess of jouissance, hence their excess of joyousness (Q.E.D.). The sense of humour of the active type is the triumph of empathy. Just as health is rare in contemporary society, so is genuine comedy rare in contemporary society; we have already cited the examples of the Marx Brothers, Charlie Chaplin, and Monty Python—we also cite the examples of Lautréamont, Molière, Aristophanes, Shakespeare, Alfred Jarry, Henry Miller, Federico Fellini, Montaigne, Beckett, Kafka, Ionesco, and Frank Zappa—who are indeed rare figures, each of whom is a genius of a far greater magnitude than Einstein, quantum physicists, and analytic philosophers combined.

Needless to say, all the joke-works of the genealogist are active-jokes. The genealogist cognizes-introjects originary nonsense, the essential and originary nonsense of history, the nonsense always already implicit in history, the nonsense always already implicit in all the suffering in history; the jouissance of the genealogist is the jouissance of all the suffering in history and of the nonsense inherent to all this suffering. The genealogist *is* the great comic author of our existence. History is a cosmic joke. Existence itself is *ontologically* a joke, an infinity of jokes, an infinite joke, the joke of infinity, the infinity itself of the joke itself, the joke itself of infinity itself, because the universe is *ontologically nonsense*, nonsense always already exists at any given time in existence, and time is infinite, an infinite loop which returns eternally. The "past," the "present," and the "future" are merely mental constructs (cf. Derrida's *Speech and Phenomena*), and for the genealogist they are all so many joke-works, because time itself is pure becoming, pure becoming itself, Becoming itself, and the totality of this pure becoming is the Eternal Return, which is best metaphorized by the metaphor of the circumference of a circle, which is also infinite, and which always leads back to the same point whether one goes forward or backward along its infinite path. Existence itself is a comedy, always already a comedy, because existence itself is always already the Eternal Return. Comedy is originary, existence itself is ontologically a comedy. Foucault writes, "Genealogy is history in the form of a concerted carnival" (FR, p. 94). The essence of life is the essence of the carnival, life *is* a carnival, especially for the genealogist. For the free spirit, existence itself is the carnival of souls, the soft parade. The labyrinth of time is the circumference of a circle experienced from the inside out (there is nothing outside of time). The genealogist affirms the Eternal Return. To affirm the Eternal Return is to affirm the ontological joke of existence itself. The affirmation of the Eternal Return is the maximalization of health, the maximalization of the active drives, the maximalization of introjection-extrajection.

The philosopher-overman is essentially a schizophrenic: the social type we could describe equally well as *Homo shakespearia, Homo rimbaudia, Homo dionysia,* and *Homo historia.* As Borges writes on Shakespeare, "No one was as many men as this man: like the Egyptian Proteus, he used up the forms of all creatures. Every now and then he would tuck a confession into some hidden corner of his work, certain that no one would spot it. Richard states that he plays many roles in one, and Iago makes the odd claim: "I am not what I am." The fundamental identity of existing, dreaming, and acting inspired him to write famous lines...The story goes that shortly before or after his death, when he found himself in the presence of God, he said: "I who have been so many men in vain want to be one man only, myself." The voice of God answered him out of a whirlwind: "Neither am I what I am. I dreamed the world the way you dreamt your plays, dear Shakespeare. You are one of the shapes of my dreams: like me, you are everything and nothing."" (Borges, SP, pp. 88-89). It is merely vanity and hubris to wish to be "one man" because all identities, including personal identities, are merely fictions of language. The formula of the philosopher-overman is Rimbaud's formula "I is an other" [*Je est un autre*]. Not only is the self an army unto itself, but the self is Becoming itself, and all of existence is Becoming itself. *What is the motivation of all life? All life wants more power. Therefore, all life is the will to power.*

The free spirit self-actualizes the infinity itself and the intensity itself, the infinite intensity, the intensity of infinity, the infinity itself of intensity itself, the intensity itself of infinity itself, of the active drives of the body without organs. The free spirit self-actualizes the infinite god-machine of infinity itself, the marvellous-machine of the Eternal Return, which is the eternal return of all subjects, all subjectivities, all mental states, all emotions. The power-machine of the Eternal Return—to be more precise, the power-machine of the *affirmation* of the Eternal Return—is the maximalization of introjection and extrajection. The power-machine of the Eternal Return is the maximalization of jouissance. The power-machine of the Eternal Return is the maximalization of empathy (empathy is a form of introjection), therefore it is the maximalization of pain-excitations and the jouissance of pain-excitations, the maximalization of the jouissance of the suffering of one's self and others, the maximalization of the forces of tragedy and comedy. Hence the high quantity of *voluptas*, euphoric reward, produced by the power-machine of the Eternal Return. The schizophrenic experiences all of history in a single day, every single day. The affirmation of the Eternal Return is the affirmation of all reality, the affirmation of the ultimate nature of reality, the emotions.

Both Becoming and the will to power necessarily imply the untruth of truth. The philosopher-overman is the self-actualization of the will to power, the self-actualization of active drives. The philosopher-overman embodies the untruth of truth itself, the philosopher-overman has self-actualized the untruth of truth itself, which is the essence of the self itself, for the self itself is the untruth of truth itself. The untruth of truth itself is fiction itself. The philosopher-overman has self-actualized the essence of fiction itself. The philosopher-overman, like Shakespeare and like Borges'

Dionysian God, is everything and nothing, everyone and no one. Nietzsche too was everyone and no one. *Thus Spoke Zarathustra* is subtitled "A Book for All and None" because it was written for one like Nietzsche, Shakespeare, and Dionysus, someone who is both "all and none," everybody and nobody, simultaneously. The free spirit has self-actualized the infinite god-machine of Chaos—which is the god-machine of Infinity, the god-machine of Chance, the god-machine of Mars, the god-machine of Dream, and the god-machine of Dionysus, the Dionysian god-machine of the Self of Interpretation-Itself—which is itself an infinity of god-machines and which engenders an infinity of god-machines. The philosopher-overman is the changeling par excellence, the changeling-god Dionysus, who is change itself, Becoming itself, the changeling who is everything and nothing. To paraphrase Jim Morrison, the philosopher-overman is "an actor out alone," but nonetheless an actor with an excess of emotions, an excess of will to power. The philosopher-overman is fully self-realized, he has realized that at bottom he is every name in history. The philosopher-overman is a god on earth, and his aim is to engender more gods on earth, more overmen. Convalescence is essentially becoming-god, health is essentially being-god.

1. As quoted in Derrida, WD, p. 278.
2. As quoted in Derrida, OG, p. 3.
3. Translated by McGowan, 1993, p. 273
4. We often use the word "paraphrase" in the sense of the concept *détournement.* The literal meaning of the word détournement in French is "rerouting" or "hijacking." Détournement, as a philosophical concept and a technique, was developed in the 1950s by the Letterist International, and later adapted by the Situationist International. Détournement was defined by the Situationists as the "integration of present or past artistic productions into a superior construction of a milieu. In this sense there can be no situationist painting or music, but only a situationist use of those means. In a more elementary sense, détournement within the old cultural spheres is a method of propaganda, a method which reveals the wearing out and loss of importance of those spheres" (*Situationist International,* June 1958). We use the technique of détournement in the service of Nietzsche's philosophy, that is to say, in the service of master morality. The project of this book is essentially the détournement of academic jargon and the writings of academic intellectuals in order to affirm master morality and Nietzsche's project of genealogy, the "transvaluation of all values." We have most prominently made détournements of Deleuze, Freud, Derrida, and Foucault. Nietzsche himself had a pragmatic understanding of the concept of détournement, although he never formulated it; one can infer this pragmatic understanding from how often he used the technique of détournement in practice.
5. *The American Night,* 1990, p. 13
6. Translated by Fowlie, 2005, p. 289
7. The formulation "Meaning is use" is attributable to Wittgenstein, or at least his translators (cf. *Philosophical Investigations*). However, as we explicate in a later section of our book (Part II, Chapter V, aphorism 43), the "neo-pragmatic" semiotic theory that "meaning is use" is implicit in Nietzsche's concept of genealogy.
8. Cf. Nietzsche's essay "On Truth and Lie in a Non-Moral Sense" and Borges' short story "Funes, His Memory."
9. "Language is the house of being" is a popular aphorism of Martin Heidegger.

10. The phrase "symbolic universe" was coined by Berger and Luckmann in their book *The Social Construction of Reality* (1966). However, we have made a détournement of it, and we use the phrase in an ontological sense (viz. the universe *is* a symbolic universe). Moreover, we have also made a détournement of "social construction" (cf. Part I, Chapter III), which we likewise mean in an ontological sense (all reality *is* the social construction of psychic drives).

11. For the semiotic doctrines that "content determines form," "form is a resultant," and "substance determines style," we are indebted to Edgar Varèse's essay "The Liberation of Sound" (1966).

12. "Things are symbols of themselves" is a popular aphorism of Chögyam Trungpa.

13. "Nothing is true. Everything is permitted." The highest doctrine of the Hashashins. The aphorism is often attributed to Hassan-i Sabbah, the leader and founder of the Hashashins.

14. We have made a détournement of Lacan's concepts "the subject of the statement" and the "the subject of enunciation."

15. This entire chapter is a détournement of Deleuze's essay "How Do We Recognize Structuralism?", which is collected in *Desert Islands*. We have made a détournement of Deleuze's vocabulary and syntax, or at least that of his translator's, in order to explicate Nietzsche's theory of forces.

16. Translated by Michael Taormina in his translation of Deleuze's "How Do We Recognize Structuralism?" in *Desert Islands*.

17. Translated by E.H. and A.M. Blackmore, 2006

18. We have made a détournement of Deleuze's concept of the "movement-image," as well his concepts auxiliary to the movement-image, namely the "impulse-image" (or "force-image"), "action-image," and "perception-image." Although a deconstruction of Deleuze's concept of the movement-image is beyond the scope of our book, the basic outline of our deconstructive reading of Deleuze's *Cinema 1* is that Deleuze makes many pedantic, hair-splitting, and unfounded distinctions between these concepts of movement-images, which in effect affirms the concept of identity, since it is on the basis of identities that these arbitrary distinctions are constructed—arbitrary distinctions which, ultimately, are a denial and self-denial of the world of the emotions. In our usage, "impulse-image," "force-image," "perception-image," and "action-image," are merely all different aspects of the same phenomenon, the movement-image, and the movement-image is essentially becoming

(just as becoming is essentially the movement-image). For a brief introduction to Deleuze's cinematographic ontology, see Martin Schwab's essay "Escape from the Image: Deleuze's Image-Ontology," collected in *The Brain Is The Screen* (2000).

19. We have made a détournement of Foucault's phrase "political anatomy," which he uses in his book *Discipline and Punish*.

20. To remove any possible doubt, I must clarify that I am *not* a Creationist. Creationism is stupid. Christianity is stupid. They are packs of lies and mountains of bullshit with no basis whatsoever.

21. To be more precise, Nietzsche theory of biological evolution is his theory of "genealogy," which we have outlined in Part II, Chapter V, aphorism 43. Chance elimination is essential to biological genealogy (evolutionary genealogy, genealogical evolution), but the details of the theory of biological genealogy remain to be worked out. However fruitful such research may be, I maintain that psychological questions are far more interesting and far more pertinent to everyday life.

22. *The American Night*, 1990, p. 13

23. We have derived our theory of the "mind-space kaleidoscope" from Cocteau's description of his own praxis of writing, as he outlines it in his book *The Difficulty of Being*: "Whenever I read a book, I marvel at the number of words I meet in it and I long to use them. I make a note of them. When I am at work this is impossible for me. I restrict myself to my own vocabulary. I cannot get away from it, and it is so limited that the work becomes a brain-twister. I wonder, at every line, if I can go any further, if the combination of these few words that I use, always the same ones, will not end by seizing up and compelling me to hold my peace. This would be a blessing for everyone, but it is with words as with numbers, or with the letters of the alphabet. They have the faculty of rearranging themselves differently and perpetually at the end of the kaleidoscope." (1966, pp. 116-117). We also owe to Cocteau the discovery that the unconscious is essentially schizophrenic, the schizophrenic unconscious. Cocteau says in an interview somewhere, "The poet is a labourer for the schizophrenic inside of us." Our Nietzschean schizoanalysis owes immeasurably more to Jean Cocteau than it does to Deleuze and Guattari.

24. We have made a détournement of Zizek's concepts "subjective violence" and "systemic violence."

25. The image on the front cover is a portrait of Friedrich Nietzsche painted by Edvard Much in 1906.

1. Nietzsche:
AC = *The Anti-Christ*
BGE = *Beyond Good and Evil*
EH = *Ecce Homo*
GM = *On the Genealogy of Morals*
GS = *The Gay Science*
HH = *Human, All Too Human*
PTG = *Philosophy in the Tragic Age of the Greeks*
TI = *The Twilight of the Idols*
TSZ = *Thus Spoke Zarathustra*
WLN = *Writings from the Late Notebooks*, trans. Kate Sturge
WP = *The Will to Power*, trans. Kaufmann and Hollingdale

(In addition, we have also cited Nietzsche's essay "On Truth and Lies in a Non-Moral Sense," as translated by Carman (2010) in the collection *On Truth and Untruth*; in this case, we have cited page numbers referring to Carman's collection of translations).

Unless otherwise noted, we have followed convention in citing Nietzsche's texts using the numbers of his aphorisms; the numbers in our citations, unless otherwise noted, refer to the numbers of aphorisms, and not to page numbers. (When citing Wittgenstein, we also refer to the numbers of his "remarks," unless otherwise noted.) Where we have cited page numbers, we have cited specific editions which are specified in our bibliography. We have worked mostly from Walter Kaufmann's translations, collected in *Basic Writings of Nietzsche* and *The Portable Nietzsche*, although the translations of Thomas Common and Ian Johnston's translation of *On the Genealogy of Morals* have also been useful to us. Moreover, on numerous occasions, we have taken liberties with the translations. Our key improvement with the translations was to translate "trieb" as "drive," which is a far more accurate translation than "instinct," which is what most translators usually opt for. Often, Nietzsche's use of "trieb" clearly signifies "impulse," "urge," "desire," i.e. "drive," and definitely not "instinctual behaviour," hence why we translate "trieb" as "drive." Our German, however, is rudimentary, to say the least, but nonetheless it is clear that Nietzsche has yet to be translated well into English, despite the truly admirable efforts of many, notably of Walter Kaufmann. Kaufmann's footnotes, especially to *On the Genealogy of Morals*, have been especially helpful in clarifying numerous details.

2. Deleuze

AO = *Anti-Oedipus*, co-authored with Félix Guattari
C1 = *Cinema 1: The Movement-Image*
DI = *Desert Islands and other Texts (1953-1974)*
DR = *Difference and Repetition*
F = *Foucault*
LS = *The Logic of Sense*
NP = *Nietzsche and Philosophy*
PS = *Proust and Signs*

3. Derrida

OG = *Of Grammatology*
SP = *Speech and Phenomena*
WD = *Writing and Difference*

We have made détournements of many of Derrida's phrases and concepts, mainly from *Of Grammatology*, most notably "unmediated presence," "system of difference and mediation," "writing," "différance," "deconstruction," and "logocentrism." Derrida does indeed deserve credit as an original thinker; however, the affirmation of difference and mediation and the critique of "unmediated presence" is always already carried immeasurably further by Nietzsche. Derrida's most original and most sublime concept is his concept of "writing"—namely, that writing is essentially a system of mediation and difference—and by implication of his concept of writing, his concept, or rather, his critique, of "logocentrism"—the fantasy of the "unmediated presence" of speech—is likewise original and sublime. However, Derrida's ethics consists of slave morality, and that is as disappointing to us as Wagner's slave morality was to Nietzsche. On the point of ethics, Derrida himself must be deconstructed, and in fact he always already deconstructs himself. A comprehensive investigation of this matter is beyond the scope of our book.

4. Foucault

D&P = *Discipline and Punish*
FR = *The Foucault Reader*
OT = *The Order of Things*

From *The Foucault Reader*, we have cited Foucault's essay "Nietzsche, Genealogy, History," translated by Donald F. Bouchard and Sherry Simon.

5. Darwin

OS = *The Origin of Species*

6. Damasio

FWH = *The Feeling of What Happens*

7. Freud

BPP = *Beyond the Pleasure Principle*
EI = *The Ego and the Id*
GPT = *General Psychological Theory*
TT = *Totem and Taboo*

8. Borges

SP = *Selected Poems*

Abraham, N. and Torok, M. (1994). *The Shell and the Kernel: Renewals of Psychoanalysis, Volume 1*. Chicago and London: The University of Chicago Press

Althusser, Louis. (2001). *Lenin and Philosophy and other essays*. (Ben Brewster, trans.). New York, NY: Monthly Review Press

Artaud, Antonin. (1976). *Antonin Artaud: Selected Writings*. (Helen Weaver, trans.). Berkeley and Los Angeles, CA: University of California Press

Baudelaire, Charles. (1993). *The Flowers of Evil*. (James McGowan, trans.). Oxford: Oxford University Press

Berger, P. L., & Luckmann, T. A. (1967). *The Social Construction of Reality: A Treatise in the Sociology of Knowledge*. London: Penguin.

Borges, Jorge Luis. (1977). "Merely a Man of Letters," Jorge Luis Borges: an interview. (Dennis Dutton, Michael Palencia-Roth, and Lawrence I. Barkove, interviewers). *Philosophy and Literature, 1*, 337-41

Borges, Jorge Luis. (2000). *Selected Poems*. (Alexander Coleman, ed.). New York, NY: Penguin Books

Bradley, Arthur. (2008). *Derrida's Of Grammatology*. Bloomington and Indianapolis: Indiana University Press

Chalmers, D. J. (2010). *The Character of Consciousness*. New York, NY: Oxford University Press.

Cocteau, Jean. (1966). *The Difficulty of Being*. (Elizabeth Sprigge, trans.). New York, NY: Coward-McCann

Cocteau, Jean. (1957). *Les Enfants Terribles* (translated as *The Holy Terrors*). (Rosamond Lehman, trans.). New York, NY: New Directions

Damasio, Antonio. (1999). *The Feeling of What Happens*. San Diego, London, New York: Harcourt

Darwin, Charles. (1888). *The Life and Letters of Charles Darwin: Volume II*. London: William Clowes and Sons, Limited

Darwin, Charles. (2003). *The Origin of Species*. New York, NY: Signet Classics

Deleuze, G. and Guattari, F. (1977). *Anti-Oedipus*. (Robert Hurley, Mark Seem, and Helen R. Lane, trans.). New York, NY: Penguin Books

Deleuze, Gilles. (1986). *Cinema 1: The Movement-Image.* (Hugh Tomlinson, trans.). Minneapolis, MN: University of Minnesota Press

Deleuze, Gilles. (2004). *Desert Islands and Other Texts (1953-1974).* (Michael Taormina, trans.). New York, NY: *Semiotext(e)*

Deleuze, Gilles. (1994). *Difference and Repetition.* (Paul Patton, trans.). New York, NY: Columbia University Press

Deleuze, Gilles. (1988). *Foucault.* (Seán Hand, trans.). Minneapolis, MN: University of Minnesota Press

Deleuze, Gilles. (1990). *The Logic of Sense.* (Mark Lester and Charles Stivale, trans.). New York, NY: Columbia University Press

Deleuze, Gilles. (1983). *Nietzsche and Philosophy.* (Hugh Tomlinson, trans.). New York, NY: Columbia University Press

Deleuze, Gilles. (2000). *Proust and Signs.* (Richard Howard, trans.). Minneapolis, MN: University of Minnesota Press

Dennett, Daniel. (1988). Quining Qualia. In *Consciousness in Contemporary Science.* (A.J. Marcel and E. Bisiach, eds.). Oxford: Oxford University Press

Derrida, Jacques. (1997). *Of Grammatology.* (Gayatri Spivak, trans.). Baltimore and London: The John Hopkins University Press

Derrida, Jacques. (1973). *Speech and Phenomena.* (David B. Allison, trans.). Evanston, IL: Northwestern University Press

Derrida, Jacques. (1978). *Writing and Difference.* (Alan Bass, trans.). Chicago, IL: The University of Chicago Press

Foucault, Michel. (1977). Preface. In Deleuze and Guattari, *Anti-Oedipus* (pp. xi-xiv). New York, NY: Penguin Books

Foucault, Michel. (1977). *Discipline and Punish.* (Alan Sheridan, trans.). New York, NY: Vintage Books

Foucault, Michel. (2010). *The Foucault Reader.* (Paul Rabinow, ed.). New York, NY: Vintage Books

Foucault, Michel. (1970). *The Order of Things.* New York, NY: Vintage Books

Freud, Sigmund. (1961). *Beyond the Pleasure Principle.* (James Strachey, trans.). New York, NY: W.W. Norton & Company.

Freud, Sigmund. (1960). *The Ego and the Id.* (Joan Riviere, trans.). New York, NY: W.W. Norton and Company.

Freud, Sigmund. (1963). *General Psychological Theory: Papers on*

Metapsychology. (Phillip Rieff, ed.). New York, NY: Touchstone

Freud, Sigmund. (1919). *Totem and Taboo*. (A.A. Brill, trans.). London: George Routledge and Sons, Limited

Guattari, F. (2000). *The Three Ecologies*. (Ian Pindar and Paul Sutton, trans.). New Brunswick, NJ: Athlone Press.

Harvey, David. (2003). *The New Imperialism*. Oxford: Oxford University Press.

Heidegger, Martin. (1979). *Nietzsche, Volume I: The Will to Power as Art*. (David Farrell Krell, trans.). New York, NY: HarperOne

Heraclitus. (1979). *The Art and Thought of Heraclitus*. (Charles H. Kahn, trans.). Cambridge, UK: Cambridge University Press

Hesiod. (1973). *Theogony*. (Dorothea Wender, trans.). New York, NY: Penguin Books

Houellebecq, Michel. (1991). *H.P. Lovecraft: Against the World, Against Life*. (Dorna Khazeni, trans.). San Francisco, CA: Believer Books

Husserl, Edmund. (1970). *The Crisis of European Sciences and Transcendental Phenomenology: An Introduction to Phenomenological Philosophy*. (David Carr, trans.). Evanston, IL: Northwestern University Press

Jenkins, Richard. (2002). *Pierre Bourdieu*. London and New York: Routledge

Kalat, J. W. (2016). *Biological Psychology* (12th ed.). Boston, MA: Cenage Learning.

Kihlstrom, J. F. (2006). Trauma and memory revisited. *Memory and Emotion* (pp. 259–291). doi:10.1002/9780470756232.ch12

Klossowski, Pierre. (1997). *Nietzsche and the Vicious Circle*. (Daniel W. Smith, trans.). London, UK: Athlone Press

Levine, Joseph. (1999). "Conceivability, Identity, and the Explanatory Gap." In Stuart R. Hameroff, Alfred W. Kaszniak and David Chalmers (eds.), *Towards a Science of Consciousness III: The Third Tucson Discussions and Debates*. Cambridge, MA: The MIT Press,

Lyotard, Jean-François. (2011). *Discourse, Figure*. (Antony Hudek and Mary Lydon, trans.). Minneapolis, MN: University of Minnesota Press

Machiavelli, Niccolò. (1992). *The Prince*. (N.H. Thomson, trans.). Mineola, NY: Dover Publications

Mallarmé, Stéphane. (2006). *Collected Poems and Other Verse*.

(E.H. and A.M. Blackmore, trans.). Oxford: Oxford University Press

Mayr, E. (2001). *What Evolution Is*. New York: Basic Books.

Miller, Henry. (1965). *Sexus*. New York, NY: Grove Press

Morrison, Jim. (1990). *The American Night: The Writings of Jim Morrison, Volume II*. New York, NY: Villard Books

Nietzsche, Friedrich. (2000). *Basic Writings of Nietzsche*. (Walter Kaufmann, trans.). New York, NY: The Modern Library

Nietzsche, Friedrich. (1974). *The Gay Science*. (Walter Kaufmann, trans.). New York, NY: Random House

Nietzsche, Friedrich. (1982). *The Portable Nietzsche*. (Walter Kaufmann, trans.). New York, NY: Penguin Books

Nietzsche, Friedrich. (1962). *Philosophy in the Tragic Age of the Greeks*. (Marianne Cowan, trans.).Washington, DC: Regnery Publishing

Nietzsche, Friedrich. (2010). *On Truth and Untruth*. (Taylor Carman, trans.). New York, NY: HarperCollins

Nietzsche, Friedrich. (1968). *The Will to Power*. (Walter Kaufmann and R.J. Hollingdale, trans.). New York, NY: Random House

Nietzsche, Friedrich. (2003). *Writings from the Late Notebooks*. (Kate Sturge, trans.). Cambridge, UK: Cambridge University Press

Ovid. (1986). *Metamorphoses*. (A.D. Melville, trans.). Oxford: Oxford University Press

Radiguet, Raymond. (2012). *The Devil in the Flesh*. (Christopher Moncrieff, trans.). Brooklyn, NY: Melville House Publishing

Reich, W. (1980). *The Mass Psychology of Fascism* (3rd ed.). New York: Farrar, Straus and Giroux.

Rimbaud, Arthur. (2005). *Complete Works, Selected Letters*. (Wallace Fowlie, trans.). Chicago, IL: The University of Chicago Press

Schwab, Martin. (2000). "Escape from the Image: Deleuze's Image Ontology." In *The Brain Is the Screen: Deleuze and the Philosophy of Cinema* (Gregory Flaxman, ed.). Minneapolis, MN: University of Minnesota Press

Situationist International. "Definitions". *Situationist International, 1*. June 1958.

Solms, M., & Turnbull, O. (2002). *The Brain and the Inner World: An Introduction to the Neuroscience of Subjective Experience*. London: Karnac Books.

Stendhal. (1957). *Love*. (Gilbert and Suzanne Sale, trans.). New

York, NY: Penguin Books

Sun Tzu. (2002). *The Art of War*. (John Minford, trans.). New York, NY: Penguin Books

Varèse, E. and Wen-chung, C. (1966). The Liberation of Sound. *Perspectives of New Music, 5* (1), 11-19.

Weinberger, J. and Stein, J. (2002). "Drive Theory." In E. Erwin (ed.), *The Freud Encyclopedia: Theory, Therapy, and Culture* (pp. 161-165). New York, NY: Routledge

Wittgenstein, Ludwig. (1969). *On Certainty*. (Denis Paul and G.E.M. Anscombe, trans.). New York, NY: Harper Torchbooks

Wittgenstein, Ludwig. (2009). *Philosophical Investigations*. (G.E.M. Anscombe, P.M.S. Hacker, and Joachim Schulte, trans.). West Sussex, UK: Wiley-Blackwell

Wittgenstein, Ludwig. (1961). *Tractatus Logico-Philosophicus*. (D.F. Pears and B.F. McGuinness, trans.). London and New York: Routledge

Xenophon. (1949). *The Persian Expedition*. (Rex Warner, trans.). New York, NY: Penguin Books

Yule, George. (2010). *The Study of Language*. Cambridge, MA: The University of Cambridge Press